Microcredit Meltdown

Microcredit Meltdown

The Rise and Fall of South Sudan's Post-Conflict Microcredit Sector

Crystal Murphy

LEXINGTON BOOKS
Lanham • Boulder • New York • London

Published by Lexington Books
An imprint of The Rowman & Littlefield Publishing Group, Inc.
4501 Forbes Boulevard, Suite 200, Lanham, Maryland 20706
www.rowman.com

6 Tinworth Street, London SE11 5AL, United Kingdom

British Library Cataloguing in Publication Information Available

Library of Congress Cataloging-in-Publication Data

Names: Murphy, Crystal, author.
Title: Microcredit meltdown : the rise and fall of South Sudan's post-conflict microcredit sector / Crystal Murphy.
Description: Lanham : Lexington Books, 2019. | Includes bibliographical references and index.
Identifiers: LCCN 2018042642 (print) | LCCN 2018044252 (ebook) | ISBN 9781498577397 (Electronic) | ISBN 9781498577380 (cloth : alk. paper)
Subjects: LCSH: Microfinance—South Sudan. | Poverty—South Sudan. | South Sudan—Economic conditions—21st century.
Classification: LCC HG178.33.S643 (ebook) | LCC HG178.33.S643 M87 2019 (print) | DDC 332.74309629—dc23
LC record available at https://lccn.loc.gov/2018042642

∞™ The paper used in this publication meets the minimum requirements of American National Standard for Information Sciences—Permanence of Paper for Printed Library Materials, ANSI/NISO Z39.48-1992.

Printed in the United States of America

Contents

List of Figures and Tables

FIGURES

TABLES

Acknowledgements

This project was supported by grants from the following institutions: The Center for Unconventional Security Affairs, The Institute for Money, Technology and Financial Inclusion, Center for Global Peace and Conflict Studies, Intel's People and Practices Research Group, UC Irvine's Department of Planning, Policy and Design, UC Irvine's Social Ecology Alumni Fund, Coalition Advocating Human Security, The Earl Babbie Research Center, Chapman University Departments of Political Science and Peace Studies, Wilkinson College of Arts, Humanities and Social Science, and Chapman University's Scholarly Creative Grant.

There are many people to thank. Foremost are those who shared their stories for this text. Most of you are not named but this really is for you.

Next are the mentors, colleagues, family and friends who supported.

Sandra Alvarez, Nevin Aiken, Robin Anderson, Amanda Apgar, Jonathan Apgar, Samuel Arthur, Natalie Baker, Cameron Birge, Arthur Blaser, Scott Bollens, Toast Boyd, Kayla Brons, Victoria Carty, Sean Carasso, John Compton, Michelle Decker, Margie Dillenburg, Brittany Estrada, David Feldman, Kevin Flynn, Patrick Fuery, Dalton Gerlach, Heather Goldsworthy, C. Ann Gordon, Sarah Hall, dream hampton, Rebekah Hendershot, Lynn Horton, Nubar Hovsepian, Jedidiah Jenkins, Ayana Johnson, Daniel N Johnson, Jason Lankow, Karen Krenis, Lisa Leitz, Sarah LeMay, Cecelia Lynch, CK Magliola, Timothy Martin, Richard Matthew, Bill Maurer, Matt Maust, Erin Mosely, Heather Murphy, Charles Murphy, Prexy Nesbitt, Reanna Ochoa, Daniel Thomas Olson, Nicole Pietrini, Taylor Pietrini, Katie Pine, Cheryl Pollard, Rajagopalan Radhakrishnan, Katherine Raines, Justin Richland, Carolina Sarmiento, Alexis Sutterman, Najeeba

Syeed, Marisa Tramontano, Emily Troshynski, Carolyn Vieira-Martinez, Jamil Zamorano Walker Smith, Athalie Waugh, Daniel Wehrenfennig, Don Will, Seanne Winslow Wehrenfennig, Tekle Woldemikael, Rebecca Zaragoza Jackson, and Tom Zoellner.

Deepest thanks to all. None of us can do it alone.

Introduction

New Countries Do Not Fall from the Sky

MICROCREDIT IN A NEW PLACE

I first heard about the dramatic changes occurring on the ground in what is now South Sudan in early 2006. I was working in Uganda and began noticing how shopkeepers were running out of what were previously abundant staples. I ordered things like beans, or soda, and was told, "It's not there." People were telling me that the reason for the shortages was Juba. "Everything is going to Juba right now." In a short time, *Juba* alone would be all the explanation necessary. "And you know what? They're getting like 7,000 Ugandan shillings for the Coke up there!" That was about four US dollars in a place where the usual soda price was 500 shillings (about 25 US cents).

Juba's economic landscape became more fascinating and pressing to me over the coming months, even though I still had yet to visit the place. I was conducting my thesis fieldwork in Adjumani, a northern Ugandan district that approaches what is now the southernmost South Sudanese border. Through this work, I was exploring problems related to microfinance experienced by Sudanese refugees who had been living in Uganda during the Second Sudanese Civil War (1983–2005). When the south of then-Sudan reopened, and refugees were mobilized for the return home, solidarity groups (loan borrowers who had guaranteed loans for one another and were accountable for one another's repayment) were defaulting on their loans en masse. There were no checks on their obligations to repay loans before departing Uganda. This, of course, was problematic for the lending institutions. Unpaid debts threatened the stability of microfinance institutions (MFI) and their ability to service those who remained local.

In that preliminary research, I explored the ways MFIs were incentivizing repayment. The MFI incentives consisted of repayment-confirmation forms that offered clients larger loans upon return to Juba. As low-tech credit scoring instruments were developed, I could not help but wonder who might use these tools, where they would store certificates of completion, and what the transaction would be like when they presented them to microcredit agencies back home in Juba.

And then I took a mental step back from the logistics of the instruments and reconsidered these individuals as people. I wondered what life would be like for current and former borrowers who would be starting life again in their home country. Would they need produce and bottled beverages from 500 miles of non-paved roads away? What exactly would they be growing or selling as part of their lives as micro-entrepreneurs? How could they afford to eat expensive produce and drink pricey bottled beverages?

Before I made my first visit to Juba, dozens of people who had been there told me that it was expensive and I would need a lot of money to get by. I was also told conflicting stories about how unsafe it was to carry large amounts of cash. Some people warned me about chronic theft; others lauded the trustworthiness of Sudanese people in general. In any case, I was told it would be simple to access the money I had in my US bank account because in a big city like Juba, like in Kampala, Uganda, there would be plenty of ATMs available.

I arrived at a city bustling with people from many different countries, dressed in numerous styles, speaking several languages, buying and selling diverse goods. But there were no ATMs. And I could not access my bank account. After two days of bouncing bus rides, with luggage still weighing down my shoulders, a pool of sweat collecting between it and my back, I stood in front of a clerk in a prefabricated shipping trailer that had been converted into a temporary hotel. I calculated in a panic. The four hundred US dollars I had on my person—enough to live lavishly in Uganda for a month—would not suffice for even one night's stay and a return bus ticket. I slept without dinner for the first time in a long time.

On my way home, and for each day of the years that followed, I thought about how exactly people coming from villages and camps forge lives in Juba. This book is dedicated to finding the answers, as much as it is to the ingenious people rebuilding South Sudan.

MICROCREDIT IN A NEW PLACE

Among the grain merchants, oil speculators and other "cowboy capitalists" who arrived in Juba immediately after the 2005 peace accords were signed, humanitarians wondered what could be done to usher the population into a secure and prosperous future. Millions of displaced persons moved home that year, and thousands of outsiders provided help and supplies for the transition. Technocrats wanted to introduce microcredit as a tool to alleviate the impending poverty.

Microcredit programs[1] give small loans to many people who are anywhere between disadvantaged and impoverished. The idea is that a little bit of start-up capital from a charity or bank will give the borrower the "push" he or she needs to bring in more income. Microcredit is believed to be socially transformative too; membership in a group-loan regimen is believed to have the potential to increase the social capital of participants and collectively empower groups of people. The borrower rises out of poverty while the provider gets more money to be able to keep providing loans. A win-win?

Sometimes. To a novice observer, microcredit appears to be a natural fit for any post-conflict recovery toolkit because it alleviates poverty and promotes social cohesion. However, microfinance has been both championed and critiqued.

South Sudan was not the first place this had been tried. Muhammad Yunus's Grameen Bank in Bangladesh popularized microcredit with small loans to the poor in the 1970s. The Grameen model was quickly deemed a success, surged in popularity, and was replicated in over 140 countries—such that lenders now provide the service to over 210 million clients worldwide. Program directors, economists, and bankers hoped the approach could be used in country after country, society after society. Even celebrities such as Natalie Portman touted the benefits of microcredit, promoting the image that microcredit programs can be a major tool in building flourishing, peaceful societies. Many looked at microcredit as a panacea for poverty. This was not all unwarranted; there has been success, after all.

However Juba is not Dhaka. South Sudan is not Bangladesh. South Sudan is no ordinary poor country. It had and continues to have particular problems, unique to its own state. Some of these were created as a consequence of civil war but others predate it. South Sudan also had particular opportunities. This book explores how individuals in South Sudan navigated the many postwar changes by aligning with available interventions, including those by the government, other states, the United Nations, and many nongovernmental organizations (NGO). Some of the changes were quite jarring, but the possibilities for forging futures were also numerous. This work centers on the nuance found in local experience.

As a doctoral researcher, political economy professor, and curious global citizen, I traveled the region between 2008 and 2013 and interviewed over 200 people. Compared to before and after this period, there was a great deal of investment and stability from violence. In the first three years, I learned of many challenges vexing the program participants and those who served them. At the time, independent statehood appeared imminent, and there was a palpable sense of hope in the air. But hope gave way to meltdown. When two of three main microcredit financial institutions in South Sudan closed shop and pulled out in 2012, it was clear that something had gone wrong in the microcredit sector. At Juba's microcredit peak, some 80,000 South Sudanese were borrowing. By 2012 there were only a few thousand receiving loans, most of which were less impoverished than marginalized. The industry had practically vanished.

This book looks at how microcredit worked, and importantly how it did not work, in South Sudan. It analyzes the reasons for why it did and did not work, and what lessons we can draw from this when implementing microcredit in other areas. The reasons behind the meltdown were complex. We can learn from these mistakes, but first we have to know what they were.

ROADMAP FOR THE BOOK

Chapter 1 "From a Galaxy Far, Far Away to the Souq" introduces the book's key concepts and situates the Juba case study in relation to the broader fields of development economics and peacebuilding. It details how the international community garnered support for developing microcredit in South Sudan and lays bare the persuasive normative appeals for efficiency of distributing finance and supporting borrower autonomy. The chapter problematizes the dissonance between the popular tropes of international development and the realities of development processes in the locations where the programs are actually based. I invite the reader to question the norm-driven (rather than evidence-driven) neoliberal assistance paradigm. This critique forms the basis for appraising claims about microcredit efficacy in chapter 2.

Chapter 2 "Does Microcredit Work?" describes exactly how analysts study what "works" in international development in general and in microcredit in particular. It discusses the problems of both institutional self-reporting and abstracted, deductive research methods. Results of past studies conflict, neither presenting clear data as to whether microcredit improves lives nor capturing the human experiences that should facilitate critical program adjustments. This critical analysis of cornerstone microcredit studies thusly demands a more robust research agenda: one using a mixed-method approach that includes the voices of the actors (both on the microcredit side and on the beneficiary side) involved.

Chapter 3 "I Can't Exchange for Dollars But Will You Talk with Me?" summarizes my approach and experience in filling in the research gap with a mixed-methods approach. Those interested in conducting similar fieldwork will find this chapter most useful. It is a commentary on recruiting and interviewing, researcher reflexivity, participant biases and expectations, and the analytical process.

Chapter 4 "Blueprints and Architects" introduces the South Sudanese microcredit story, including its guiding architects, their particular visions for what was possible, and what scaffolding of support they put into place to achieve their visions. It describes the approaches replicated by the MFIs, including the standardized group-lending scheme and interest rates. Chapter Four brings to life the long-running debate of the dueling approaches to microcredit: the poverty lending approach that would service the poor through subsidies, and the commercial model that would service people who are less poor but would be commercially solvent. The two major MFI actors in Juba each represented one pole of the debate, allowing the reader to see how each method worked out in Juba's challenging context. Implementation was more complex than any post-conflict best practice brief could anticipate.

Chapter 5 "Cookie Cutters and Meeting People" follows what happens when organizations attempted to replicate the successes of a tool implemented in one context and applied it to a starkly different context. It analyzes how model replication missed the mark through the prism of microcredit's first step: joining a group. The microcredit models replicated in Juba unwittingly precluded some participants. By deploying the standard-issue group loan procedure in Juba, the institutions practiced what I term "de facto preferential lending." Loans went to people with intact social networks, while independent returnees had a harder time getting microcredit. Applying this loan filter in Juba undermined the development goals the lenders had set out to achieve. Post-conflict microcredit can and must attend to the social ties and fissures that result from war.

Chapter 6 "What's Trust Got to Do with It?" shifts the focus to the people who used microcredit in South Sudan. It delves into the ways borrowers navigated the co-borrowing process, specifically the nuanced social dynamics of the group repayment. It analyzes how Juba borrowers evaluated potential peer groups prior to joining, and how they managed relations during the loan cycles. Borrower processes for determining trust and conditioning payments were robust and ongoing processes, with outcomes that transcended simple repayment. While some borrowers were content to discipline and enforce payments, more frequently they rejected any conversion of social ties toward economic ends. Borrowers practiced what I term "social anti-capital;" driven by sympathy and compassion, many borrowers prioritized maintaining social ties over creating the social tension required to recover money from each other.

Chapter 7 "Borrower Breakdowns" scales back and reviews the greatest challenges for former and continuing borrowers, and how they were addressed. Juba microcredit users toggled between the import system, the retail market system, and the loan system—each with its own social, temporal, and cost intervals. The chapter documents how borrowers made sense of credit within a postwar economy that was constrained greatly by hyperinflation and import dependence. An examination of the practical limitations experienced by participants alongside their responses to them, suggests that microcredit was not hopeless but was in need of specific changes to accommodate the local constraints.

Chapter 8 "They Think Food Grows on Trucks" returns to the industry view, this time of the local staff and management. Employees diagnosed their clientele with cases of a so-called dependency syndrome, marked by poor attitudes and failure to exhibit proper levels of independence. While the dependency trope is effective at garnering support from Western audiences, this local stereotyping impeded a proper diagnosis of the immediate needs of borrowers. The chapter interrogates allegations of dependency in light of the many structural conditions in contemporary South Sudan, confronts the complicated nature of social interdependence inherent to lending and processes of development, and calls on the reader to rethink the ideal of self-sufficiency.

Chapter 9 is what I call an "Autopsy." It zooms our lens into the 2012 turning point when the Juba microcredit industry was departing from poverty lending in Juba. The autopsy of the crash includes reflections from former members of the sector, describing the culprits in closer detail. The most powerful drivers of the microfinance industry resolved to eschew the hard work of financing the poorest, instead shifting its goalposts toward institutional sustainability and profits. Ultimately, the chapter shows how the MFIs were beholden to their own internal systemic dependencies, including their debt ratings, requirements from headquarters, and problematic metrics for success.

And lastly, in the Conclusion I close the book by summarizing what unfolded in Juba microcredit, highlighting the sector's departure from its initial intention to finance the poorest members of society. The chapter recommends what practitioners can do to avert the problems we saw in Juba. Tailoring programming to local circumstance is the key, and the chapter outlines some specific strategies for this based on the lessons learned in the text. For microcredit to achieve its goal of getting capital to the poor, it needs to let go of the black-and-white, charity versus banking binary it finds itself in. Microcredit needs to go gray. The book closes with a call for transparency in order to better inform donors and investors about the variety of microcredit they are funding. Finally, I advocate filling the gap in subsidized grant funds to make the loans affordable, responsive, and effective in challenging post-conflict settings.

PRIOR PRESCRIPTIONS FOR SOUTH SUDAN

For many decades, the odds have been stacked against what is now South Sudan—the youngest country on earth—but in 2005, people all over the world began to see hope. It was then that the north and south ceased civil war and Southern Sudan was granted semi-autonomy and then an opportunity to become an independent state six years later. This marked the start of a new era. But the "new peace," a refrain heard often around town at the time, was not a blank slate for South Sudan. The disconnection between planned recovery efforts by people in power and more locally directed approaches created a reality where even the best strategies seldom saw the fruition they intended. Citizens, subject to state prescriptions for centuries, responded with creativity and resistance.

Many challenges for South Sudan were products of political or economic factors, but others originated in sheer geography. Landlocked between Republic of the Sudan, Ethiopia, Kenya, Uganda, Democratic Republic of the Congo, and Central African Republic, South Sudan faced several obstacles to development vis-à-vis its sometimes-tense relationships with neighboring countries and difficulties reaching global markets.

Prospects for South Sudan now rest on shoddy foundations that were formed even before the colonial period. Historian Douglas Johnson attributed the beginning of the North-South disparities in the state to the Turco-Egyptian regime in the eighteenth century. Southern economies did not develop at the same pace as the north when "the dramatic expansion of slave-raiding and slave-owning" began to take effect.[2] Egyptian powers controlled Sudan intermittently during the western "Scramble for Africa." This was especially significant in the 1880s, when Egypt's struggling political system met the Mahdist Islamic Sudanese regime. Millions of civilians died in famine and in war; the economy was decimated. In 1899, a young Winston Churchill wrote one of the most famous accounts of this period in his *The River War: An Historical Account of the Reconquest of the Soudan*. He argued that Egyptian rule of the Sudan "was not kindly, wise, nor profitable. Its aim was to exploit, not to improve the local population. The miseries of the people were aggravated rather than lessened: but they were concealed."[3]

It is unsurprising that Churchill's account of late nineteenth-century Sudan focused on justifying, even encouraging, Britain to step in and "give peace to warring tribes, to administer justice where all was violence, to strike the chains off the slave, to draw the richness from the soil, to plant the earliest seeds of commerce and learning, to increase in whole peoples their capacities for pleasure and diminish their chances of pain."[4] "What an enterprise," he wrote, "that an enlightened community may attempt is more noble and more profitable than the reclamation from barbarism of fertile regions."

Churchill was not alone in painting the Sudanese people as backward. Pre-colonial accounts almost universally described the region's indigenous economies as fundamentally different from the pro-merchant *ethos* spreading down from Europe. Kuir Garang has criticized the ways in which the South Sudanese ideas have been "historically downplayed" and "projected as uncultured and uncivilized."[5] This tale of backwardness elicited intervention by outsiders time and again throughout the region's history.

The Anglo-Egyptian Sudan administered by both the UK and Egypt (1899–1956) created social divisions that have endured into the present day. British administrators used ethnic, religious, and linguistic differences between the north and south to justify treatment of the two regions as separate colonies. By 1930, this was formalized into the Southern Policy.

The south was the loser in almost every contest during the colonial era, and its inhabitants did not always comply with rules handed down to them. In 1922, colonial governors forbade merchants from traveling to the south. Residents profited from the cash exports of beeswax, honey, ivory, tobacco, and coffee only if they did business with illegal non-Sudanese traders.[6] Another folly, known as the Zande Cotton Scheme, began in 1946, when the "insatiable postwar demand for cotton" created a surge in profits for the Sudanese governments.[7] This inspired administrators to move 50,000 Azande from their villages in today's southwestern South Sudan into artificial towns like Torit to harvest and spin cotton. While the scheme was profitable in the short term for the administrators, Azande people themselves did not prosper. Their preference for the agrarian way of life, coupled with unsatisfactory pay, eventually provoked mass riots.[8]

The South Sudanese have both resisted and adopted new, imported economic traditions. E. E. Evans-Pritchard described social organization and exchange in his 1930s ethnography of Nuer in South Sudan, a cornerstone piece of anthropology.[9] He portrayed a society whose economy revolved around the inherited cattle wealth and transfer of brides. Few Nuer, he wrote, "understood the concept of currency; fewer still understood the impersonal principles of market exchange; and literally no one parted willingly with a cow for money." Occasional exchanges with Arab merchants worked, even though they were characterized as gift giving that created a sense of obligation to reciprocate. The process included "no idea of price and currency in our sense" but rather connoted spiritual values of ransom and sacrifice.[10]

As colonial rule was coming to an end, administrators reported opposition in the south to Islamic governance. British officials were said to have considered creating separate governments for northern and southern provinces, however the consensus of British and Sudanese delegates at the 1947 Juba Conference was that the south was too "weak" and "backward" to govern itself.[11] Instead, the British-led Conference announced that north and south would become one state, governed by an administration in the north.

Meeting minutes, confidential at the time, explained:

> The main consideration is that the Sudan, though a vast country in area, is small in wealth and population, and if the Sudan is ever really to become self-governing and self-dependent it must not be divided up into small weak units. Those who prepared the report believe that the sooner Southern and Northern Sudanese come together and work together, the sooner they will begin to coalesce and cooperate in the advancement of their country. This belief is sincerely and genuinely held by many Northern Sudanese, and they hope that by including Southern Sudanese in the future Assembly, the process of unification will be hastened. I am confident that their recommendations are based on the very highest motives, and think they do not seek opportunities of exploiting backward tribes in the South.[12]

The beginning of post-colonial Sudan entailed so stark a southern disadvantage that war began almost immediately. In 1953, southerners held only four of 800 seats in the legislature and by independence in 1956, the self-governance clauses that southern representatives had demanded as a condition for a unified Sudan were absent from the constitution. The subsequent First Sudanese Civil War lasted fifteen years and ended with the recognition of some southern autonomy. Though considerably less than the federal autonomy the Southern Sudan Liberation Movement sought, the south became the Southern Regional Government with the signing of the 1972 Addis Ababa Agreement. The Regional Assembly could request, but not ensure, southern exemptions from legislation contrary to regional desires.[13]

Increased security in the interwar period (1972–1983) opened new trade networks. Cattle epidemics and food shortages gave rise to the rapid development of trade circuits, namely hide exports for grain imports.[14] This period, wrote Sharon Hutchinson, marked the broader Southern acceptance of new ways of "earning": cattle could be purchased with cash rather than inherited, wage labor could be attained outside of the region (most often in Khartoum), and token gifts like bright clothing could be used for bride-wealth purchases.[15] With external influences came not only new economic patterns but also new vocabulary used to describe, frame, and conceptualize them. Whereas Evans-Pritchard in 1956 described that there was just a single verb to signify both the acts of buying and selling in many Nilotic languages,[16] Hutchinson observed that by the 1980s, the acts of buying and selling, for example, were linguistically distinct.[17]

The Second Sudanese Civil War started in 1983 in response to President Gafaar Nimiery[18] putting *Shari'a* Law into effect in both the north and south. This law defied the limited southern autonomy that had been established with the Addis Ababa Agreement. When Omar al-Bashir and his officers gained control of Khartoum in 1989, they aimed to build a "New Sudan" organized by Islam, by the *Shari'a* as interpreted by the National Islamic Front, and by the Arabic language. John Garang was leading the Sudanese People's Liberation Movement (SPLM) in a fight for a single democratic Sudan, but the SPLM members largely aimed for self-determination or an independent state. After a decade of factionalism, Garang and the SPLM eventually coalesced on the ideal of southern self-determination.

The Second Sudanese Civil War halted many of the interwar transformations of the southern economy. Rural territories in the region were abandoned, and tense relations with northerners further curtailed trading. Military planes coming through Khartoum were necessary to deliver goods from outside the south, and most goods were sold to those affiliated with the Sudanese government. Rarely did imports reach those without contacts or living in rural areas. Costs fluctuated greatly through the mid-1990s until transnational NGOs began to deliver goods and pay their employees in kind. Prices soon steadied as a result of this, and local "peace markets" emerged, as in Bahr el Gazal, a large town near the northern border, and stimulated small-scale localized trade.[19] Any economic stimuli that appeared during the conflict periods, furthermore, were sporadic as it depended greatly on outside factors.

One local fixture is worth mentioning: the biscuit is now ubiquitous in South Sudan. You can find biscuits anywhere—from the fancy air-conditioned Indian-owned supermarkets to the smallest of cardboard trays held by hawkers on rural village roadsides. The least-hospitable tea server would be reprimanded if they offer tea without sugar, but the second-worst offense is to serve tea without a biscuit. Servers are asked for the "companion," should they forget. This sweet snack was first integrated into the diet in South Sudan with the arrival of colonizing Britons devoted to afternoon "tea time," and is an emblem of market society transformation. The biscuit is one of many material objects Sudanese residents appropriated and adapted for themselves, applying new cultural meanings in the process. Shifts like these regularly occur not only in physical form but also in language use and nonverbal customs, in order to effectively communicate. In times of transformation, communities use objects and symbols functionally. Commodities, ideologies, labels, and behaviors appropriate the past into the new present so as to satisfy desires. Their endurance through transitions demonstrates that the appropriators find the thing—the vocabulary, the commodity, and so on—worth co-opting for some purpose. However, and as this story will show, the ways these processes are negotiated largely depends on the actors involved and the resources available to them.

JUBA'S NEW PEACE

On January 9, 2005, the Comprehensive Peace Agreement (CPA)[20] between the Government of National Unity in Khartoum and the Sudan People's Liberation Movement in the south was signed. This came after the second north-south civil war that had begun in 1983 had claimed the lives of over two million civilians, and exiled four million Southerners to Uganda, Ethiopia, Kenya, Democratic Republic of the Congo, Central African Republic, and Egypt.[21] The CPA was a commitment to "the right of the people of Southern Sudan to self-determination" through democratic governance of the country that "is founded on the values of justice, democracy, good governance, respect for the fundamental rights and freedoms of the individual, mutual understanding and tolerance of diversity within Sudan as a whole."[22] The Government of South Sudan was established with an interim constitution signed that December, making Juba the capital of Southern Sudan.[23] The signing of the CPA marked the beginning of a remarkable transformation.

The Republic of South Sudan was established in 2011 with a referendum supported by over 98 percent of the population. The title of James Copnall's 2014 book, *A Poisonous Thorn in Our Hearts: Sudan and South Sudan's Bitter and Incomplete Divorce*, says a lot about the ongoing challenges. The economic outlook for South Sudan places it behind the north and further behind most of the world, however if you were to walk the aisles of the markets today, what you would see is perhaps more meaningful, and more hopeful, to the South Sudanese than anything written in grim headlines. Markets now carry trinkets that are not desperately needed. Vegetables in every hue of the rainbow traveled long journeys to be there. You might hear laughter in dozens of languages. Despite the evident shortcomings, there are new prospects for opportunity for the many of those who call post-conflict Juba home.

Defining the post-conflict period can be difficult, even when there are clear indications that hostilities have ceased. In this text, the post-conflict period refers to 2005–2013. This is from when South Sudan signed a peace agreement with the North in 2005, until late 2013 when internal conflict ignited the South. That another conflict followed the Sudanese Civil War complicates the usage of the post-conflict term here. Data collection for this text took place in Juba during this period while the microcredit sector existed and through its disappearance in 2012. My last visit focused on gathering field level information for this project was in the summer of 2013. It is important to note that the conflict that began in December 2013 was *after* the MFI doors were shut. Historians might be tempted to write off the MFI failures as a consequence of the new, internal conflict: that would be historically inaccurate. Nevertheless,

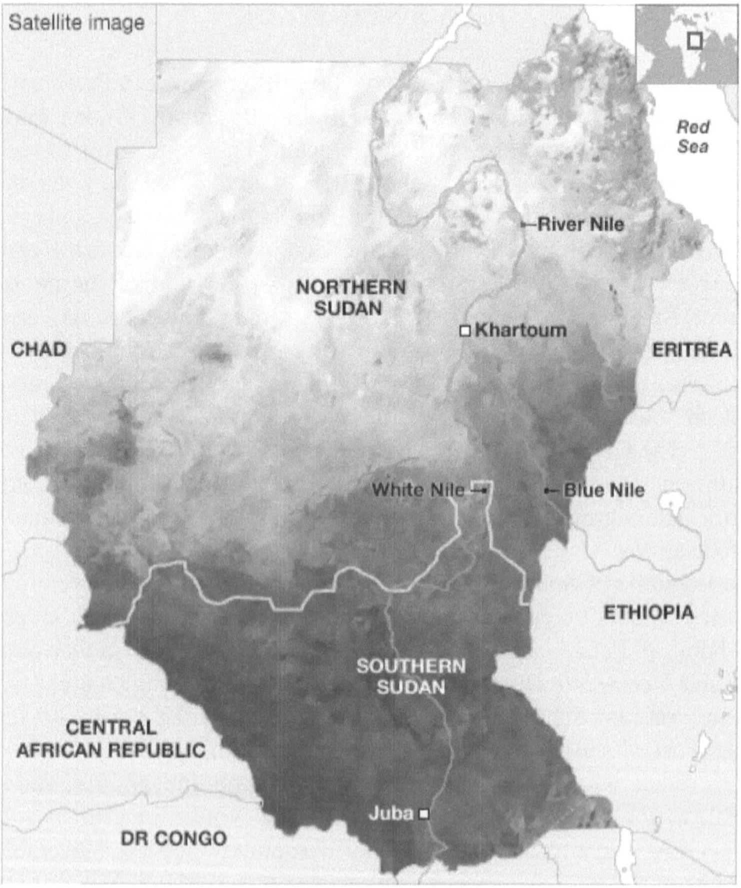

Figure I.1 Map of Sudan with 2005–2011 Boundaries. *Source:* BBC, "South Sudan Country Profile." (2011).

when I use the term "post-conflict" to describe the social or economic context in South Sudan during that period, the definition requires some further finesse.

Any post-conflict venue has a number of features—social, economic, political, and others—that shape it. Several factors that have been observed to characterize post-conflict economies both at the local and at national levels include the following: lost lives, lost livelihoods, lost human capital, lost income, broken or altogether lost political institutions, little rule of law, devastated industry and physical infrastructure, and fractured social capital. Importantly, the specific measures of these losses vary substantially from one conflict to the next, and some people experience gains from certain conflicts. For instance, though both classify as post-conflict, a low-income country like

Liberia experiences the legacy of war in a different way than a middle-income country like Serbia does. Several factors moderate a post-conflict economy.[24] These include the duration and intensity of the conflict, the degree to which institutions and infrastructure were destroyed (and how long they had existed prior to the conflict), how and whether citizens were able to endure the conflict locally or abandon the area, whether the state had abundant resources (curses of mismanaged environmental abundance or degradation), and so on. Of course, war causes significant changes in the structure of the economy. Though there may be major reductions in certain industries, there may also be production increases in specific, informal, and sometimes even illicit activities.[25] It also transforms political institutions.[26] While it is not possible to trace every shift as a direct response to the conflict, the opportunities created by war—and the end of war—are often clear.

To simplify this very complex matter, when I use the adjective "post-conflict" in this text to describe some part of the story in South Sudan, I do not intend to address all of the possible ramifications of the transition toward peace, but rather to highlight some noticeable experiences of the larger Juba community. This includes the different ways that people described problems based on where they were during war, what they expected Juba to be like on their return, and what they believed was influencing their living conditions.

This text uses a grounded definition of the post-conflict. Instead of matching what features were observable in South Sudan against one of many available preexisting frameworks, I draw on the features described to me by participants throughout my fieldwork for further analysis. Accordingly, this definition of post-conflict is centered on the Juba experience of post-conflict, and these categories will be elaborated upon throughout the text. Some of these elements serve as background context, whereas others, as will be shown, were seen as the orienting analytical features of what occurred with the microcredit industry. The four main types of relevant post-conflict features that the local residents reported, and I witnessed first-hand, are as follows:

- The demographic disruption associated with the return of refugees, internally displaced persons, capitalists, and aid workers hailing from fragmented social networks created largely outside the country during the conflict;
- The institutional changes associated with nascent state and local governance, nascent legal frameworks, and reliance on international actors for social services;
- The high costs associated with rebuilding deteriorated physical infrastructure, including buildings and accessible roads;
- The unequal access to resources and opportunity among Juba citizens.

The peace agreement meant large population flows into the South. People returned to South Sudan by taking advantage of a variety of initiatives when possible. A year after the signing of the peace agreement, the United Nations High Commissioner for Refugees (UNHCR) transported the first official Sudanese repatriation convoy of refugees from Kenya, beginning a period of voluntary repatriation to South Sudan. Between the 2005 signing and 2009, the International Organization for Migration (IOM) estimated that North-South and South-South return movements had transported almost two million people.[27] About 10 percent of returns were organized with UNHCR, the Government of National Unity, and the Government of Southern Sudan. The remainder of repatriates residing around regional urban centers, such as Khartoum, Nairobi, and Kampala, returned largely by their own means, or what the IOM categorized as "spontaneous" returns.[28]

By the 2008 Population and Housing Census of Sudan, there were 8.26 million residents in Southern Sudan;[29] however, those figures were hotly contested in light of the impending vote on southern independence. The Southern Sudan Assembly Resolution No. 95/2008 complained that Khartoum's central bureau of statistics refused to share the raw census data. The results indicated surges in northern regions such as Darfur and included Southern internally displaced persons. The Government of Southern Sudan resolved "to totally reject the Sudan fifth population and housing census results of 2008 which shall be null and void and shall not be used for any national planning whatsoever, least of all 2010 national and 2011 referendum."[30]

Despite this disagreement, South Sudan's population undeniably grew after the CPA, especially in the capital city of Juba. Juba and its surrounding southern *payams* (local districts) had been sparsely inhabited during the Second Sudanese Civil War; only between 50 and 150 thousand people lived in all the southern territories.[31] After the first census was taken in 2008, there was an average annual population growth rate of 4.3 percent. There was another population surge with the 2011 independence. In the two years after independence, Juba's population was estimated to have more than doubled. As this book goes to press, South Sudan's population is estimated to be 11.3 million.[32]

From certain vantages, the economy steadily improved since the late 1990s. Sudan underwent growth in the interwar period and a boom into the new, relatively more peaceful millennium. Capital and earnings poured into the country at rates comparable to more economically powerful counties such as India, Kenya, and Senegal. Average income in Sudan was twice as high as those of Benin and Bangladesh. In the years following the CPA, it rose and almost always remained over the thousand-dollar-per-annum mark (Figure I.2).

Quantifying historical conditions in South Sudan remains challenging because the country-level data is obscured by data from territories that have changed over time. In other words, data from the World Bank and Population Reference Bureau are arranged by country, and do not distinguish the southern particularities including conflicts fought in the south, the effects of industry, and the impacts of infrastructure decimation. Furthermore, the data covering South Sudan alone reference only a few years in time.

State-level figures that aim to describe South Sudanese livelihoods can shroud as much as they reveal.[33] Although we have combined data for the bulk of their histories, there is only a small window (2008–2013) through which we can view Sudan and South Sudan separately in terms of gross domestic product (GDP). Sudan GDP remained fairly consistent and experienced some growth during the post-conflict period. On the other hand, South Sudan GDP per capita virtually halved the year after independence, from $1,814 down to $957, then began to recover in the following year (Figure I.3).

Why were poverty-reduction interventions rolled out when South Sudan GDP was triple the "dollar per day"[34] metric definition of poverty? GDP figures smooth average incomes across those that reaped the most from oil

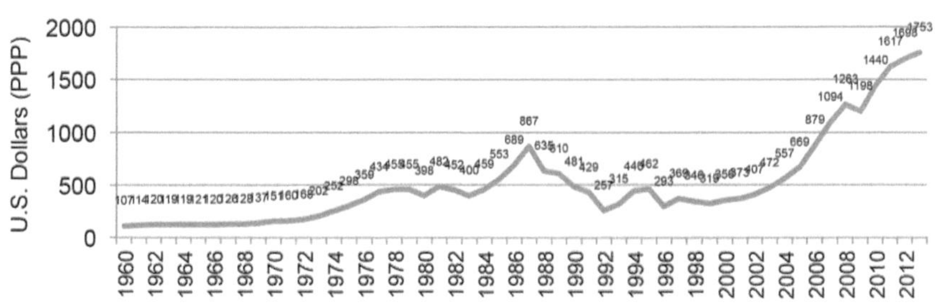

Figure I.2 Sudan GDP Per Capita, 1960–2013 (PPP). *Source:* Data from World Bank, "World Bank Open Data." (2014). GDP Per Capita, considering Purchasing Power Parity.

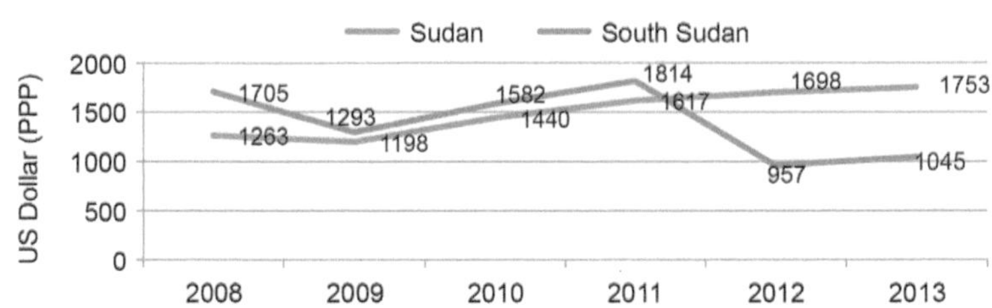

Figure I.3 Sudan and South Sudan GDP Per Capita, 2008–2013. *Source:* Data from World Bank, "World Bank Open Data." (2014).

revenue (to the order of millions and billions).[35] More than half of the country was living below the poverty line.[36]

South Sudan's population experiences significant rates of inequality. Its Gini Coefficient, the measure of income distribution deviation among individuals within a country, was 45.5 in 2013.[37] (Whereas a Gini score of zero represents total equality among members of a given society, 100 represents total inequality among the population.) In 2013 South Sudanese income inequality was comparable to Qatar, Malaysia, and Kenya. This was substantially more unequal than places whose inequalities are renowned like China (37) and India (33.6) but quite less than South Africa (65.5). The substantial income disparity in post-conflict South Sudan was apparent to the naked eye. It was home to millionaires driving Hummers and extremely poor people struggling to stay alive.

The most commonly cited explanation for such high inequality in South Sudan involves oil, both a resource blessing and a curse. Newfound crude oil exports contributed greatly to South Sudan's economic expansion starting in 1999, however other sources of income did not follow suit. In 2015, the World Bank thus deemed South Sudan the most oil-dependent country on earth; oil comprised 60 percent of its GDP and virtually all of its exports.[38] However, the majority of the population did not participate in the oil industry. This scenario is often called a resource curse—when economies with abundant resources paradoxically plummet; they are commonly explained as occurring when the spoils are distributed unevenly.[39] This theory assumes that the state is the primary mechanism for producing inequality, among other precarious suppositions.[40] Nevertheless, it is safe to say that in South Sudan, the state did not use the money for much that directly enhanced the economic capacity of its average citizen.

South Sudan gained access to a share of the oil revenue as mandated by the CPA in the early part of 2006. Once this happened, the south earned revenue from the north on the sales of oil through its pipeline linking reserves to the global market. Those who ran refineries earned income directly from petroleum sales and reaped in the benefits. A handful of multinational firms also profited by helping transport, refine, and export its share of the oil. The oil revenue from the Machakos protocol was delivered straight to the SPLM government, but the revenue went mostly to Government of South Sudan (GOSS) employees and security personnel.[41] That left the rest of the population without.

Survivors of the civil wars were not entirely without skills or capital, but were still experiencing the devastating effects of wars. By 2009, just over a quarter of the population aged fifteen and above was literate. Only 16 percent of the overall female population was literate—among the lowest levels in the world.[42] Men that had trained for military service were stereotyped as avoiding other employment, but jobs were not easy to come by. Eighty-five percent of the working population engaged in non-wage work, mostly (78 percent) in agriculture, which accounted for just 15 percent of the country's output.[43] Those who idealized cattle herding, agriculture, or private enterprise had little means to do so with any profitable outcome. Capital was scarce.

ECONOMIC LIFE IN THE NEW SOUTH SUDAN

Establishing a state is no small task. The GOSS was hampered by its national priorities. Some 40 percent of the national budget was spent on its public sector and a "vast and growing army," which only accounted for 8 percent of the GDP.[44] In light of this, several countries, multilateral organizations, and NGOs stepped in to fill the void in social services.[45] Total assistance to South Sudan was an estimated US $1.6 billion annually, and external assistance came out to more than 15 percent of South Sudan's total GDP, and close to half all government revenues. In 2012, the largest donor states included the United States (US $472 million), followed by the United Kingdom (US $96 million) and Sweden (US $47 million).[46] The Multi-Donor Trust Fund South, which pooled funds from the Netherlands, Norway, United Kingdom, European Commission, Sweden, Germany, Denmark, Finland, Italy, Iceland, Greece, Canada, Spain, and Egypt, allocated over US $100 million per year after the CPA signing.

Through all of this, South Sudan received roughly $100 in aid per capita, yet people were still struggling.[47] The reason for this was that not everyone had the same idea about the best ways to spend it.

In Juba, local government agencies as well as multilateral, NGOs worked to stimulate business and smoothen the economy through the transition into sovereignty. Urban planning efforts in Juba were implemented to establish marketplaces in recent years, but illustrated the old adage against "too many cooks in the kitchen." Several areas were designated for markets around the town, but it quickly became overly populated and traffic-filled. To relieve the pressure, planners expanded roads by demolishing several major trading posts. This put vendors in very difficult positions. The 2008 thoroughfare construction project, for instance, resulted in last-minute evictions of vendors from their places of business. In response to the evictions, vendors had to make choices about where to work next, and with whom.

Cultural diversity in Juba meant residents were constantly navigating different social and economic systems. The south is comprised of over sixty groups and cultures, each having unique values pertaining to economic life. Dinka is the dominant ethnic group, numbering over a million. Nuer comprises the second-largest distinctive group, and then the smaller groups include Shilluk, Bari, Luo, Zande, and Madi. Each of these groups had distinctive customs that related to appropriate ways of transacting, as well as a rich network of people they trusted and with whom they did business.

This is not to say that ethnic relationships formed within these networks were the most important or even most salient when discussing market life. Ethnic groups were salient for life, for language, for the assumptions that one can make when meeting, greeting, sharing, or hosting for any South Sudanese. But none of the South Sudanese encompassed singular identities. These ethnic relations or networks overlapped with many other types of relations or networks. Networks created by displacement both inside and outside the country were, for many purposes, far more influential for daily life than ethnicity.

Language, for instance, impacts people's prospects in all kinds of interactions. Although South Sudan's official language is English, much business throughout the country is done in Juba Arabic, a regional vernacular, as a majority of the population was raised with Arabic as the *lingua franca*. But South Sudanese are also commonly fluent in several other languages, including KiSwahili or French, depending on where they were during the war. Additionally, citizens of South Sudan almost always speak a national mother tongue from where they hail. Over seventy languages are spoken today in South Sudan.[48]

The knowledge of several languages fosters communication efficacy and creates opportunities for the South Sudanese. All languages are valuable for citizens; likewise, while people have personal relationships with the different languages they use, they privilege none. Rather, they choose to speak the language that is the most effective to communicate, given a specific context. At the end of the civil war, Juba markets were swarmed with multilingual buyers and sellers engaged in code switching, navigating the economic systems, and negotiating across multiple languages—some of which were only recently acquired in exile.

Everyone came to Juba after the war with different resources and aspirations. Those who underwent "organized return," including people from Internally Displaced People camps, received targeted assistance upon arrival. Another segment elected to return to their homeland on their own and arrived without sponsorship. A 2009 report by the IOM described how locating the "spontaneous" returnees, "posed one of the greatest challenges to the international community and authorities aiming to support this massive population movement."[49] In either case, South Sudanese were returning to a "home" they never knew, or at least one they did not recognize, as it was vastly different from the one they had left two decades earlier. Either way, repatriates faced a new economy they needed to negotiate in; even those who remained in town faced a new economic landscape to navigate due to the newcomers, the international organizations aiming to facilitate peace operations, and the consequential market changes.

South Sudan's "high-risk, high-reward" atmosphere presented great prospects for investors in a place that, as one journalist pointed out, "needs everything."[50] Business soared in southern "virgin business towns," while Juba was labeled a "boom town" by East African news sources that encouraged Ugandans, Somalis, Ethiopians and Congolese to seize investment opportunities in the region.[51] Despite being low-ranked on the World Bank's "ease of doing business" scale (159th among 183 economies),[52] prospects were endless for tenacious businesspeople. The housing needed construction and the roads needed paving. Not only were imported supplies required for these projects but also food for all those doing the jobs. "This was cowboy capitalism in its rawest state, unfettered by well-established rules, taxes, or insurance policies," read a Boston Globe article in 2013.[53]

But international systems created obstacles for entrepreneurs. Economic sanctions on Sudan from the west—for humanitarian violations including the alleged harboring of terrorists by the north—limited access to the goods required to nurture growth in the south during the Interim Period (2005–2011) between the CPA and independence. Once South Sudan gained independence, it was freed from almost all international sanctions on Sudan. The United States, for example, authorized oil and technology industry activities in the South by December of its first year as a nation.[54]

Nascent markets also meant low levels of domestic production. Thus, South Sudan relied greatly on imports from neighboring countries. Traders thus played an important role in the local economy. Cleophas Lado once described the "polyopoly" of the *Jebella* traders as the "absolute masters of the political economy of scarcity." The cash crops they traded created "unprecedented opportunities for capital accumulation and consequently unequal gain among members of society."[55] Traders with *lorries*—trucks—continued reaping significant profits in this distressed context, while those without lorries paid dearly. The poor in Juba who did not own some means of production were largely relegated to importing goods for retail.

The need for trading across borders made currency exchange an inevitable problem, as money transfer was an integral part of the process of buying and selling. Cross-border currency prices thus became one of the biggest challenges for anybody doing business in Juba. Those who managed to get their hands on US dollars had stability against the vast fluctuations in South Sudanese Pound values.[56] The pound's value against the USD, for example, rose from 2.09 in December of 2008 to 7.2 in March of 2015.[57] Devaluation benefitted investors, but strangled residents who relied on—now costlier—imports for most goods. And even while many savvy South Sudanese navigated between currencies with ease, another problem lurked beneath the surface, which cost many others: the black market for currency.

Finance Minister Aggrey Tisa Sabuni complained that the black market originally evolved because foreign currency was "insufficient to satisfy demand."[58] Others blamed the short supply of foreign currency on corruption committed by officials and foreign-exchange managers.[59] Dollars from central bank reserves were reported missing, and officials were accused of selling their reserves early onto the black market.[60] For many, this black market was a symbol of broken promises in South Sudan.

Currencies were also not trusted. To explain this, I will share one of my personal experiences with currency exchange. In 2008, I sought to change Uganda shillings to either US dollars or Sudanese pounds because those were the only two currencies accepted by my hotel manager. I went to a small foreign exchange bureau building right in the center of town with signboards reading, "BUY" and "SELL" just like those seen at international airports. The teller said she could not exchange in "that way." In other words, she could have exchanged from pound to dollar, or dollar to pound, or several other options, but not from *shilling* to dollar or pound. Without saying it explicitly, the reason was simply that she could not buy Uganda shillings at a profitable rate. So, she sent me to the "bus park." (I learned later that the forex[61] traders with the best rates were invisible to the untrained eye.) I followed directions to a row of vendors sitting under rainbow umbrellas, covered in red dust, adjacent to an empty garbage dump. Each vendor had behind him a crate or small table, upon which sat an open-backed clear box filled with stacks of various monies. Several vendors' umbrellas shaded friends who were keeping them company.

After approaching several tables, a Kenyan friend of mine identified one that appeared "somehow good"—in other words, the best option. I ended up at Kampala Coach bus station offices. The traders were Buganda bus operators from central Uganda. The units of math between the currencies were dissimilar, and thus the math involved was quite complicated. After some confusion with my own calculations (too many thousands), I left with a 1.2 pound: 1 shilling rate. My one million Uganda shillings (roughly 500 US dollars) became 1,200 pounds. Each of the five men surrounding the stall counted the stack, passing the money between his hands twice to verify the amount. Ten others watched from afar. Compared to International Exchange rates, I lost about 20 cents on the dollar, or a sum of 88 dollars total through the exchange. I may have lost 20 cents on the dollar, but that is nothing compared to what people in South Sudan lost in the war and the failed aid policies thereon after.

This book will take readers through the insider, outsider, and observer perspectives of the South Sudanese microcredit endeavor. What you will probably find is that all the failings were in many ways predictable. Each group we examine had a history, a culture, and a logic all of their own. The surprises appear when we compare expectations across the different actors: what planners expected from practitioners, what practitioners expected from borrowers, and what borrowers expected to gain from participating. We learn that flashpoints of dissonance arose not only from the cultural differences between the outsiders and the insiders, but from dynamics internal to the international organizations, and internal to the process of making and receiving microcredit on the ground in post-conflict South Sudan. The differences in viewpoints and expectations created practical limitations. With this resulting friction, not everyone had the same power to devise accords.

NOTES

1. The term "microfinance" can include the use of various financial instruments—including savings and insurance—that target the poor. While much work has been done to promote and study varieties of microfinance, the providers of microcredit in Juba were primarily (if not exclusively) in the business of lending. Thus this book focuses on *microcredit*, which is the borrowing instrument.

2. Douglas H. Johnson, *The Root Causes of Sudan's Civil Wars: Peace or Truce* (Kampala: Fountain Publishers/James Currey, 2011), 4–5.

3. Winston Churchill, *The River War: An Historical Account of the Reconquest of the Soudan* (London: Longmans, Green & Co, 1900), 20.

4. Winston Churchill, *The River War: An Historical Account of the Reconquest of the Soudan* (London: Longmans, Green & Co, 1900), 19.

5. Kuir ë Garang, *South Sudan Ideologically: Tribal Socio-Democracy, SPLM Ideologues, Juba Corruptocrats, Khartoum Theocrats and their Time-Frozen Leadership* (Calgary: The Nile Press, 2013), 5.

6. Douglas H. Johnson, *The Root Causes of Sudan's Civil Wars: Peace or Truce* (Kampala: Fountain Publishers/James Currey, 2011).

7. Robert O. Collins, *A History of Modern Sudan* (Cambridge: Cambridge University Press, 2008), 60.

8. Cleophas Lado, "Some Aspects of Rural Marketing Systems and Peasant Farming in Maridi District, Southern Sudan." *Transactions of the Institute of British Geographers* (1988), 364.

9. Edward Evan Evans-Pritchard, *The Nuer: A Description of the Modes of Livelihood and Political Institutions of a Nilotic People* (Oxford and New York: Oxford University Press, 1940), 1969.

10. E. E. Evans-Pritchard, *Nuer Religion* (Oxford: Oxford University Press, 1956), 221–224.

11. Kenneth Okeny, "The 1947 Juba Conference." *Northeast African Studies* 13, no. 1 (1991), 47, wrote that the decision to create a single Sudan was already decided in 1946 "without consulting Southern opinion, the Administration reversed

its Southern Policy and began instead to implement a policy of uniting the North and the South. However, not all British officials in the South supported the move; so to avoid embarrassment, the Civil Secretary convened a conference in Juba in June 1947 to ascertain the views of Southerners."

12. B. V. Marwood, "Juba Conference 1947 Conference Recordings." (1947).

13. See Johnson 2011 analysis of Minutes of Conference on the Southern Sudan held in Addis Ababa between Sudan Government and Southern Liberation Movement, 1972.

14. S. E. Hutchinson, *Nuer Dilemmas: Coping with Money, War and the State* (Berkeley and Los Angeles: University of California Press, 1996), 64.

15. Although these were variously adopted by western and eastern Nuer.

16. Edward Evans Evans-Pritchard, *Nuer Religion* (Oxford: Oxford University Press, 1956), 221–224.

17. S. E. Hutchinson, *Nuer Dilemmas: Coping with Money, War and the State* (Berkeley and Los Angeles: University of California Press, 1996), 59.

18. Also transliterated *Nimeri.*

19. USAID, *A Guide to Economic Growth in Post-Conflict Countries.* Office of Economic Growth, Agriculture and Trade. (Washington, DC 2009).

20. Also called the Nairobi Comprehensive Peace Agreement.

21. JAM Sudan, *The Report of the Sudan Joint Assessment Mission (JAM): Framework for Sustained Peace, Development and Poverty Eradication* (March 2005).

22. Government of the Republic of Sudan and the Sudan People's Liberation Movement. *Chapeau of the Comprehensive Peace Agreement* (New York: United Nations Peacemaker, 2004).

23. Between 2005 and July 2011, also known as the Interim period, the region was called Southern Sudan and its government, the Government of Southern Sudan.

24. See Michael Pugh, "The Political Economy of Peacebuilding." *International Journal of Peacebuilding* 10, no. 2 (2005). Michael Pugh, Mandy Turner, and Neil Cooper, *Whose Peace?: Critical Perspectives on the Political Economy of Peacebuilding* (Critical Perspectives on the Political Economy of Peacebuilding) (Palgrave Macmillan UK, 2008).

25. Frances Stewart and Valpy FitzGerald, "Introduction: Assessing the Economic Costs of War." In *War and Underdevelopment*, edited by Frances Stewart, Valpy FitzGerald, and Associates (Oxford: Oxford University Press, 2001).

26. See James K. Boyce and Madalene O'Donnell, *Peace and the Public Purse: Economic Policies for Postwar Statebuilding* (Boulder, CO: Lynne Rienner, 2007).

27. IOM "Sudan Spontaneous Return Tracking Report." (2009), 3.

28. IOM "Sudan Spontaneous Return Tracking Report." (2009).

29. According to Population Census Council. "The 5th Sudan Population and Housing Census" (2008).

30. Isaac Vuni, "South Sudan Parliament Throw Outs census Results." (*Sudan Tribune,* 2009).

31. Population estimates during the war understandably vary. Wiki-census estimated about 80,000 people lived in the south.

32. World Bank, "World Bank Open Data." (2014). GDP Per Capita, considering Purchasing Power Parity.

33. Benaiah Yongo-Bure, *Economic Development of Southern Sudan* (Lanham: University Press of America, 2007).

34. The World Bank changed its definition of the poverty line to $1.25 per day in 2009. See Martin Ravallion et al., *World Bank Economic Review* (2009).

35. See Stiglitz, Sen and Fitoussi, *Mis-Measuring Our Lives: Why GDP Doesn't Add Up* (New York: The New Press, 2010) for a discussion on the shortcomings of GDP.

36. UNDP, "Human Development Reports." UN Development Programme, Income Gini Coefficient (2013).

37. UNDP, "Human Development Reports." UN Development Programme, Income Gini Coefficient (2013).

38. World Bank, "South Sudan Overview." World Bank, South Sudan (2015).

39. See Jeffrey Sachs and Andrew Warner, "Economic Reform and the Process of Global Integration" (1995).

40. Cyril Obi, "Oil as the 'Curse' of Conflict in Africa: Peering through the Smoke and Mirrors." *Review of African Political Economy* (2010). See Michael Watts, "Crude Politics: Life and Death on the Nigerian Oil Fields" (*Niger Delta Economies of Violence Working Paper*, 2009) and Kairn Klieman, "U. S. Oil Companies, The Nigerian Civil War, and the Origins of Opacity in the Nigerian Oil Industry, 1964–1971." *Journal of American History* (2012) for other critiques of the resource curse theory.

41. World Bank, "Sudan at a Glance." World Bank Development Data (2009).

42. World Bank, "World Bank Open Data." World Bank, Data (2014).

43. World Bank, "World Bank Open Data." World Bank, Data (2014).

44. IRIN, *South Sudan: Briefing – Live Without Oil* (Juba: IRIN News, 2012).

45. Refugees International, "South Sudan: Urgent Action Needed to Avert Collapse." Refugees International (2009).

46. Global Humanitarian Assistance, "South Sudan Key Figures 2012" (2014).

47. Bertelsmann Stiftung, *South Sudan Country Report* (Gütersloh: Bertelsmann Stiftung BTI, 2014).

48. Gary F. Simmons and Fennig, Charles D. *Ethnologue: Languages of the World, 20th edition.* (Dallas, Texas: SIL International, 2013).

49. IOM, "Sudan Spontaneous Return Tracking Report" (2009), 3.

50. Farah Stockman, "The Wild West in South Sudan: Cowboy Capitalists Rush into World's Newest Nation, as Locals Struggle—and Politicians Take a Cut." (*The Boston Globe,* 2013).

51. Sudan Tribune, "East Africans Drive Business in 'Boom Town' Juba." (*The Sudan Tribune,* 2006).

52. World Bank, "Project Information Document (PID) Appraisal Stage: *Private Sector Development Project Report* no. AB 6781, (2011).

53. Farah Stockman, "The Wild West in South Sudan: Cowboy Capitalists Rush into World's Newest Nation, as Locals Struggle—and Politicians Take a Cut." (*The Boston Globe,* 2013).

54. OFAC, *South Sudan Sanctions Program* (2012).

55. Cleophas Lado, "Some Aspects of Rural Marketing Systems and Peasant Farming in Maridi District, Southern Sudan." (*Transactions of the Institute of British Geographers,* 1980), 36.

56. Mading Ngor, "South Sudan Pound Rises after Qatari Bank Import Deal." (*Thomson Reuters,* 2012).

57. Trading Economics, "South Sudanese Pound 2008-2014." Trading Economics, South Sudan (2015).

58. P. Moi, "Dual Exchange Rate Privileged a Few – Tisa." (*The New Nation,* 2014).

59. Sandrai Adel, "Devaluation of South Sudanese Pound: A Sound Economic Policy in Unsound Economic Environment." (*The Sudd Institute,* 2013).

60. Radio Tamazuj, "South Sudan Importers Discouraged by Dollar Scarcity." (*Radio Tamazuj*, 2014).

61. "Forex" is a term used to describe foreign currency exchange.

Chapter 1

From a Galaxy Far, Far Away to the Souq

Tracing the neoliberal tradition

"Microfinance has become a buzzword of the decade," wrote Matthew Swibel for Forbes in 2007, "raising the provocative notion that even philanthropy aimed at alleviating poverty can be profitable to institutional and individual investors. Instead of merely writing a check (then writing it off), why not make a tidy profit from a short-term, high-interest loan, most for under $200, so that a Mexican seamstress may buy a new sewing machine?"[1] With or without the motive of making a profit, the idea of microfinance reconciles well with the modern moral, capitalist ideology. Even Jeff Sachs and Bill Easterly, leading public scholars of poverty who see eye-to-eye on almost nothing about how poverty can be solved, have both praised the business of microcredit.

Indeed, since the late 1970s, microfinance outreach has been colossal, with some 3,600 institutions serving more than 210 million clients around the globe—from Bangladesh and India to South Africa and Haiti.[2] Born in Bangladesh, microfinance entered the public limelight in 1996 when David Bornstein's *The Price of a Dream* touted the Grameen Bank innovations based on credit rather than charity. Ten years later, Grameen's founder, Muhammad Yunus, won the Nobel Peace Prize for this game-changing idea. This honor brought further international attention to the economic innovation. Microfinance continued gaining popular support by (especially Western) investors and development practitioners in the developing world.[3]

Microfinance has attained this growth mostly due to its careful and successful framing as a cure-all by appealing to deep-seated ideals held by policymakers, individual donors, and practitioners. It is cast as a powerful, and convenient, alternative to the state-centered, dependence-inducing aid paradigm. Microcredit or microloans are loans made to the enterprising poor. When they function properly, the loans alleviate poverty as individuals borrow, invest, and earn enough to pay back the debt.[4] The poor that receive microloans are not considered "beneficiaries" of the aid industry; they are instead regarded as "clients" of microfinance investors. As long as borrowers are held accountable for repaying borrowed funds, investors can ensure that their clients do not become "lazy" or "dependent." Proponents say this encourages a swift change from "expecting relief" to experiencing "sustainable development."[5] Microfinance helps the needy in the right way according to the ideals of many policymakers, donors, and practitioners and thus sells itself as a solvent business.

HOW DID MICROCREDIT GET TO SOUTH SUDAN?

In the mid-nineteenth century, one of Switzerland's leading businessmen and social activists Henry Dunant began advocating for medical services for wounded soldiers. The nascent International Committee of the Red Cross (ICRC) argued that once wounded or captured (i.e., incapable of fighting), soldiers should be deemed neutral and worthy of receiving help. The ICRC promoted the rights of wounded soldiers and prisoners of war as an issue not of nationality, but of humanity, for the first time on a global scale, opposing references to immobilized soldiers as either friend or foe. So powerful was this idea that in the following year (1864), thirteen countries adopted the first Geneva Convention on those wounded in battle. Originating in the Red Cross's lobbying, these international laws on warfare, the Geneva Conventions and the Hague Laws, still exist today. Early twentieth-century humanitarian strategies tapped into a moral sense public obligation to this new vision of neutral victims. World War I posters repeated compassionate imagery of angelic nurses and catchphrases including, "Do Your Part" and "The Best Mother in the World." Other slogans included "All You Need is a Heart and a Dollar" and "In the Name of Mercy Give!" For over a century, poster advertisements not only asked for monetary donations but also pled for the contributions of knitted socks and more.[6] Since then, kinds of aid and the means of soliciting it have changed significantly.

The twentieth century saw not only the rise of charitable giving but also an increased understanding that charity work can be done well or poorly. Leaders in the field began gearing their work toward the most effective ways to "be humanitarian." Donors in some spaces began growing skeptical of those who provide care. Professionals and scholars chastised others for what economist Abhijit Banerjee referred to as "lazy giving," ignoring the outcomes of charity while thinking "that giving is good and the more money the better." This made it so "one need not think too hard about how the money is spent."[7] In the last decade, economist William Easterly as well as many others has not been shy to decry that, indeed, too many well-intended dollars have been wasted on too few results.[8]

Such began the feverish search for a more thoughtful and responsible approach to helping others around the world. This quest was reminiscent of American philosopher John Dewey's early twentieth-century reflections on philanthropy, elucidating a desire to do the right thing, the right way. Deliberation and thoughtfulness could be the antidote to harmful spending.[9] This desire to combine intelligence with intention, while still promoting the good of others, grew in the Western imagination into the twenty-first century, becoming what professor Ananya Roy called "millennial development"—evoking "the modern, Western self who is not only aware of poverty's devastation but is also empowered to act upon it in responsible ways."[10] It became clear that people who wanted to help had many different ideas about how to do it, and these ideas about the nature of the problems led to widespread trends in attempted solutions. To understand how microcredit became the popularized "cure" to poverty, we must first understand the cultural history of the program architects.

NEOLIBERAL IDEOLOGY IN ECONOMIC DEVELOPMENT

The ideas about giving responsibly that gave rise to microcredit's popularity generally starts with the question of who should help, and then—how. Long-running debates regarding the role of markets in development processes scaffold these questions. When I use the term "neoliberalism" herein, I refer to the broader, culturally ensconced logics that advocate market-based policies. I use the term "neoliberalism" when tracing the recurring ideational features that shape and connect multiple parts of the Juba case; this group of ideas is a major part of the context within which the policymakers and donors operated, as well as the borrowers. Indeed, many others have eloquently disputed the veracity of neoliberalism—either as practice or as a cogent ideology.[11] Few, though, would argue that some overlapping tenets persist and reformulate among various publics and continue to shape real policies. Features of this cultural-ideological neoliberalism transfer through multiple units of analysis in this case. The most pervasive idea among them conjures the "invisible hand" concept taught in Western secondary schools; the notion of equilibrium or an ideal level of sustainability without intervention is key. In this paradigm, the problem of poverty is exacerbated by welfarism, charity, and the like. The ideal solutions can be achieved through individual or possibly social, but never public responsibility. The second stream of ideas is interrelated: the solution for an uneven playing field is a standardized template for economic prosperity that should work for everyone. Third, and also interrelated, is the notion that the problem of poverty is centrally about the absence of capital. Within this third feature is the belief that wealth capital is separate from the social and individual.

Although these debates date far further than a century prior, the more recent, "developmental state" concept serves as a useful entry point to illuminate the context at hand. Mid-twentieth-century development economists posited the notion that less-developed countries were caught in a poverty trap due to "circular and cumulative causation"[12] that could only be broken with a "big push"[13] of highly active state intervention. Those who adopted this school of thought advocated for foreign aid, national financial assistance, and protectionist trade policies to deal with the failures of the market to adequately employ, provide savings opportunities, and offer access to larger markets. Even economist John Maynard Keynes—who generally agreed with the classical view that the market could find the equilibriums of wages, price, and employment—conceded that when market failure does occur, government intervention is required to restore equilibrium (particularly that of full employment). In effect, as Robert Gilpin suggests, this recognized that classical economics did not contain a uniform prescription. Instead, "Keynesianism supported the fundamental assumption of development economics that less developed economies were different from developed economies, and therefore the state should play a central role."[14]

Perhaps the biggest challenge to practicing these ideas appeared with the emergence of the World Bank (WB) and International Monetary Fund (IMF), financial institutions both formed at the end of World War II at Bretton Woods. As the Cold War waged, reform policies that reduced the role of the recipient states became the dominant doctrine guiding international assistance. This doctrine came to be known as the Washington Consensus, which, according to John Williamson, marked the end of an "apartheid which claimed that developing countries came from a different universe" and brought them into the "orthodoxy" of an open, market-based economy and macroeconomic discipline.[15] The Washington Consensus "eventually came to be perceived, at least by its critics, as an overtly ideological effort to impose 'neoliberalism' and 'market fundamentalism' on developing nations."[16] Accordingly, these institutions disbursed Structural Adjustment Policies (SAP), or standardized loans and subsidy packages given directly to the governments of poor countries, conditioned on factors such as the opening of markets and the privatization of industries.

Eventually the Structural Adjustment Policies earned a long list of indictments. Global development expert Nancy Birdsall's thirteen-year study of SAPs in Pakistan offers a superb example of such criticism. In it, she observed that Pakistan had only experienced marginal improvements in certain growth metrics, but had overall undergone stagnation and even a decline in social indicators—like education enrollment rates—during and after the implementation of structural adjustment policies.[17] Walden Bello described how "adjusted and readjusted for nearly 20 years, Manila simply could not climb out of a deepening hole," which included its stagnation and destruction of environmental resources.[18] Naomi Klein's declaration that the IMF "shock therapy" in Bolivia instead deepened poverty by leaving hundreds of thousands without jobs, pensions, or social services offers another example.[19]

There were two dominant explanations for the travesty in regions like these. Many claimed that the World Bank and IMF market solutions failed because of corrupt recipient governments. Rent-seeking autocrats, they claimed, did not see to it that the new neoliberal structures positively impacted the lives of their vulnerable populations.[20] State-directed assistance was criticized for being permissive of elite capture[21] and was thought to actually "increase the honey pot to be contested."[22] Indeed, when considering the various types of foreign aid through states, Easterly argues that "bad governments can sabotage even the most well-intentioned aid programs."[23] Even ordinary citizens have thus become distrustful of governments. For instance, 63 percent of Americans strongly disagree with the statement that African governments improve the living conditions of the citizens of Africa.[24] This is because the contemporary Western imaginaries of aid, both at the popular and professional-bureaucratic level, assume African political leaders to be corrupt. Because of this widely adopted mentality, there is a push to avoid governments altogether when attempting to distribute assistance in African regions.

The efficacy of markets themselves has remained the subject of much tumultuous debate among people in the field. The IMF became convinced the SAPs failed not because of the nature of liberal markets, but because their "reforms were uneven and remained incomplete."[25] Economist Joseph Stiglitz suggests a different rationale, contending that the IMF was an instrument of "market fundamentalism" that ignored the science suggesting neoliberalism was not by itself an efficient tool; instead, he pointed out that market imperfections abound and called for intervention accordingly.[26] Whereas the Washington Consensus asserts that markets alone can alleviate poverty, the Post-Washington Consensus recognizes that the failure rests partly with the market model itself, and acknowledges that the unfettered market cannot solve all problems.[27] Practitioners have been less responsive to this explanation.

While the utter faith in markets that had been exhibited in the Washington Consensus was slightly tempered by some policymakers, it lives on with Western publics who enjoy the "winning side" of its effects in their own lives. The seduction of free markets is an ongoing sentiment in Western culture—especially when states that get involved in them seem to do everything wrong, argue Fred Block and Margaret R. Somers.[28] Dani Rodrick has observed this enduring romance as it applies even to among professionals who are crafting policy: "how difficult it is to wean the World Bank's country specialists away from the Washington-Consensus, laundry-list, best-practice approach to reform."[29]

At the turn of the twenty-first century, protests surrounding failure of shock therapy led to the split between IMF and the World Bank under James Wolfensohn.[30] In his *Goodbye Washington Consensus, Hello Washington Confusion?* Rodrik points out how the World Bank 2005 report "Economic Growth in the 1990s: Learning from a Decade of Reform," renounced a one-size-fits-all set of best practices. The report emphasized, with humility, that not all neoliberal reforms are good, and implementing more of them is not necessarily the solution.

But the Wolfensohn contextualization of the "state as the problem" versus the "neoliberal model as the problem" did not settle the debate on how to help the poor. Instead, it focused on bypassing the state for provisioning aid, and unrolling development programs in different ways. On Julia Elyachar's telling, social safety nets devised from the Structural Adjustment Policy fallout pushed the neoliberal rhetoric toward the individual: "A development strategy built around the needs of the people, and based on communities and small enterprises, was believed to be a palliative to the ills that globalization-as-development has wrought."[31] Ben Fine observed a similar enthusiasm over the potential to be found in the "social capital" unit of analysis.[32] In both cases, the penchant for outsourcing the work of development to the poor themselves seemed to be able to skirt the original questions. This logic set the stage for microcredit's role in the World Bank and other development agency agendas.

THE ROOTS OF MORAL INDUSTRIOUSNESS

Theories of poverty on the individual unit of analysis—perceiving economic status to be determined by personal choice—have deep roots in the Western consciousness. Not only did these ideas shape the ways in which humanitarian assistance eventually came to target individuals but they also became a key referent for donors entering into the aid landscape.

The Protestant Reformation was a response to shifts in social understandings brought on by the Renaissance, changes in geo-politics, colonialism, and economics, played out on a broad religious stage. The overarching theological disputes came down to whether or not men and women needed the Catholic Church—including its priests and popes—as mediators to God. Protestantism, in its various manifestations, emphasized that it was personal faith that merited salvation. However (and here is the important part for our inquiry purposes), true faith was marked by good deeds.

The Parable of the Talents, told by Jesus of the Christian faith, was about a rich man who delegated the management of his wealth to three servants. Two wisely invested their money, doubled it, and were rewarded. One, however, received less money than the others, did not invest it, and the master reprimanded him.[33] This example of the servant, who failed because of unwisely burying his coins, was an indictment of negligence, established in contradiction to the virtue of hard work. Later, this story was reinterpreted by largely protestant communities as the virtues of hard work through the means of capitalism. The enduring cultural remnants, transcending the pews, became an important driver of Western capitalism as analyzed by political economist Max Weber in *The Protestant Ethic and the Spirit of Capitalism.*[34]

In his 1630 sermon, "A Model of Christian Charity," John Winthrop characterized charity as first a mandate to be an industrious capitalist capable of earning and providing for oneself. He describes one who neglects charity as "worse than an infidel who through his own sloth and voluptuousness shall neglect to provide for his family." In other words, excess should be given or lent to the poor. This anti-sloth prescription was intended for the rich, not the poor, but over time, the mindset shifted. The Protestant work ethic, centered on industriousness, spread as an expectation of virtually all economic classes. Weber marks the shift as occurring at the end of the seventeenth century, when the Puritan battle cry became: "Giving alms is no charity." Protestants appealed to sixteenth-century theologian and reformer John Calvin, who had expressly forbidden begging "on the part of one able to work, is not only the sin of slothfulness, but a violation of the duty of brotherly love according to the Apostle's own word."[35] It was this period that the Puritans, Calvin's theological heirs, began building a system of workhouses for the unemployed.

From Reformation to American colonialism, the idea of poverty went from being a modernization flaw to being evidence of individual moral failure. These ideas pervaded domestic solutions to poverty in the West and spread around the world through the word of colonizers and missionaries. Anthropologists Jean and John Comaroff point out how, for example, the Methodist mission originating in late eighteenth century carried with it an implicit message "of salvation attainable through arduous and methodical self-construction. Its rhetorical forms were cast in the factory and the foundry, and its model of orderly process was that of the self-regulating market . . .what had become a moral economy."[36]

Historian Michael Katz traced American notions that the poor—rather than the economy, or the state—were culpable for their condition to the late eighteenth and early nineteenth century.[37] According to Katz and Stern, when the resources for redressing poverty are scarce, helpers have to decide whose needs, and which ones, are legitimate. This means prioritizing some needs over others. Accordingly, they wrote, a line "drawn partly with moral criteria, has tried with very imperfect success to distinguish between the deserving and undeserving poor. In one form or another, this distinction has persisted and still shapes policy."[38] Similarly, Viviana Zelizer showed how the (im)morality assigned to the "underclass" worked out in American welfare assistance when it changed from in-kind food to food stamps (vouchers exchangeable only for food) to other more liquid forms of cash. New surveillance policies highlighted the fear that poor people would misappropriate cash assistance.[39] The poor were conceptualized as undeserving because of their lack of responsibility; charity itself was thus indicted for reinforcing rather than stopping this immorality.

Charity in its various forms, including social welfare programs, was seen to create perverse incentives—mostly dependency on the system, counter to imperatives of moral industriousness. Fraser and Gordon traced the genealogy of the term "dependency" as an ideological term as a postindustrial individual pathology with a moral character.[40] In his 1976 presidential campaign, Ronald Reagan told the story of a Chicago welfare recipient arrested for fraud with "eighty names, thirty addresses, twelve Social Security cards . . . collecting veteran's benefits on four non-existing deceased husbands."[41] Although social scientists overwhelmingly found that the lazy and fraudulent were in the minority, the fraudulent "Welfare Queen" became among the most circulated stories[42] to build a particular political agenda.[43] Few were immune to the new mythology. Take for example the great lengths sociologist Charles Murray went to in the 1980s and 1990s to "prove" that black unwed mothers have more kids to get more welfare benefits.[44]

This notion that poverty is an individual problem that cannot be addressed by dependency-inducing aid still endures now in modern political-economic-religious circuits. In 2014, American megachurch pastor Rick Warren spoke alongside Rwandan President Paul Kagame. A theme during the event was that Kagame had applied the philosophy of Warren's best-seller, *The Purpose Driven Life*, in his approach to Rwanda's impressive development after the genocide of 1994. In sermon as well as in his writing, Warren offers a highly individualist approach to personal and spiritual development. Warren touted his church's practical role in Rwandan development through support of entrepreneurial programs: "they don't need a hand out. They need a hand up, to do it themselves."

In the twenty-first century, the popular American conversation around aid paints recipients as dangerously dependent. Frances Fox Piven offers a superb summary of this, "the nineteenth-century view [was] that poverty is the result of moral breakdown, and moral breakdown is encouraged by helping the poor. Crusaders looked about them, saw the vast misery and disorganization created by industrial conditions, and concluded that the problem was that too-liberal charity was encouraging the immorality of the poor."[45] Where aid has been provided for long periods of time, this view permeates; in particular, it persists in the spaces where the consequences of colonialism and conflict remain unresolved.

WHAT THE DONORS BELIEVE THE POOR NEED

You might wonder whether Muhammad Yunus found himself in the pews of a Calvinist church while studying economics at Vanderbilt University, before returning to his native Bangladesh to found the Grameen Bank. "When we want to help the poor, we usually offer them charity," he wrote in his book *Banker to the Poor*. "Most often we use charity to avoid recognizing the problem and finding a solution for it. Charity becomes a way to shrug off our responsibility. Charity is no solution to poverty. Charity only perpetuates poverty by taking the initiative away from the poor."[46] As such, microcredit emerged as a response tapping into these mores – the poor can improve their own fates through capitalism. The microcredit movement finds itself under the umbrella of the broader movement labeled "social entrepreneurialism."

Social entrepreneurs assert that social good can be done in a fashion that promotes positive change, but that it should never be pure charity. Indeed, within the language of the movement, "empowerment" occurs when "beneficiaries" are instead considered "clients." Clients can pay for their benefits, and investors can then earn profits. David Bornstein's popular 2004 book, *How to Change the World: Social Entrepreneurs and the Power of New Ideas*, showcased innovative, problem-solving people who "view the villagers as the solution, not the passive beneficiary. They begin with the assumption of competence and unleash resources in the communities they're serving."[47] This view asserted the capacity of poor peoples to discern what they needed, and social entrepreneurs were thereon after poised to support their visions. In this framework, those distributing the loans service the broader sociopolitical project of enhancing the poor's industriousness.

Business professor and founder of the social entrepreneurship academic field J. Gregory Dees wrote about the unresolved tension between the "two cultures" he saw at play in social entrepreneurship: "On one side, we have the age-old culture of charity that is tied to heart and steeped in moral traditions from around the world. On the other, we have the more modern culture of problem solving that is tied to head and emerged as part of the scientific, industrial, and now entrepreneurial age."[48] (I note that Dees began this article with a quote admiring Yunus's wisdom.) Social entrepreneurship in general, and microcredit as an instance of it, plays to both desires. Dees warned, importantly, that the tensions that exist in these projects—giving versus markets, sacrifice versus investment—are strong and yet must work hand-in-hand.

So the market side of the social entrepreneurship narrative goes thus: one need not feel bad for making money while doing the good work of empowering the poor. In this perspective, the needy are consumers. C. K. Prahalad and Stuart Hart's 2002 *The Fortune at the Bottom of the Pyramid*[49] presented an explicit treatise to recognize the untapped market potential of the world's poor from this view. Products, from small bottles of Johnson and Johnson shampoo to even housing, could be sold to the poor. Not only are there prospects for investing in the poor, but a human security rationale behind it, too: investment at "the bottom of the pyramid . . . means lifting billions of people out of poverty and desperation, averting the social decay, political chaos, terrorism, and environmental meltdown that is certain to continue if the gap between rich and poor countries continues to widen."[50] The appeal to invest was almost irresistible.

In theory, a spectrum exists between outright giving and expecting a full return on investment; social entrepreneurs stake out positions along the spectrum. The World Bank's Consultative Group to Assist the Poor (CGAP)'s piece on this topic delineated between two veins: "impact first" and "finance first" investors.[51] Impact first investors might accept lower returns on investments as long as social outcomes, such as educational attainment or health gains among recipients, are high whereas finance first investors would not. Jacqueline Novogratz, whose Acumen Fund invests in developing world entrepreneurs, describes such investment as the "opposite of old-fashioned charity." Like the other social entrepreneurs, she suggests that financial returns are important. However, she also argues that success in microfinance ought to include social returns for the recipients of investment as well. More socially minded investors joined responsible "impact investment" vehicles. Similar funds are collected by entities such as the Omidyar Network, Rockefeller Foundation, Aspen Network of Development Entrepreneurs, and the Bill and Melinda Gates Foundation, to name a few. How do microcredit supporters settle on exactly how to help—in other words, which method yields the best result?

FRAMING MICROCREDIT

Poverty is complex, and how to address it is even more so. Historically grounded theories such as Immanuel Wallerstein's World-Systems suggest that core or wealthy countries grew at the expense of poor, peripheral ones.[52] Karl Marx blamed the inherent violence of capital accumulation by the ownership class, and despite the enormous body of scholarly work that has subsequently argued this, the villains are still mostly unclear to the average person. Slavoj Žižek commentated on the irony of trying to help from within the very capitalist structures that created poverty in the first place.[53] Even without feeling responsible for the suffering taking place elsewhere, many people usually still guilt through the awareness of distant suffering.[54] But this suffering is part of a complex, systemic problem, and if these issues are beyond comprehension for the public, how do we begin to redress them? Psychologist Arie Kruglanski would describe this dilemma as the need for cognitive closure.[55]

Donors are also sensitive to frames that describe their beliefs about the nature of poverty. Jessica Jackley, co-founder of Kiva, a popular website that collects loan funds from individual lenders, says her organization "runs on heartstrings" Although the phrase "have a heart" still recruits, it does not as much as it did before. The appeal once held to assist victims of war has changed along with the popular and intellectual paradigms on the nature of poverty itself, and part of this is due to the fact that victim problems are now different. I would argue that it is now easier for the international community to sympathize with enemy combatants (Geneva Conventions on prisoners of war) than it is with the less emergent poor. Devising solutions to poverty is not so straightforward as what has for a century been enshrined in international law. Emergencies imply a sort of worthy, blameless victim as inculcated by a coterie of aid agencies and international mandates. The causes of poverty are much less straightforward than the bomb someone launched at you, or the hurricane devastation.

Simplifying helps get through the disorientation. As a practical matter, agencies that are looking for public support must frame their messaging so as to pique the right sensibilities in prospective donors. Marketing charity is as old as the field of psychology as there is a rich academic history in Communication Studies that illuminates the power of simplification in order to increase engagement.[56] Communications about assistance can only ever address the "'what to do' question in a selective way" says Lilie Chouliaraki.[57] Robert Entman offers an overview on how the framing itself can diagnose, evaluate, and prescribe. "To frame is to select some aspects of a perceived reality and make them more salient in a communicating text, in such a way as to promote a particular problem definition, causal interpretation, moral evaluation, and/or treatment recommendation for the item described."[58] The microfinance institutions, and their public-facing fundraising agencies, advertise with prospective donors in mind. If framed correctly, their campaigns express their activities in ways that tap into preexisting constructs about the cause of the need, to convince consumers that this is a respectable way for them to participate. The framing is threefold.

The first part of microcredit reductionist framing is what Anke Schwittay calls the "Financialization of Poverty." Because the "structural complexities of global poverty could easily become overwhelming and inhibit action, presenting its problem in a simplified, financial way makes it wieldy and actionable."[59] She argues that such a simplifying sleight of hand, however, sheens over the multifaceted, complex, and intrinsically personal stories of poverty. Furthermore, Schwittay echoed Peter Edward's concern that the now-ubiquitous World Bank's $1-a-day global poverty lines—purely income-based—are mono-dimensional, reinforcing "poverty's universalizing definition as a common condition shared by poor."[60] Schwittay charts how these financially reductionist notions of poverty mobilize finance-specific interventions, "because only as a financial problem can poverty be alleviated by financial means."[61] Yunus himself relayed that "the poor know that credit is their only opportunity to break out of poverty"[62] was case in point.

The second microfinance frame characterizes the qualities that "make" the poor to be more like the rich. Throughout the twenty-first century, donors wondered how to get people into the right cultural mindset. "If the poor would only understand," wrote Majid Rahnema, "what historically brought the people of the North to higher standards of living and greater political, economic and technological power, they, too, would no longer hesitate to take the main highway of development."[63] Microfinance proponents adopted this frame when deploying the "discipline as empowerment" trope, referring to the need for the poor to gain a sense of economic discipline. Microcredit has tremendous appeal because it can, in one fell swoop, assure the poor access capital as well as their responsibility. This rhetoric can be seen in the celebrity endorsements of the programs as well as the web promotional campaigns; these spokespeople calcify and spread powerful frames that spur contemporary public engagement with causes. The singer Bono advocated, "You know that mantra, 'Give a man a fish, he'll eat for a day, teach a man to fish, he'll eat for a lifetime?' It's missing something: microfinance is the fishing rod, the boat, the net, etc. Cash and dignity, side by side . . . . Maybe the mantra should be: Give a man a fish, he'll eat for a day. Give a woman microcredit, she, her husband, her children and her extended family will eat for a lifetime."[64] Bono has been a prominent voice in the public conversations around aid and development in recent years, but he is not the only one pointing to microcredit as a silver bullet.

Actress Natalie Portman likewise joined the ranks of celebrity-believers in microcredit. The lending model itself piques heart-and-mind strings for so many neoliberal-minded ears. When asked in an interview why she chose to work with microcredit (of all organizations), she explained, "It's a pretty wonderful idea. . . . And it is a simple concept and really successful, and its proven itself over the years."[65] As if scripted by Pastor Rick Warren, the

Portman video advertising microcredit began with "Lend a hand" written on a US dollar bill.[66] Portman's praise for microloans efficacy draws heavily on descriptions about the lending model—the idea of it—itself. She spoke of how borrowers can ascend within the system, "after women have been with FINCA for a while and have proven their responsibility." Proven responsibility, in this context, is empowering, so the story goes.

The third microfinance frame is exemplified by Portman's praise that "it's sustainable," compared to vanishing aid donations of yore: "you go in once to a village, you put money in once, and that money continues forever." This happens because "the women pay back their loans with interest at such incredible rates—it's like 97, 98 percent—it's better than wealthy people in the United States—the money continues and it turns over three times a year, so one amount of money serves three women every year—and their families of course."[67] The allegedly high repayment rates pervade the public conversation around microcredit as evidence that it works.[68] Not only does the repayment rate trope imply that borrowers are disciplined and their priorities are right, but it also plays to the perception that the assistance can perpetuate without (immorality inducing charitable) subsidy.

Much of the microcredit zeal has been born from tapping into moral financial ideas in the absence of proof and sometimes even in direct contradiction to actual findings. Dichter deftly stated that microfinance is an "immature and unproven field, anyone can say almost anything, and with the public relations surrounding the field, most of it goes unquestioned."[69] The Star Wars actress is but one of many celebrities advocating for microfinance from the limelight. Advocacy and social networks have led Western donors to websites offering public investment in microfinance, and this in turn fostered more zeal.

Microfinance institutions and their funding intermediaries use catchphrases that pique the interest of their specific cultural donor community. They know their audience well enough to characterize their work through tropes that are effective and affective. Themes common to their websites include messages of empowerment, agency, and discipline through the monitoring of clients. For instance, the Grameen Foundation's slogan is "Empowering people. Changing Lives. Innovating for the world's poor." The notion that microfinance is "life changing" suggests, in the semiology of philanthropy, that communities change for the better, not worse. The phrase is paired here with the term "empowerment," which has nothing short of magical valence in the popular culture of assistance despite much contention around the term in academic and some practitioner circles.[70] Depending on whom you ask, and how power is defined, empowerment can mean many different things. Jessica Rowlands names a few, describing how empowerment can represent changes that allow communities to challenge systemic constraints, increase solidarity to challenge underlying assumptions, or increase "individual capacity and opportunities for access."[71] Given the individual (if not isolating) nature of microenterprises promoted in microfinance,[72] I interpret the industry's use of the term to leverage Rowlands's last point. Microcredit empowerment dwells within notions of individual capacity; it has little to say about borrowers mounting power or collaborating to take on the system. Indeed, these are individual borrowers getting loans to run their individual businesses. If disempowerment is when one is lacking opportunity to access resources, finance is deemed the only factor missing for each individual life to improve.

In this frame, the poor can all do great things that are worth funding. The subtext quite loudly attends to the notion that without this particular tool, the poor are unable if not unwilling to help themselves. Microfinance "helps people to help themselves," wrote Global Partnerships on their mission statement webpage.[73] FINCA similarly explains how participants "can affect their own development."[74] Another organization extended the ethos to incontestably responsible parents: loans "enable them to provide for their families with dignity and send their children to school."[75] Messages extolling self-reliance are everywhere.

MFI lingo thus speaks to the public's concern with the poor's pathological dependency. Bangladeshi NGO BRAC does so explicitly, stating what is good about this new path in contrast with the alternative. "Poverty must be tackled from a holistic viewpoint, transitioning individuals from being aid recipients to becoming empowered citizens in control of their own destinies."[76] By obtusely contrasting the before-and-after picture of dependency, their message is quite effective. Practitioners and propagandists celebrate the active, working, laboring, and productive qualities facilitated by the loans.

Words are not the only way the appeal is made about these logics of borrower worthiness and blissful autonomy. The language of microfinance persuasion transcends letters. Shameem Black explains how the photos and descriptions of borrowers on Kiva's website "guarantee" an "emotional return" from sentimental lenders by "singl[ing] out ambitions that resonate with middle-class Western ideals, such as paying for children's education, expanding a business, and improving the security of one's home."[77] Anke Schwittay analyzed the visually mediated elements of Kiva and CGAP's photo contest within this industry as well. She shows how snapshots taken by Kiva Fellows are carefully staged so as to show borrowers active in their places of work and smiling.[78]

Through these rhetorical processes, billions of dollars were raised around the world to funnel into microlending. Loan monies hail from states, citizens, and corporations alike as microfinance became popular among both private and public actors. Governments now do microfinance as part of bilateral foreign aid deals, and they also organize through World Bank, IMF, and other pooled funding vehicles. Public funding dominates two-thirds of microfinance investment overall (US $17 billion in 2012), according to CGAP, but private funding is growing at even faster rates.[79] Private actors such as Citibank, Sergey Brin, and Larry Page have invested noteworthy sums,[80] even while 1.5 million individuals take to Kiva's online platform to lend in small amounts.

The money raised has outpaced scientific basis for microcredit's effects on the lives of its borrowers. As we will explore in the next chapter, there exists no conclusive verdict on microfinance in "typical" developing societies. Indeed, criticisms of poverty finance have grown in recent years, in part due to lack of conclusive data. Even less is known about its appropriateness for underdeveloped and developing societies in the wake of conflict.[81] Still, practitioners continue to establish microfinance operations in the wake of wars, and test the limits.

MICROCREDIT AS PEACEBUILDING

In the aftermath of war, peacebuilding emerges among matters of first importance. Societies once caught in the throes of civil conflict often tend to repeat the cycle, popularly cacheted as the "conflict trap." Although alternative analyses, like that of Christopher Cramer, have suggested that conflict might actually serve to produce new and potentially positive opportunity from the chaos,[82] Economist Paul Collier et al. posit that post-conflict countries face a high risk of future conflict and need to rectify the economic decay inherited from wartime. Fast growth has potential for conflict prevention in post-conflict societies, because in the long run it diversifies economic extremes through increased income levels of the poorest.[83] This is especially important when considering that economic deprivation can be a source of civil strife in societies where economic disparities coincide with geographic, ethnic, religious, or tribal forms of social identity.[84] Therefore, as economic disparities are reduced, the general welfare of divided societies can improve, and become less prone to violence. In that vein, past UN Secretary General Kofi Annan stated that "every step taken towards reducing poverty and achieving broad-based economic growth is a step toward conflict prevention."[85] Annan's comment represents the core of peacebuilding logic examined in this book.

Origins of the liberal peacebuilding paradigm bear mention. Rooted in the international relations tradition of liberal institutionalism, liberal peacebuilding came to posit that supporting liberal economies with market structures and democratic policies is the best recipe for effective post-conflict peacebuilding.[86] Much like neoliberalism in general, the "liberal peacebuilding" concept has informed so many policies and programs in "fragile and conflict-affected states" after the Cold War, that Roger Mac Ginty referred to the paradigm as preserving a "near monopoly" on peacebuilding operations.[87] Mac Ginty and others worry that the "highly standardized" liberal peacebuilding model cannot be sensitive to the nuance of each war affected population; its application, suggest other researchers, can result in superficial changes at best, or corruption and inequalities at worst.[88] In light of the inconsistent realization of these ideas, others charge that the liberal peacebuilding discourse is "essentialist and misleading," bearing little resemblance to the actual mechanisms at work in wealth production (e.g., a Marxist argument that capitalism keeps wealth among the bourgeoisie) and therefore not an existing project at all.[89] Nevertheless, the dominant liberal peacebuilding paradigm set the stage for microfinance in multiple important ways.

As with capitalism in general, the alluring reductionism of a path to peace, which entailed a rolled-back state, persists throughout the time-honored institutions that deliver postwar rehabilitation assistance. Thus Graham Harrison argues that the IMF and World Bank presence in conflicted countries is "paradoxical." The SAPs advocated by both organizations, he argues, undermine opportunities for the recipient state to foster its public legitimacy through social provisions. Despite the IMF's narrow focus on finance, the Bank has recognized that state investments (in areas including infrastructure and rule of law, among others) are needed for the markets to improve conditions for people after war. But, despite its rhetorical nod toward statebuilding, Harrison argues that the Bank ultimately depoliticized aspects of war like political violence and governance, such that "one could cut all references to conflict out of the [Bank's] State and Peacebuilding Fund (SPF) documentation and identify a fairly orthodox and generic World Bank program of neoliberalism and good governance."[90]

How is larger-than-life liberal faith applied in practice, such that postwar recovery can be achieved? "In short, international organizations and NGOs are drawn together by a common policy framework of liberal peacebuilding; however, they are very often divided in terms of specific programmatic orientations and priorities."[91] Anna Ohanyan describes this condition as "conflicted concord," wherein visions align but implementation does not.[92]

The pressure to homogenize the "relief to development continuum" grew within this time period. Debates about how to tackle poverty after conflict have pitted advocates of relief, sustainable development, and state building strategies against one another.[93] Until very recently, the post-conflict assistance paradigm had followed a phased approach in which humanitarian relief, reintegration, democracy training, and infrastructure aid were treated as discrete and sequential efforts, almost always in that order, leaving economic support until later stages of aid. But increased evidence found that these phased tactics were actually impeding recovery by creating gaps in donor budgets.[94] Donors grew increasingly concerned that aid was cultivating dependency among beneficiaries. Some even began suggesting that development start as soon as a country reopens after conflict, bypassing the short-term strategies of immediate aid efforts.[95] The praxis of large transnational institutions began to prioritize growth-focused interventions much sooner than had been done in the past by former standards of the aid industry.

This shift in institutional policymaker perspective occurred just as the romance with microfinance had taken root in society as an exemplary anti-poverty tool. Microfinance, now seen as a force for development, is being applied to push people out of the relief-receipt demographic. Its application to achieve the liberal peacebuilding vision takes as given the odds of neoliberal success, expecting to surmount poverty regardless of the context.

Microcredit rhetoric not only presumes that loans enhance incomes in generally poor countries but also claims that microcredit contributes to peace. This faith-based logic emphasizes microcredit's role in fostering social cohesion by uniting people who are different in the group-loan process. microfinance is a social process. Public relations operatives praise how loans empower and create bonds; shared liability group loans are called "solidarity" groups, and this group convening has a "role in social and political reconciliation . . . through encouraging inter-ethnic economic activities, or by building trust through multi-ethnic community banks or solidarity group lending."[96]

That microcredit could be seen as an important instrument for peacebuilding[97] is certainly an exciting extension of the conflict trap and dependency theories, but grounds for these claims are unclear. For instance, Susanne Alldén found that microcredit programs in Cambodia and Timor-Leste worked well for some but not for all recipients, due to several internal and external conditions.[98] Geetha Nagarajan and Michael McNulty have pointed out how some achievements in postwar microcredit experiments have "convinced many of its use as a promising intervention mechanism in conflict situations to reactivate the damaged economy" but emphasized that there was no consensus about what worked among them.[99] There is still much to learn about the contexts in which credit programs are rolled out, as well as the models used to provide them.

THE WORKING OUT OF FAITHS

Proponents of microfinance were unwavering in their belief about what poor people needed long before they reached South Sudan. The "public transcript" of microcredit tells us how industry leaders and advocates popularized their logic, but the industry was not a monolith. Behind the scenes are sharp differences of opinion around the issue since the 1980s. Divergent lending practices that have serious consequences for the participants have followed this riff, and it is far from clear that microcredit supporters understand that they are casting their vote in one camp or the other. This case study adds testimony to that riff—one that is growing within the donor structures that buttress the global microfinance complex. These historically rooted ideologies informed policies, which then faced another set of negotiations when implemented at the ground level, thousands of miles away from where the ideas originated.

Here in South Sudan, knowledge of microfinance's "hidden transcripts" becomes very important. Aminur Rahman suggested that behind the empowerment claims were a myriad of ways that microfinance agents monitored and disciplined systematically vulnerable Bangladeshi women.[100] Ananya Roy uncovered a different form of hidden transcript of microfinance; in the halls of policy makers, she highlighted the disconnect between the complicated ideologies of the architects of the public transcript, and the public transcript they put forth.[101] Roy's book, *Poverty Capital* traces what at first blush seems like a distinct rivalry between the Washington model of microfinance and the Bangladesh model. While the Washington model emphasizes commercializing MFIs, profits, and sustainability as a first priority, the Bangladesh model instead asks not what lending can do for donors solvency, but what credit can do for the "poorest of the poor."

The Washington Consensus propagated by global financial institutions emphasized the neoliberal overhaul of whole states, and that view reverberated in the shaping of South Sudanese economic policy. What Roy referred to as "the Washington Consensus on microfinance" was buttressed by institutions like the World Bank, its education arm Consultative Group to Assist the Poor (CGAP), and most USAID administrators. These institutions advocated for the microcredit industry to be as market-driven as possible, many having noticed opportunities to turn noteworthy profits on the loans. Still others focused on opportunities to charge higher interest rates as a way to extend government subsidies.[102] As a corollary, such a policy shift would leave out the poorest clients as they would be considered a prohibitively risky population to invest in. It reimagined microlending to slightly less but "economically active" poor people as a process that would trickle down benefits.

On the other side, the Bangladesh Consensus on microfinance advocates created "Microfinance Plus," also called "Poverty Lending," a program that placed microfinance in the broader landscape of social protection for the poor, and thereby required attention to training and services alongside credit provision.[103] The Bangladesh view on poverty realized relatively early that not all poor people were ready for full-fledged microloans. Modifications from the original Bangladesh loan formats, such as Grameen II, instituted flexible repayment schedules that could accommodate a greater variety of market activities. BRAC, another major Bangladeshi microcredit provider, offered loans packaged with health and enterprise training. Such modifications continue to be the subject of debate, with commercial credit purists decrying such strategies.

Roy called the "battle of these paradigms . . . a fierce and important battle for the soul of microfinance."[104] On one side, microfinance is a market-oriented bank and on the other, it is part of an NGO-development organizational structure. Neither side has been exempt from critique. The commercial model is charged with predatory lending, and the poverty model for costliness and creating dependence on donors. This paradigm battle was also fought in South Sudan.

All of the ideas and monies supporting microfinance in South Sudan were imported, as was everything sold by borrowers (atypical to most everywhere else such loans are given). The two biggest actors on the MFI scene represent the poles of the Washington and Bangladesh microfinance ideologies, though several other interwoven actors had different ideas about what to do along with the amalgam of state and non-state actors involved in the provision of credit. Incentives were thus both economic and moral.

This book observes a test—on the battlefield of ideas—to see if one side, both, or neither had anything to offer a hyper-everything postwar economy in South Sudan. After all, the world in which their experiments occurred was much more nuanced than their historical ideologies alone could explain. The field-level staff had mandates to follow and were, to varying degrees, inculcated into their companies' different cultures before they began to interface with those who might be clients. Borrowing from what Tim Mitchell calls techno-politics, "the projects themselves formed the science."[105]

Microfinance in South Sudan included the workings-out of faith and doubt through experimentation on the poor. It seemed to have started as a well-intended campaign. However, like the "poorest of the poor," those living in many post-conflict countries are risky borrowers. They are expensive to service and their businesses are not sure to succeed. This experiment tested the boundaries of the ideas. There were hiccups on the ground, and there were hard external pressures. Costs of providing finance rose quickly, and when MFIs found themselves at a fork in the road, they had to choose: either be sustainable businesses or subsidize loans to remain inclusive. At their founding in 2002 and 2006, each MFI took a different route, and by the year 2012, their differences were dramatic.

The high costs of servicing these post-conflict poor moved unresolved debates on lending methods to the front and center. Industry leaders absorbed and recreated ideologies in their praxis. They had to decide what products the poor would receive in light of rival mandates to service them in a way that was financially sustainable. This is where push came awkwardly to shove. If the poor are not like the rich, do you forsake them for those who are less risky and do not need donations? If the poor need something different from loans to get out of poverty, then what is it? In other words, if the poor are or should be like the rich, then what is required to bring them into the folds of capital?

Finally—is it possible that what the poor need cannot be learned in Washington, DC, or Dhaka? The problem with much of the theorizing that drove the material reality of what became not-so micro of credit in South Sudan is that it was built on historical foundations far from the practice. Donors can be skeptical of the pathologies of the poor, but so too can recipients judge what is given. South Sudanese people are not simply subjects of development. They have willingly experimented with programs offered, including microcredit. They have developed opinions based on those experiences. They have also been willing to push back against programs that do not work for them.[106] And while many development practitioners believe that their coping techniques and resourcefulness can be capitalized upon to achieve organizational aims,[107] selling new ways to earn a living first requires learning what is actually needed from the poor themselves. Recipients have insight into which programs will work for them, yet the global community has had a more difficult time assessing success beyond its ideological frameworks.

NOTES

1. Matthew Swibel, "The World's Top Microfinance Institutions." *Forbes* (2007).

2. Larry R. Reed, *State of the Campaign Report*. State of the Campaign (2015).

3. Muhammad Yunus, *Banker to the Poor: Micro-lending and the Battle Against World Poverty* (1999), Morduch 2003, 2005.

4. Joanna Ledgerwood, *Microfinance Handbook: An Institutional and Financial Perspective* (1999); Muhammad Yunus, *Banker to the Poor: Micro-lending and the Battle Against World Poverty* (1999); Marguerite Robinson, *The Microfinance Revolution: Sustainable Finance for the Poor* (2001). The field of Microfinance operates on the income-based measure of poverty. While the field of Microfinance finds common ground on the $1 a day measure of poverty, there is much criticism that incorporates other aspects into a definition of poverty. See Ajit Bhalla and Frederic Lapeyre, "Social Exclusion: Towards an Analytical and Operational Framework" 1997; Partha Dasgupta, *An Inquiry into Well-Being and Destitution* (1993); Naila Kabeer, "Beyond the Poverty Line: Measuring Poverty and Impoverishing measures" 1995 and Amartya Sen, *Development as Freedom* (1999); Anke Schwittay, *New Media and International Development: Representation and Affect in Microfinance* (2014).

5. John Beijuka, "Microfinance in Post-conflict Countries: The Case Study of Uganda." (*International Labor Organization*, 1991), 1. See also Dale Adams,

Douglas Graham and J. D. Von Pischke, *Undermining Rural Development with Cheap Credit* (1984); Dambisa Moyo, *Dead Aid* (2009).

6. See, for example, Lisa Malkki, *The Need to Help: The Domestic Arts of International Humanitarianism* (Durham and London: Duke, 2015).

7. Abhijit Vinayak Banerjee, et al., *Making Aid Work* (Cambridge: MIT Press, 2007).

8. William Easterly, *The White Man's Burden: Why the West's Efforts to Aid the Rest Have Done So Much Ill and So Little Good* (New York, NY: Penguin Press, 2006). See also Dambisa Moyo, *Dead Aid: Why Aid Is Not Working and How There Is a Better Way for Africa* (New York: Farrar, Straus and Giroux, 2009).

9. John Dewey, *The Middle Works* (Edwardsville, IL: Southern Illinois University Press, 1983).

10. Ananya Roy, *Poverty Capital: Microfinance and the Making of Development* (New York and London: Routledge, 2011), 12.

11. See James Ferguson, "Formalities of Poverty: Thinking about Social Assistance in Neoliberal South Africa." *African Studies Review* (2007).Alfredo Saad-Filho and Ben Fine, "Thirteen Things You Need to Know About Neoliberalism." *Critical Sociology* (2016).

12. Gunnar Myrdal, *Economic Theory and Underdeveloped Region* (London: University Paperbacks, Methuen, 1957).

13. P. N. Rosenstein-Rodan, "Problems of Industrialisation of Eastern and South-Eastern Europe." *The Economic Journal* 53 (1943).

14. Robert Gilpin and Jean M. Gilpin, *Global Political Economy: Understanding the International Economic Order (*New Jersey: Princeton University Press, 2001), 311.

15. John Williamson, "Did the Washington Consensus fail?" Outline of speech at the Center for Strategic & International Studies (Washington, DC, 2002).

16. Dani Rodrik, *Goodbye Washington Consensus, Hello Washington Confusion?* (Cambridge, MA: Harvard University, 2006).

17. Nancy Birdsall, Adeel Malik, and Vaishnav Milan "Poverty and the Social Sectors: The World Bank in Pakistan 1990–2003" (Washington, DC: World Bank Operations Evaluation Department, 2005).

18. Walden Bello, "Is the Structural Adjustment Approach Really and Truly Dead?" *Business World* (1999).

19. Naomi Klein, *The Shock Doctrine: The Rise of Disaster Capitalism* (New York, NY: Picador, 2007).

20. William Easterly, *The White Man's Burden: Why the West's Efforts to Aid the Rest Have Done So Much Ill and So Little Good* (New York, NY: Penguin Press, 2006).

21. Jean-Philippe Platteau and Frédéric Gaspart, *Disciplining Local Leaders in Community-Based Development.* Centre for Research on the Economics of Development (CRED), (Namur, Belgium: University of Namur, 2003).William Easterly, *The White Man's Burden: Why the West's Efforts to Aid the Rest Have Done So Much Ill and So Little Good* (New York, NY: Penguin Press, 2006); Dambisa Moyo, *Dead*

Aid: Why Aid Is Not Working and How There Is a Better Way for Africa (New York: Farrar, Straus and Giroux, 2009).

22. Herschel I. Grossman, "Foreign Aid and Insurrection." *Defense Economics* (1992); Collier, et al., *Breaking the Conflict Trap: Civil War and Development Policy* (Washington, DC: World Bank 2003), 138.

23. William Easterly, *The White Man's Burden: Why the West's Efforts to Aid the Rest Have Done So Much Ill and So Little Good* (New York, NY: Penguin Press, 2006), 136.

24. Chapman University, American Fear Survey, 2015.

25. Anoop Singh, et al., "Stabilization and Reform in Latin America: A Macroeconomic Perspective on the Experience Since the Early 1990s." *International Monetary Fund* (2005), 14.

26. Stiglitz 1998; Nobel Media, "Joseph E. Stiglitz — Biographical." Nobel Media AB (2014).

27. Observing that countries that had some countercyclical safety net programs fared better when these shocks came, Nancy Birdsall and Francis Fukuyama forecasted in Foreign Affairs in 2011 that "emerging-market and low-income countries are likely to . . . trad[e] the flexibility and efficiency associated with the free-market model for domestic policies meant to ensure greater resilience in the face of competitive pressures and global economic trauma. They will become less focused on the free flow of capital, more concerned with minimizing social disruption through social safety net programs, and more active in supporting domestic industries. And they will be even less inclined than before to defer to the supposed expertise of the more developed countries, believing—correctly—that not only economic but also intellectual power are becoming increasingly evenly distributed."

28. Fred L. Block and Margaret R. Somers, *The Power of Market Fundamentalism: Karl Polanyi's Critique* (Cambridge, MA: Harvard University Press, 2014).

29. Dani Rodrik, *Goodbye Washington Consensus, Hello Washington Confusion?* (Cambridge, MA: Harvard University, 2006), 8.

30. Julia Elyachar, "Empowerment Money: The World Bank, Non-Governmental Organizations, and the Value of Culture in Egypt." (2002) citing the World Bank.

31. Julia Elyachar, "Empowerment Money: The World Bank, Non-Governmental Organizations, and the Value of Culture in Egypt." (2002), 496.

32. Ben Fine, "The Developmental State Is Dead-Long Live Social Capital?" *Development and Change* (1999).

33. Matthew 25 Bible New King James Version.

34. Max Weber, *The Protestant Ethic and the Spirit of Capitalism* (Taylor & Francis e-Library, 1904/2005).

35. Max Weber, *The Protestant Ethic and the Spirit of Capitalism* (Taylor & Francis e-Library, (1904/2005), 108–9.

36. Jean Comaroff and John Comaroff, "Christianity and Colonialism in South Africa." *American Ethnologist* (1986).

37. Michael B. Katz. *The Undeserving Poor: America's Enduring Confrontation with Poverty, Fully Updated and Revised* (Oxford: Oxford University Press, 2013).

38. Michael B. Katz and Mark J. Stern, "Poverty in Twentieth-Century America." *America at the Millennium Project Working Paper #7,* (2001).

39. Viviana Zelizer, *The Social Meaning of Money: Pin Money, Paychecks, Poor Relief, and Other Currencies* (Princeton: Princeton University Press, 1994).

40. Nancy Fraser and Linda Gordon, "A Genealogy of Dependency: Tracing a Keyword of the US Welfare State." *Signs: Journal of Women in Culture and Society* (1994).

41. *New York Times* 1976, 51.

42. Michael B. Katz, *The Undeserving Poor: America's Enduring Confrontation with Poverty, Fully Updated and Revised (*Oxford University Press, 2013).

43. Martin Gilens, *Why Americans Hate Welfare: Race, Media, and the Politics of Antipoverty Policy* (Chicago: University of Chicago Press, 2000). See also Paul Krugman, "Republicans and Race." *New York Times* (2007).

44. Charles Murray, "Does Welfare Bring More Babies?" *Public Interest* (1994).

45. Frances Fox Piven, "Foreword to Schram, S. F." In *Words of Welfare*, edited by Sanford Schram, p. xii (Minneapolis and London: University of Minnesota Press, 1995), 12.

46. Muhammad Yunus, *Banker to the Poor: Micro-lending and the Battle Against World Poverty* (New York: Public Affairs, 1999), 237.

47. David Bornstein, *How to Change the World: Social Entrepreneurs and the Power of New Ideas* (Oxford: Oxford University Press, 2004).

48. Gregory J. Dees, "A Tale of Two Cultures: Charity, Problem Solving, and the Future of Social Entrepreneurship." *J Bus Ethics Journal of Business Ethics* (2012).

49. Followed by Prahalad's 2004 Bestselling book by the same title.

50. C. K Prahalad and Stuart L. Hart, "The Fortune at the Bottom of the Pyramid." *Strategy + Business: Corporate Strategies and News Articles on Global Business, Management, Competition and Marketing* (2002).

51. Estelle Lahaye, Ralitsa Rizvanolli and Edlira Dashi, "Current Trends in Cross-Border Funding for Microfinance." *CGAP* (2012).

52. Immanuel Wallerstein, *The Modern World-system: Capitalist Agriculture and the Origins of the European World-economy in the Sixteenth Centenary* (Berkeley: University of California Press, 1974).

53. Slavoj Žižek, *First as Tragedy, Then as Farce* (London: Verso, 2009).

54. Lilie Chouliaraki, "Distant Suffering in the Media" (2008), 3.

55. Arie W. Kruglanski, *Lay Epistemics and Human Knowledge: Cognitive and Motivational Bases* (New York: Plenum, 1989).

56. See, for example, Robert Entman, "Framing: Toward Clarification of a Fractured Paradigm." *Journal of Communication* (1993).

57. Lilie Chouliaraki, "Distant Suffering in the Media" 2008.

58. Robert M. Entman, "Framing: Toward Clarification of a Fractured Paradigm." *Journal of Communication* (1993), 52.

59. Anke Schwittay, *New Media and International Development: Representation and Affect in Microfinance* (New York: Routledge, 2014), 7.

60. Peter Edward, "The Ethical Poverty Line: A Moral Quantification of Absolute Poverty." *Third World Quarterly* 27 (2006), 381.

61. Anke Schwittay, *New Media and International Development: Representation and Affect in Microfinance* (New York: Routledge, 2014), 4.

62. Anne Schwittay, *New Media and International Development: Representation and Affect in Microfinance* (New York: Routledge, 2014), 7 citing Yunus (1999: 59).

63. Majid Rahnema, *Poverty in Wolfgang Sachs The Development Dictionary 2nd Edition* (London and New York: Zed Books, 2010), 185.

64. As quoted in Sam Daley-Harris, "State of the Microcredit Summit Campaign Report 2005." *The Microcredit Summit Campaign* (2005).

65. Marianne Schnall, "Conversation with Natalie Portman." n.d.

66. Bill Higgins, "Natalie Portman Gets Behind Microfinance for Third World." *Pret-a-Reporter* (2011).

67. Marianne Schnall, "Conversation with Natalie Portman." n.d.

68. Note: Repayment is good for MFIs seeking to cover costs, but says little about the fate of borrowers. Repayment rates are a sticky figure that can shroud what it took beyond the MFI's gaze to achieve them (including taking out loans elsewhere, and getting further into debt and borrowers being coerced). See, for example, Gehlich-Shillabeer (2008) and Rahman (1999).

69. Thomas Dichter, *What's Wrong with Microfinance?* (Warwickshire: Practical Action Publishing, 2007), 5.

70. See Cecilia Luttrell and Sitna Quiroz, "Understanding and Operationalising Empowerment." ODI Working Paper, 2009.

71. Jessica Rowlands, *Questioning Empowerment: Working with women in Honduras* (Oxfam Publishing, 1997).

72. See Julia Elyachar, "Empowerment Money: The World Bank, Non-Governmental Organizations, and the Value of Culture in Egypt." *Public Culture* (2002).

73. Global Partnerships, "About us." Global Partnerships, About Us, n.d.

74. FINCA, "Mission and Vision.", n.d.

75. Enterprise Development, "We're on a Mission to Help the Poor End Poverty." n.d.

76. BRAC, "Creating Opportunity for the Poor." BRAC, Home, n.d.

77. Black 2009, p. 277 as cited in Anke Schwittay, *New Media and International Development: Representation and Affect in Microfinance* (New York: Routledge, 2014), 278.

78. Anke Schwittay, *New Media and International Development: Representation and Affect in Microfinance* (New York: Routledge, 2014).

79. Estelle Lahaye, Ralitsa Rizvanolli and Edlira Dashi, "Current Trends in Cross-Border Funding for Microfinance." *CGAP* (2012).

80. Jim Hopkins, "Ebay Founder Takes Lead in Social Entrepreneurship." *USA Today* (2005).

81. Geetha Nagarajan, *Developing Microfinance Institutions in Conflict Affected Countries: Emerging Issues, First Lessons Learnt and Challenges Ahead* (Geneva: Enterprise and Cooperative Development Department, ILO, 1997) noted how few instances of post-conflict microfinance there had been, and still fewer research projects done to draw conclusive findings at the time.

82. Christopher Cramer, *Civil War is Not a Stupid Thing: Accounting for Violence in Developing Countries* (London: Hurst & Co, 2006).

83. Paul Collier, et al., *Breaking the Conflict Trap: Civil War and Development Policy* (Washington, DC: World Bank, 2003).

84. Bryan Caplan, *The Myth of the Rational Voter: Why Democracies Choose Bad Policies,* (Princeton, NJ: Princeton University Press, 2007).USAID, *A Guide to Economic Growth in Post-Conflict Countries* (Office of Economic Growth, Agriculture and Trade, Washington, DC, 2009), 8.

85. Quoted in Lakhdar Brahimi, *Report on the Panel on United Nations Peace Operations,* 2000, para. 27.

86. Rolland Paris, *Building Peace after Civil Conflict* (New York: Cambridge University Press, 2004).

87. Roger Mac Ginty, *No War, No Peace: The Rejuvenation of Stalled Peace Processes and Peace Accords* (London: Palgrave Macmillan, 2016).

88. Oliver Richmond, "'Beyond Liberal Peace? Responses to "Backsliding."' In *New Perspectives on Liberal Peacebuilding*, edited by Edward Newman, Roland Paris and Oliver Richmond (Tokyo: UN University Press, 2009).

89. Jan Selby, "The Myth of Liberal Peace-Building." *Conflict, Security & Development* (2013).

90. Garrison Harrison, "Financing Peace?" In *Peacebuilding, Power, and Politics in Africa*, edited by Devon Curtis and Gwinyayi A. Dzinesa (Athens: Ohio University Press, 2012), 166.

91. Diane Stone "The Policy Research Knowledge Elite and Global Policy Processes." In *Non-state Actors in World Politics*, edited by D. Josselin and W. Wallace (New York: Palgrave, 2001). as cited in Anna Ohanyan, *NGOs, IGOs, and the Network Mechanisms of Post-conflict Global Governance in Microfinance* (New York, NY: Palgrave Macmillan, 2008), 5.

92. Anna Ohanyan, *NGOs, IGOs, and the Network Mechanisms of Post-conflict Global Governance in Microfinance* (New York, NY: Palgrave Macmillan, 2008).

93. Oliver Richmond, "The Dilemmas of Subcontracting the Liberal Peace." In *Subcontracting Peace: The Challenges of the NGO Peacebuilding*, edited by Richmond and Carey (Burlington: Ashgate, 2005).

94. Stephen Lewarne and David Snelbecker, "Economic Governance in War Torn Economies: Lessons Learned from the Marshall Plan to the Reconstruction of Iraq." *USAID* (2004).

95. Mary B. Anderson and Peter J. Woodrow, *Rising from the Ashes: Development Strategies in Times of Disaster* (Boulder: Westview Press, 1989). Margaret Buchanan-Smith and Simon Maxwell, "Linking Relief and Development: An Introduction and Overview." *IDS Bulletin*, (1994).

96. Dave Larson, *Searching for Differences: Microfinance Following Conflict vx. Other Environments* (Bethesda: Development Alternatives, 2001), 5.

97. Genevieve Sheehan, "Microfinance as a Pathway to Peace and Reconciliation: A Case Study from Sri Lanka." *International Perspectives on Peace and Reconciliation* (Melbourne: University of Melbourne, 2003).

98. Susanne Alldén, "Microfinance and Post-conflict Development in Cambodia and Timor-Leste." *Sojourn: Journal of Social Issues in Southeast Asia* (2009).

99. Geetha Nagarajan and Michael McNulty, *Microfinance Amid Conflict: Taking Stock of Available Literature* (Accelerated Microenterprise Advancement Project, 2004).

100. Aminur Rahman, *Women and Microcredit in Rural Bangladesh: An Anthropological Study of Grameen Bank Lending* (Boulder: Westview Press, 1999).

101. Ananya Roy, *Poverty Capital: Microfinance and the Making of Development* (New York and London: Routledge, 2010), 12.

102. Marguerite S. Robinson, *The Microfinance Revolution: Sustainable Finance for the Poor,* (Washington, DC: The World Bank, 2001).

103. Ananya Roy, *Poverty Capital: Microfinance and the Making of Development* (New York and London: Routledge, 2010).

104. Josh Leon, "Poverty Capitalism: Interview with Ananya Roy." *Foreign Policy in Focus* (2011).

105. Timothy Mitchell, *Rule of Experts: Egypt, Techno-Politics, Modernity* (Berkeley, CA: University of California Press, 2002), 37.

106. See Cleophas Lado, "Some Aspects of Rural Marketing Systems and Peasant Farming in Maridi District, Southern Sudan." *Transactions of the Institute of British Geographers* (1988).

107. See Julia Elyachar, "Empowerment Money: The World Bank, Non-Governmental Organizations, and the Value of Culture in Egypt" (2002).

Chapter 2

Does Microcredit Work?

The limits of what we know

There is a story I heard many times in the field. The details vary but the moral was consistent. In an African country, the women of a village must walk several miles to get fresh drinking water and carry it back home. Along came an NGO, which dug a new well right in the middle of town. This, they said, would save time and energy for the women. The well-meaning outsiders returned a couple of months later and found the well broken. So they repaired it. They returned again a year later to learn that it had yet again broken. They were puzzled that the community would take such poor care of their well, boasting that the engineering should have endured for quite some time. When repairing it the second time, they discovered that the well had been broken intentionally—someone had thrown a wrench into the gears.

The truth was that the women who had the most to gain from the nearby well had sabotaged it because their walks to the distant well were their only breaks from their children and their only chance to talk without interruption. They did not like losing their communal time.

This tale serves as a fable to development practitioners. The good intentions of outsiders are no match for what autonomous people themselves want and need.[1] Writing for the World Bank, Judy L. Baker has said, "Despite the billions of dollars spent on development assistance each year, there is still very little known about the actual impact of projects on the poor."[2] Oftentimes, interventions are conceptualized in faraway places by people who think very differently about what they posit enhances well-being. Those who seek to be charitable need to understand beneficiary desires.

Some might say the money for that well was wasted. The well itself originated with a Western charity that wanted to provide the community with a basic necessity for life: drinking water. Many people organized to raise fund, engineer, and install that well, believing their contributions would help Africans; this was, as we learned, not the case.

But this fable goes far beyond one well, and describes a macro-level problem with aid. The aid business, to start, is gigantic. In 2013 alone, US global charitable giving to poor countries totaled US $335.17 billion, US $200 billion of which came from private donors.[3] Between the Official Development Assistance, other official flows,[4] and private sources, the United Kingdom's capital outlay to developing countries totaled US $68.25 billion in 2012.[5]

There is a wide gap between intentions and effects in this phenomenon of helping. Moreover, there is woefully little known about the giving and receiving ends of this dynamic process. When living standards in sub-Saharan Africa are as poor as they were fifty years ago (in terms of GDP per capita),[6] critics like William Easterly lament that the US $2.3 trillion dollars the West spent in foreign aid during the last fifty years has been largely a waste of money[7]—just like the well. If we knew what strategies worked, they would have been already implemented, and circumstances would have improved in poor countries. However, donors are compelled to give for different reasons, and those motivations are rarely informed by what has worked. To further complicate this, there are innumerable variables in considering what has worked, when it has, and where.

Western plans for Africa often missed the mark. The continent is littered with abandoned agricultural and hydrological infrastructure left to rot in the sun after donors lost interest. Decisions made in Amsterdam or New York ignored the feelings of those "closest to the well" in an attempt to convince their donors that their scientific progressive strategies will actually work. The extent of the failures is difficult to chart, since donor states and multilateral organizations seldom, if ever, publish the scope and results of their activities abroad, even though a veneer of transparency comes from publishing dollar amounts. Keeping track of impact across the board is a notorious challenge, and the best science for microfinance and other international assistance programs is still not widely applied, or circulated to those prepared to fund it. We know woefully little about how well some interventions work in comparison to others, but there have been several notable attempts to improve our understanding. Because of this, some conclusions are apparent.

HOW WE KNOW WHAT WE KNOW ABOUT POVERTY INTERVENTIONS

Though little is known about the success of development intervention across the map, one research consortium that has made strides in this arena is Innovations for Poverty Access (IPA).[8] Comprised of prominent faculty from

Yale, MIT, Harvard, and others, IPA has assembled various research projects to test the efficacy of several types of interventions, ranging from anti-malarial mosquito nets to savings programs. The organization is popular, inside and out of academia, and provides particularly useful insights into trends in favored methods.

IPA research teams draw heavily on a practice called Randomized Control Trials (RCTs). This, many agree, is the "scientific gold standard," used across a variety of disciplines. In this method of experimental research, one group gets a treatment—say a medication—and another groups gets a control—either nothing, or a placebo in some cases. Using this approach on sample sizes of large numbers is the science for determining causality. In other words, we have to compare people who "have" and "have not" to know what is responsible for the remedy.

IPA researchers, together with institutional affiliates, perform these kinds of studies all over the developing world, and they have uncovered some truly remarkable findings. For example, I recently received a charming email update from them that challenged me: "Most people get this easy quiz wrong—will you?" appeared in the subject line. The quiz was introduced with a comment that "One of the best ways to improve the lives of the poor is through education but poor children in developing countries often miss school for several days of the school year. Several programs have been designed to get and keep kids in school so they learn effectively." The quiz asked if I knew which of three options, based on "thorough rigorous testing from several programs," is "extremely cost-efficient as well as highly effective in keeping kids in school." Is it:

A. School Uniforms

This program offers students a free uniform to reduce a family's school-related expenses and associated stigma with sending a child to school improperly dressed.

B. Girls Merit Scholarships

This program covers the cost of a girl's education so that her hard work is rewarded with more opportunities in the future.

C. Deworming Pills

This program provides deworming treatments at existing schools for common parasitic worm-related infestations.

According to IPA's research, deworming pills (a surprise to me at the time) had the biggest impact in keeping girls in school.[9] The difference in impact between programs was no small matter, either. Every US $100 spent on deworming medicine added 13.9 years in school, whereas the other two interventions combined did not improve attendance by even a full year.

By comparing the benefits of various interventions against people who receive none, scientists are beginning to measure what it is that works. These findings are novel and could be helpful for donors and policymakers to better direct funding. At the same time, this is not the absolute truth in what works for aid recipients.[10] The results are limited in their ability to explain critical nuances of development programming when put into practice. In other words, we still have a long way to go.

WHAT WE KNOW ABOUT MICROFINANCE IMPACT

Microfinance has a mixed track record among its hundreds of millions of participants around the world. Upon its inception in Bangladesh in the 1970s, microfinance gained incredible fame for its purported ability to heal a host of ills related to poverty. Formal finance requires collateral, but when studying economics at Vanderbilt, Muhammad Yunus thought there could be another way. Seeing that the definition of poverty, the lack of *financial capital*, presented an obstacle to creditworthiness, he suspected *social capital* could serve as a substitute. He developed microfinance loans to poor people in his native Bangladesh, whereby group members could co-guarantee loans in *lieu* of collateral or credit scores. Group loan contracts have members pay if others miss a payment. Borrower social pressure to repay loans, according to this logic, contributes to over 95 percent of microloans repaid in full and on time. It is these high repayment rates that are central to popular claims about microfinance success.

When the founder Muhammad Yunus and his Grameen Bank won the Nobel Peace Prize in 2006 "for their efforts to create economic and social development from below,"[11] popularity surged beyond the policy community to reach ordinary citizens. Rising skepticism of microfinance's positive impact claims began in the early 2000s[12] but critiques were largely confined to academic journals. Microfinance garnered some US $16 billion in 2007 and rose steadily to US $34 billion in 2014, according to CGAP Funders Survey estimates.[13] David Roodman traced the increased number of microfinance investment vehicles from twenty-three in the year 2000 to over one hundred by 2008.[14] Across donor regions, there was a noteworthy upward trend over the time period discussed in this book.

Yet academic studies yielded mixed findings about microfinance outcomes. From the earliest research, there was a pervasive interest in several relevant factors. Though syntax varies by case study, researchers sought to understand the scope of impact in quantifiable terms—the science of measured outcomes. In particular, they focused their scrutiny on the amount of clients served (often with a gendered headcount to measure the empowerment of women), repayment rates (demonstrating fidelity of borrowers and solvency of MFIs whereby "anything below 95 percent is considered unsatisfactory" by donor organizations[15]), and financial metrics (whereby increases in income and/or consumption signify poverty alleviation).[16] What follows is an overview of the most significant studies exploring these factors.

To begin, Hulme and Mosley (1996), in researching microcredit's influence on poverty alleviation, focused their inquiry on outcomes in terms of changes in income. They found that better-off borrowers made the biggest improvements in terms of incomes, but the poorest did not benefit in the same way. When compared to control groups that received no loans, most people with incomes below the poverty line ended up with *less* income after borrowing microloans.[17] They found that microfinance institutions by and large serve the "not-so-poor" over the very poorest, even though institutions boasted their assistance to the latter group the most.[18] Many MFIs began focusing their lending, in tandem with this research, on the average poor compared to the ultra-poor,[19] but this was not only by institutional design. Even self-selected groups of borrowers were less inclusive of the poorest.[20] In all, while these research projects originally set out to understand the impact of microcredit in terms of borrower wealth, they failed to consider the important reality of how poor people gain access to credit.

Similarly, in studying microcredit impact in terms of economic measures in Bangladesh, which included a sample size of more than 1,500 participants, Pitt and Khandker (1998) used World Bank survey data in a quasi-experimental cross-sectional approach, comparing borrowers with other villages that met the membership requirements. They found that overall only 5 percent of borrowers lifted themselves out of poverty—defined as having increased assets and expenditures.[21] Some scholars saw this as too modest,[22] given that lending reached a quarter of the population. Scholars also worried the result missed factors that could have been relevant.[23] But their project was novel because it also found that consumption varied by gender. For women borrowers, consumption rates due to microfinance were approximately 18 percent, whereas for men it was 11 percent. This reinforced the donor culture of giving preference to female borrowers, as they were believed to provide for their families better than men would with the newfound wealth.

Khandker (2005) followed up on those borrowers a few years later. By comparing survey datasets of borrowers receiving distinct treatments, he assessed that microfinance contributed only marginal improvements for borrowers. Comparing data from almost 1,800 Bangladeshi households in 1991 and 1992 to 2,600 households (the originals plus new villages) seven years later, he found average cumulative returns rose as much as 21 percent for female borrowers. "The results are resounding," he wrote. "Microfinance continues to reduce poverty among poor borrowers and within the local economy, albeit at a lower rate. Moreover, because of better economic conditions, the gains in real consumption were much higher for both program participants and non participants over the study period."[24] Khandker's studies were very influential in garnering popular support for microcredit.

In time, other scholars questioned the validity of the microcredit research opus. One example of the many emerging critiques was the inclusion criteria—how much land was held by participants. This factor ended up being a bigger determinant than analysts had planned for in their analysis. In practice, adjusting the model to include land holding essentially rendered the prior outcomes moot.[25] These articles were highly technical, but the crux of the matter: having a large amount of land might influence how much and how well a person does with microcredit. ("How much" and "how great an influence" are subject to where the analysts draw the lines.) And of course, there was the ongoing concern as to whether retrospective, quasi-experimental methods from such a database could aptly determine success in the same way as a randomized control trial.

The first major randomized evaluation that set out to understand the impact of microcredit group loan products was launched in more than a hundred slums in Hyderabad, India, in 2005. Between the launch of the evaluation and 2013, researchers compared half of the slums that were randomly selected for an MFI with those that had not been. The studies found that borrowers with greater opportunity for microcredit access were no more likely to start any new business, although they were more likely to invest in existing business, and start several at once. Overall, borrowers demonstrated no increase on consumption in the short and longer follow-up terms. Three to four years after the initial expansion, the researchers "found no changes in any of the development outcomes that are often believed to be affected by microfinance, including health, education, and women's empowerment."[26] These results contradicted many prior speculations about the "miraculous" effects of microcredit. Roodman and Morduch (2009) did a perfect job posing the questions raised by these inconsistencies. "Has the impact of microcredit varied over time and place? Is the key that the Bangladesh studies were longer-term? Or is the difference in methods?"[27]

Meanwhile, other studies questioned if it was even appropriate to examine the impact of microcredit through the narrow prism of consumption. Evidence emerged to reveal what is now called "debt recycling." For example, using a variety of research techniques including semi-structured surveys, group discussion, and participant observation of seventy-four borrowers, Gehlich-Shillabeer (2008) found that the poorest people used loans directly for consumption rather than investing in their businesses. It turned out that what borrowers consumed, and when, mattered to their individual success. Moreover, she also found that borrowers frequently (approximately 60 percent in the Bangladeshi case study) took out multiple loans from other institutions to pay off their debt owed to one another.[28] Many concluded that this cycle perpetuates poverty or hardship among borrowers rather than enabling them to escape from these conditions.[29] The typical institutional level of analysis, which looks primarily to repayment rate, failed to observe such dynamics. While some wrote off these findings as anecdotal to its limited sample size, Gehlich-Shillabeer's study was nevertheless groundbreaking for a country renowned for having microcredit services available to virtually its entire adult (and some adolescent) populations.

There was also the lingering question of how well borrowers did over the longer term. Karlan and Zinman (2009) evaluated the impacts of the expansion of individual liability credit in the Philippines, generally tailored for a class above the poorest for whom group liability loans are designed. They found that loan recipients, compared to their control group counterparts, did not experience an impact on household income or consumption after a year-and-a-half time span. The researchers deduced that some lasting investments were being made, however they were unable to discern that participant investments were occurring in the business activities that microfinance purports to foster. Instead, the size and scope of businesses in which owners had received individual loans had shrunk. Though the study found that statistically, borrowers were more likely to send a relative to school, it found "no evidence of improvements in measures of subjective well-being; if anything, the results point to a small overall decrease."[30] Karlan and Zinman conceded that while the results were meager for the relatively upper-class borrowers they observed, "the fact that we find little evidence of effects on those with lower-income within our sample frame does not bode well for arguments that impact is biggest on those who are poorer."[31]

Crepon, Devoto, Duflo and Pariente (2011) found from their randomized evaluation in rural Morocco that microcredit significantly increased access to credit.[32] In that study, they found on average no changes in terms of consumption, family health, or education rates as measured by studies elsewhere. However, their analysis uncovered one distinction between borrowers that had particularly noteworthy influence in livelihood outcomes. When separating borrowers by whether or not they had preexisting self-employment at the time the intervention began, they found that borrowers without prior self-employment activities increased consumption, especially on food and durable goods, but yielded no improvements in business outcomes. On the other hand, borrowers who were self-employed at the beginning of the study decreased consumption but were more likely to expand the scope of their businesses. When averaging results from all participants' net changes in investment to businesses and personal investment, the nuance between the winning and losing choices were lost.

One recent study compared various microcredit models including loans, cash grants, and a combination of business skills training paired with programs in 1,550 micro-entrepreneurs in Uganda. Fiala (2013) performed an ordinary least squares regression[33] accounting for a range of characteristics (individual ability and patience levels, gender, family pressure as measured by proximity, and regional market effects). The programs and their hybrids were evaluated with follow-ups in the short run (six to nine months). Outcomes measured business output—specifically profits—as the main variable of interest. Comparing different survey arms that received one of the four randomly assigned treatments or a control of no intervention, the author found after nine months that loans (standard to the commercialized microcredit model implemented everywhere) yielded no impacts. Men who received loans supplemented with business training yielded on average a 54 percent increase in profits from their businesses, while no increases were seen for women. In fact, women who received either the loans with business training, or just the grants, experienced losses in incomes.[34] Furthermore, despite increased income for several men, there were no findings of increased consumption, savings, or expenditures on their children's health.[35]

Overall, these studies contradict each other when it comes to microcredit ability to cure poverty. While income and consumption rose in some places, it declined in others. Microcredit worked better for some demographics than others, in certain locations. In most countries, the poorest of the poor did not experience the positive outcomes that the moderately poor did. In some areas, women's lives improved with microcredit, but in others, they worsened. What remain are questions about what accounts for these vast variations. Do they relate to local markets, the preferences of the intended beneficiaries, or something else altogether?

SHORTCOMINGS OF POPULAR MICROFINANCE MEASUREMENT APPROACHES

No study can do it all. Several qualities about the research described above pose limits to knowing how microfinance changes lives. The past analytical approaches are marked by a tendency to use quantitative data and randomized evaluations, and use primarily financial or pre-defined proxy metrics to explain social phenomena. Each of these trends in research increases knowledge about how microcredit works and yet fails to show *why* it works this way.

Reductionist, closed-ended data that is run only through statistical analyses dominates international development research. Microfinance research is no exception. Early evaluations were critiqued for lacking respondent selection and longitudinal results because they were done in single settings and without control groups.[36] Early research could track before and after changes, but could not discern whether the transformations were due to the microcredit programs themselves or other factors too.[37] Since then, researchers have tried to improve their methods with a move toward RCTs in this arena. New findings are produced through replicating study designs across various sites, and using "large n" statistics to compare effects among those who received credit with control groups who did not.

Meanwhile, some scholarship evolved beyond the financial frames. There has been a recent move toward utilizing alternative indicators to know whether or not programs are successful with respect to social parameters. One example of such use of indicators to measure social progress is the concept of "women's empowerment,"[38] which counts variables like birthrates and education. The donor and policy assumption is that if women are doing well, or are empowered, they would seek more education and have fewer children. For example, one important study of the two biggest providers, Grameen and BRAC in Bangladesh, evaluated the outcomes on the following "indicators of women's empowerment: mobility, economic security, ability to make small purchases, ability to make purchases, involvement in major household decisions, relative freedom from domination by the family, political and legal awareness, and participation in public protests and political campaigning." The study said that women improved according to those frameworks.[39] However, competing studies demonstrated that sometimes the variables they used in tests did not explain the social dynamics that also played into the women's increased access to capital. Phenomena as complex as "intrahousehold power relations" must be evaluated with serious involvement of the borrowers themselves, argued Naila Kabeer.[40]

Some of these reductionist measurement strategies shrouded real social problems. For example, in keeping with the above gendered empowerment logic, while many scholars claimed women were growing empowered by microfinance, Aminur Rahman (1999) found that participants who came into new funds and/or increased autonomy were more likely to be involved in domestic disputes.[41] Issues also arise when microcredit procedures clash with local norms. Lamia Karim's 2011 ethnography, for example, cites examples of how most Bangladeshi microloan users were not in fact the women in the borrowing program, but their husbands, and the failure to repay microloans resulted in amplified shame on the poor women.[42]

And then there is the story of the largest public failure of microfinance in history that occurred in Andhra Pradesh, India. In 2010, accounts of multiple borrowers committing suicide made their way to mainstream media, revealing that hundreds of borrowers had grown desperately unable to meet the demands of the loans. Philip Mader explained that "Indian microfinance institutions pursued reckless growth at all costs and ignored all warnings in a particular environment inherited from the past."[43] Whereas many of the hallmark studies about microfinance success vis-à-vis high levels of repayment originated in this part of Southeast Asia, they had not noticed what was happening at the individual livelihood unit of analysis. Borrowers constantly found themselves poorer than before engaging in microcredit, as they were unable to satisfy the demands of the loan terms. The pressure from the lenders and co-borrowers proved too great. Like the 2008 Gehlich-Shillabeer study described earlier that had found that borrowers were recycling their debt, here institutional-level and even individual-level research failed to see the predicaments affecting borrowers, too. Occurrences like these support the arguments of Milford Bateman: microfinance may work for the financiers who see profits and the MFIs who see employment, but not necessarily the poor.[44]

Microcredit is not just a bank from which people borrow money, only interacting when depositing money or cashing out. When engaging in microcredit, borrowers are responsible for making payments if a colleague fails to make his; in this way, it is highly social. Because of this, and because poverty is more complex than economic constraint, researchers have tried to understand how the social dynamics involved in group-lending work.

CASE STUDY OF A CASE STUDY

In 2005, Dean Karlan, founder of IPA, conducted a study to learn about the relationship between social capital and borrower propensity to repay group loans and save money.[45] At the individual level, literature preceding his work has defined social capital as a composition of the social skills and networks that enable an individual to overcome imperfect information problems and form contracts with others.[46] The study sought to test claims made by the microcredit industry that the group-lending structure makes use of borrower social relations to improve repayment rates. To test these claims, he needed to find evidence that high social capital directly correlated with higher repayment rates. While these rates could be counted, social capital is not as easily quantified; as a result, Karlan needed to use social capital scales to quantify the qualitative concepts into statistical algorithms. To do this, he utilized preexisting and well-known metrics from the General Social Survey (GSS) following Glaeser et al. (2002), who argued that responses to the questions predicted trustworthy (but not trusting) behaviors, which are good for socioeconomic functioning.[47] The three GSS questions they asked were as follows: (1) "Generally speaking, would you say that most people can be trusted or that you can't be too careful in dealing with people?" (2) "Do you think most people would try to take advantage of you if they got a chance, or would they try to be fair?" And (3) "Would you say that most of the time people try to be helpful, or that they are mostly just looking out for themselves?"

Answer choices were limited and discreet. Subjects had to agree, disagree, or give a neutral response. In addition to these survey questions, Karlan carried out a game that simulated both trusting and trustworthy behaviors among participants.[48] Karlan ran a statistical regression analysis on the answers against the behaviors observed during the game, and found significant relationships between social capital and financially trustworthy behaviors. Positive responses to the GSS questions (i.e., I agree that most people can be trusted) predicted higher rates of group loan repayments and savings. In short, he argued that social capital enhances both repayments and savings. The GSS questions, in his project, predicted trustworthy but not trusting behavior.

Then in 2011, along with his colleague Sendhil Mullainathan, Karlan applied that same framework to see whether those who had strong feelings associated with having high predictive power in explaining social capital would be better at repaying individual loans, as compared to the group loans in the previous study. In this second study in the Philippines, the correlation did not hold. Those metrics of social capital did not correspond with improved repayment among individual borrowers.

It is puzzling that there would be such a stark difference between the two studies. One explanation may be that when borrowers have strong associations, or high social capital, they are less inclined to shirk, and more inclined to find ways of making payments, even when goings are tough. The researchers' explanation for the difference in findings between the two studies was similar. "This may be because social capital makes people less likely to default when the burden falls on people within their network, as is the case with group lending. However, in the case of individual loans, the burden falls on the bank, which is likely to be outside of a subject's social network."[49] To better understand the difference in findings, it is important to notice two important factors that changed between the two studies: the country context and the loan product being tested. The authors linked the different results to the different products under scrutiny. In their conclusion, they argued that the unique finding was due to the difference in perceived obligations of an individual loan compared to the group loan. But we still cannot account for the cultural and economic differences between the two countries. Indeed, the authors admit there is a lot of complicated "murkiness" within the data. Many questions went unanswered. For instance, why would people be less likely to pay back a bank than their peers? What leads anyone to pay others back? Does trust or trustworthiness relate to borrowing?

PARSIMONY AND SCOPE

There are many choices involved in crafting research. There is an understandable desire for metrics that can be replicated across contexts, so that hypotheses can be better tested out, but these benefits come at a cost. What is being realized over time is that the most succinct variables fall short in explaining the real externalities experienced by loan recipients.

Most experiments deployed in economics and sociology are deductive rather than inductive from the outset. This means that because almost any study founded in knowledge of the field will be grounded with a hypothesis beforehand. Deductive methods like those mentioned in the earlier section require researchers to assign discrete questions they anticipate will speak to the issues addressed by the hypothesis. The questions in turn elicit codified responses. Yet there are limitations with this method as the analysis is thus bound by data collected in anticipation of a specific hypothesis. In other words, having a hypothesis in mind already will tend to yield results that fit within the original parameters. As a result, the interpretation of outcomes beyond those parameters only produces conjecture.

My main quarrel with the ethics of research trials here has to do with the fact that even well-respected researchers quiet the voices of their subjects. Though some economists and psychologists believe people often say differently than they mean,[50] reducing participants' experiences and opinions to distilled variables does not fill the knowledge gap sufficiently. Participants' lived experiences matter. The research community has gotten in the habit of creating tests or analogs that can be measured; however, we are counting and anticipating, not listening.

NOTES

1. This story is so common that it is probably true, though I have yet to find the source. It was even told in the 2016 film *Whiskey Tango Foxtrot*. There are studies that have yielded similar outcomes. Some studies have also demonstrated how intended beneficiaries adapt the goods to their own ends. For examples, see Phillip C. Kottak, "Culture and Economic Development," *The American Anthropologist,* 92, no. 3. (1990); Alok Kumar Sanjay and Vivek Gupta, "Gyandoot: Trying to Improve Government Services for Rural Citizens in India eTransparency Case Study no. 11 (2000).

2. Judy Baker, *Evaluating the Impact of Development Projects on Poverty: A Handbook for Practitioners* (The World Bank, 2000).

3. Charity Navigator, "Giving Statistics." Charity Navigator, Index, n.d.

4. Other Official Flows (OOF) is defined by the UK government as "flows to developing countries by the official sector which do not satisfy both criteria necessary for ODA (i.e. can either be non-concessional and convey a grant element of less than 25 per cent or non-developmental purposes or both)."

5. DFID, *Statistics on International Development* (Department for International Development, National Statistics, 2013).

6. Benno Ndulu, et al., *Challenges of African Growth: Opportunities, Constraints and Strategic Directions* (Washington, DC: The World Bank, 2007).

7. Willian Easterly, *The White Man's Burden: Why the West's Efforts to Aid the Rest Have Done So Much Ill and So Little Good* (New York, NY: Penguin Press, 2006).

8. To see an overview of their reports, I suggest looking at their webpage: http://www.poverty-action.org

9. Innovations for Poverty Action, "School-Based Deworming." http://www.poverty-action.org/deworming.

10. In fact, the hallmark deworming study from Kenya based on evidence from the late 1990s was recently called into question. See Michael Clemens and Justin Sandefur, "Mapping the Worm Wars: What the Public Should Take Away from the Scientific Debate about Mass Deworming." (*Center for Global Development*, 2015).

11. "The Nobel Peace Prize 2006". *Nobelprize.org*. http://www.nobelprize.org/nobel_prizes/peace/laureates/2006/.

12. Hugh Sinclair, *Confessions of a Microfinance Heretic* (San Francisco: Berrett-Koehler, 2012).

13. Matthew Soursourian and Edlira Dashi, *Current Trends in International Funding for Financial Inclusion*. CGAP Donor Brief (Washington, DC: CGAP Publishing, 2015).

14. David Roodman "Charting Growth." 2011.

15. Malcom Harper, "What's Wrong with Groups?" In *What's Wrong with Microfinance?* edited by Thomas Dichter and Malcolm Harper (Practical Action Publishing in association with GSE Research, 2007) in Dichter, T., Harper, M. (Eds), p. 39.

16. See also Shah Nawaz, "Microfinance and Poverty Reduction: Evidence from a Village Study in Bangladesh." *Journal of Asian and African Studies* 45, no. 6 (2010), which analyzes the roles of subsidy within the measurement constructs of the "welfarist" and "institutionalist" approaches.

17. David Hulme and Paul Mosley, *Finance Against Poverty* vol. 2 (London and New York: Routledge, 1996).

18. Paul Mosley and David Hulme, "Microenterprise Finance: Is There a Conflict Between Growth and Poverty Alleviation?" *World Development* 26, no. 5 (1998).

19. Sergio Navajas, et al., "Microcredit and the Poorest of the Poor: Theory and Evidence from Bolivia." *World Development* 28, no. 2 (2000).

20. Richard Montgomery, "Disciplining or Protecting the Poor? Avoiding the Social Costs of Peer Pressure in Micro-credit Schemes." *Journal of International Development, Special Issue, Sustainable Banking with the Poor* 8, no. 2 (1996).

21. Mark M. Pitt and Shahidur R. Khandker, "The Impact of Group Based Credit Programs on Poor Households in Bangladesh: Does the Gender of Participants Matter?" *Journal of Political Economy* 106, no. 5 (1998).

22. David Roodman and Uzma Qureshi, "Microfinance as Business." *Center for Global Development 2*, (Washington, DC, 2006).

23. David Roodman and Jonathan Morduch, "The Impact of Microcredit on the Poor in Bangladesh: Revisiting the Evidence." *Journal of Development Studies* 50, no. 4 (2013).

24. Shahidur R. Khandker, "Microfinance and Poverty: Evidence Using Panel Data." *Bangladesh World Bank Economic Review* 26, no. 2/3 (2005), 285.

25. David Roodman and Jonathan Morduch, "The Impact of Microcredit on the Poor in Bangladesh: Revisiting the Evidence." *Journal of Development Studies* 50, no. 4 (2013).

26. Esther Duflo et al., "The Miracle of Microfinance? Evidence from a Randomized Evaluation." (*National Bureau of Economic Research,* 2013).

27. David Roodman and Jonathan Morduch, "The Impact of Microcredit on the Poor in Bangladesh: Revisiting the Evidence." *Journal of Development Studies* 50, no. 4 2013).

28. Mareen Gehlich-Shillabeer, "Poverty Alleviation or Poverty Traps? Microcredits and Vulnerability in Bangladesh." *Disaster Prevention and Management* 17, no. 3 (2008).

29. John D. Von Pischke, *Finance at the Frontier: Debt Capacity and the Role of Credit in the Private Economy* (Washington, DC: World Bank Publications, 1991).

30. Dean Karlan and Jonathan Zinman, "Expanding Microenterprise Credit Access: Using Randomized Supply Decisions to Estimate the Impacts in Manila." (2009).

31. Dean Karlan and Jonathan Zinman, "Expanding Microenterprise Credit Access: Using Randomized Supply Decisions to Estimate the Impacts in Manila." (2009), 4.

32. Bruno Crepon, Florencia Devoto, Esther Duflo and William Pariente, "Estimating the Impact of Microcredit on Those Who Take It Up: Evidence from a Randomized Experiment in Morocco." *Economics* (2014).

33. This analysis is used to test if there is correlation happening between linear variables using a line of best fit.

34. The negative effects were more pronounced among women from the north whose economy is substantially more challenging than the central region.

35. Nathan Fiala, "Stimulating Microenterprise Growth: Results from a Loans, Grants and Training Experiment in Uganda." *SSRN Electronic Journal* (2013).

36. See Dean S. Karlan, "Teaching Entrepreneurship: Impact of Business Training on Microfinance Clients and Institutions." *Review of Economics & Statistics* 93, no. 2 (2001). Beatriz Armendariz and Jonathan Morduch, *The Economics of Microfinance* (Cambridge: Massachusetts Institute of Technology Press, 2005).

37. Cristina Elisa Orso, "Microcredit and Poverty. An Overview of the Principal Statistical Methods used to Measure the Programme Net Impacts." *POLIS Working Paper* (2011), 10.

38. See Susy Cheston and Lisa Kuhn, "Empowering Women through Microfinance." in *Pathways Out of Poverty: Innovations in Microfinance for the Poorest Families* (Bloomfield: Kumarian Press, 2002).

39. Syed M. Hashemi, et al., "Rural Credit Programs and Women's Empowerment in Bangladesh." *World Development* 24, no. 4 (1996).

40. Naila Kabeer, "Conflicts Over Credit: Re-Evaluating the Empowerment Potential of Loans to Women in Rural Bangladesh." *World Development* 29, no. 1 (2001) and Naila Kabeer, "Resources, Agency, Achievements: Reflections on the Measurement of Women's Empowerment." Development and Change. 30, no. 3 (1999).

41. Aminur Rahman, *Women and Microcredit in Rural Bangladesh: An Anthropological Study of Grameen Bank Lending* (Boulder: Westview Press, 1999). Juliet Hunt and Nalini Kasyanthan, "Pathways to Empowerment Reflections on Microfinance and Transformation in Gender Relations in South Asia." *Gender and Development* 9, no. 1 (2001). Guy Levé, *The Encyclopedia of Card Play Techniques at Bridge* (Toronto: Master Point Press, 2007).

42. Lamia Karim, *Microfinance and its Discontents: Women in Debt in Bangladesh* (Minneapolis: University of Minnesota Press, 2011).

43. Philip Mader, "Rise and Fall of Microfinance in India: The Andhra Pradesh Crisis in Perspective." *Strategic Change* 22 (2013).

44. Milford Bateman, *Why Doesn't Microfinance Work?: The Destructive Rise of Local Neoliberalism* (London & New York: Zed Books, 2012).

45. Dean S. Karlan, "Using Experimental Economics to Measure Social Capital and Predict Financial Decisions." *American Economic Review* 95, no. 5 (2005).

46. Karlan used Francis Fukuyama, *Trust: Social Virtues and the Creation of Prosperity* (New York: Free Press, 1995) and Elinor Ostrom, *Governing the Commons: The Evolution of Institutions for Collective Action* (Cambridge: Cambridge University Press, 1990) frameworks for his operationalizing.

47. Barney G. Glaeser, et al., "Measuring Trust." *Quarterly Journal of Economics* 115 (2000).

48. He did this to close the loop between the Trust Game theories and the social capital tests hitherto used in the field. While his report analyzed the relationship

between the two experiments, this summary in this text only outlines the portion that was replicated in another study. In short, the Trust Game assumes Player A is trusting player B trustworthy by giving the player A an opportunity to pass money to player B in hopes that player B will return some or all of it. Karlan additionally examined how variables between participants mediated the outcomes of trusting and trustworthy behaviors, including how close they live to each other, and church attendance.

49. Udo Schüklenk, "Protecting the Vulnerable: Testing Times for Clinical Research Ethics." *Social Science & Medicine* 51, no. 6 (2000).

50. Daniel Kahneman and Amos Tversky, "Prospect Theory: An Analysis of Decision Under Risk." *Econometrica* 47 (1979).

Chapter 3

I Can't Exchange for Dollars But Will You Talk with Me?

Learning in a different way

Checking premade boxes with a yes or no will not suffice. Understanding how ideas shape and are shaped by practice is integral to understanding how poverty alleviation efforts work. This work needs to occur both within and outside "the formal boundaries" of the development industry.[1] Few studies have mapped ideologies within the social worlds receiving microcredit, and the context of their findings may be specific to the situations in those sites. Given that so little is known about the experience of microfinance culture in post-conflict societies, the focus of this case is at the local implementation within one postwar country.

The findings presented by this text suggest that new methods can better illuminate the social dynamics that underpin development than the mainstay of past MFI studies. These methods are better able to identify the lived realities of policies put in practice. This chapter describes the grounded, qualitative methods of this project as a roadmap for the evidence shown in the text. This account of my research process illustrates not only the challenges, opportunities but also joys of this work.

POSTPOSITIVE MOVEMENT IN UNDERSTANDING POVERTY ALLEVIATION

William Easterly, one of the world's foremost international development economists, was recently asked why aid fails.

He explained that

> The critical thing that makes foreign aid fail so often—and this is really heart-breaking—is simply that the poor who are the intended customers of foreign

aid, just like you are the intended customer of the Pepsi Corporation when they sell you Pepsis. . . . But unlike your relationship with Pepsi, the poor have no right to complain and no right to turn down the product if they don't like it. The poor just get foreign aid foisted on them by these ill-informed "experts," and there's no feedback from the poor—whether they're satisfied or not, whether their money even reached them or not.[2]

While his use of the phrase "no right to complain" might be not true of every case, his point does speak to the division between so-called givers and receivers. There is occasional feedback from the poor in regard to interventions, but it is slight and rare. In light of this, we have to grapple with the fact that overall we know little about poor peoples' preferences, despite the continual outpouring of financial support into programming.

Typical program evaluations can only show part of the picture of the everyday lived experience of people using microfinance interventions. Their experiences may not be understood or articulated by program participants in strictly economic terms of repayment or arrears. Trite as the adage might be, money does not buy happiness. Nobel Prize winning economist Amartya Sen aptly pointed out in his groundbreaking *Development as Freedom* that "real incomes can be rather poor indicators of important components of well-being and quality of life that people have reason to value."[3] Similarly, Clifford Geertz, in his ethnographic writings on Indonesian economics, described development that focuses on per-capita income as "highly misleading" when faced with the inherently embedded social processes that foster, sustain, and are affected by measurable income. Noting the tendencies of economists to focus on the macro level, and cultural anthropologists to focus on the micro, he proposed that

a really effective theory of economic growth will appear only when the social process and take-off approaches are joined in a single framework of analysis, when the relationships between the broad changes in social stratification, or political structure, or cultural values which facilitate growth, and the specific changes in levels of saving and investment we hold to cause it can be related to one another.[4]

Understanding the nuance of local ideas about what constitutes "well-being" is central to bridging this divide. Therefore, we need to practice other ways of learning how exactly participants construe and make use of the services being offered them.

J. K. Gibson-Graham, a pair of scholars who critique the obsession with capitalism as the only analytical frame, encourage us to "deconstruct familiar economic representations" to see what is beneath the figurative tip of the iceberg.[5] Money, after all, is not exclusively a store of value, but has deep relational meaning and frequently unanticipated ways of being used.[6] It is for this reason this project stepped out of traditional microfinance research methods whose foci are mostly economic, centering instead on not only whether it works but describing *how*.

PROJECT METHODOLOGY

Seeking a more nuanced picture of the social life with microloans than is visible in the current literature, I spent the summer months of 2008, 2009, 2012, and 2013 in Juba, South Sudan. To accomplish my research goals, I relied heavily upon anthropological—instead of economic—methodologies. I observed daily activities at microfinance branches, including disbursements to and repayments from current clients. I accompanied MFI field officers on home visits to clients and "outside" marketing visits. I spent time in local businesses, familiarizing myself with quotidian business practices, conveniently facilitating interviews with other Juba residents not affiliated with microfinance institutions.

The text that had informed research design largely treated information as if it were perfectly arranged and ready for the taking. All one needed to do was go and get it. The very brief methods sections in the studies I was reading explained little about how previous scholars carried out their projects from day to day. Many ignored the fact that research is a process that cannot occur without participation.

This project design began with a commitment to Grounded Theory, which is the process of learning and data collection starting with broad questions that allow data to emerge, and then later require the researcher to theorize in accordance to what emerged. It is a decidedly inductive method that systematically analyzes responses in order to develop codes, and hypotheses, and eventually theory. In that practice, I employed open-ended interviews and conducted observations, rather than focusing on predefined variables. I set out to resist using the leading questions or the reductionist variables used by other scholars that tried to anticipate elements that might influence how microcredit "works." Instead, I wanted participants to name their own interests along the way. As years of this project went on, open-coded responses to early interviews informed more honed, specific interviews and surveys. I will often in the next sections refer to the early and later years of this project when referencing approaches that relate to the iterative nature of the grounded research method.

WHAT ARE DATA?

This study's data are unique in two respects: it uses less-than-traditional sources and it uses less-than-traditional means of collecting the data from said sources. Because agencies are incapable of knowing what happens beyond the data they selectively collect as they disburse and receive payments, there are limitations to the data they can provide for understanding their impact on borrowers. We learned in the earlier example of recycled debt that microfinance institutions themselves were unable to see everything that happened for the borrowers. Therefore, this study set out to expand the scope of data sources beyond what was reported by microfinance institutions.

I had to triangulate varied sources of knowledge about the programs, to "attempt to map out, or explain more fully, the richness and complexity of human behavior by studying it from more than one standpoint."[7] To do this, this project not only sampled institutional personnel, people who were borrowing at the time of meeting, but also surveyed at length people who lived in targeted areas but did not use microfinance or had previously used it. Indeed many have acknowledged that important differences can exist between the people who participate and those who do not.[8] The process also led me to triangulate the interview data that were created alongside what was available from the MFIs and their supporting agencies. As stated, the original aim of this project was to understand *how* microcredit functioned in a post-conflict society. Yet this story changed as the events on the ground developed. Thus second set of data, or the materials that helped shape the local story into the larger final story arc about what happened to the Juba industry, will be described below.

The primary data collected were not the institutional data relating to portfolio size and repayment rates that were discussed above but instead were created through personal experiences in the form of interviews and through participant observation. My method for data collection is too rare in development research: I talked to people. Real human beings told me their experiences and opinions. And I listened. Though it sounds very simple, I will not say it was easy.

SAMPLING FOR INTERVIEWS

To learn how Juba microcredit functions for all stakeholders, the main groups or sub-samples that I sought out were microfinance recipients and microfinance industry personnel. While in Juba, I interviewed people from various backgrounds and levels of affiliation with development programs, and microfinance in particular. I conversed with microfinance institution staff and executives, asking about their economic and social goals, as well as their incentive structures. I also spoke with several people involved in the microfinance donor and coordination communities. I explored the clients' and former clients' perspectives on finance. My aim was to situate microfinance within larger conceptions of assistance, money and banking, in Juba and in general. Given that Juba is a cosmopolitan city in the sense that South Sudanese and others who inhabit it lived elsewhere during the last two decades, I expected this was no small order.

Since I did not embark on this project with a deductive research question, I did not focus my interviews on any particular population subset while in the field. Moreover, some sample groups I anticipated encountering were easier to access, and others were harder. Because of this, the interviews are not evenly distributed among the constituents relating to microfinance in Juba. Though the sample groups were not statistically evenly distributed, they were rich with information (Table 3.1).

The MFI staff and managers were among the most interested in the study and were eager to participate. We engaged in long meetings and occasional meals, and they were very transparent in our conversations. Many offered contacts with their colleagues and brokered interviews for me. I interviewed and/or shadowed five managers and thirteen staff, including field officers, research administrators, and clerks.

There are times where I specified staff by name, and others where I concealed their identities. Where named, it was when they had been specifically asked. Where concealed, I acknowledge losing some analytical power. This was an ethical choice I made due to the nature of some of the more controversial topics being discussed.

All client identities were assigned pseudonyms throughout. At the time of interviews, they were not asked to which MFI they had belonged. This was intentional, so as to foster a confidence in me and to relieve fear of reprisal if they spoke out against any person or agency. As with the choice to refrain from linking staff names to their institutions, this choice traded some degree of analytical precision as well.

The majority of the microfinance industry in South Sudan went underwater between 2010 and 2011. In light of this shift on the ground, I thought it important to add an additional sample set of people who previously had borrowed but no longer did. I interviewed sixty such individuals in 2012 and 2013.

Table 3.1 Interview Data Sources by Type

Type	*Count*
MFI management	5
MFI staff	13
MF donor-coordinators	8
Current borrowers	85
Former borrowers	70
No MFI affiliation	22
Total	203

Source: Author.

BEGINNING A FIELD STUDY

I had a lot of ideas about how the field research would go, and not all of them were accurate. Before traveling to Juba to officially begin fieldwork, I had visited one MFI, met with its staff, and met a handful of their beneficiaries. I knew from online research that there were approximately 20,000 borrowers through six registered MFIs in Juba, a city whose population was growing with repatriates so quickly that the population doubled in the first year after the 2005 Comprehensive Peace Agreement, and again by another year later.

Respondents were courted for the study in various ways. Some of the interviews were scheduled in advance, while others were sampled through snowball techniques, and still others were impromptu. Accessing participants was more complicated than many fieldwork writings indicate.

I spent an embarrassingly long few days of my first fieldwork trip to Juba initiating conversations with people who entered the restaurant at the compound where I was staying. Very quickly, after some basic "getting to know you" questions, I tried asking if people had been exposed to microcredit. It was apparent that people thought this was strange, and while some told me their experiences, many did not want to. Early on I realized that asking such questions, though the content was trivial, entailed talking about money matters, which was sometimes seen as intimate. Moreover, I realized immediately that asking to tape interviews was not the best choice. I needed to modify my approach, acknowledge that an outsider must earn trust, and then develop rapport.

Meanwhile, I tried to find who was formally involved in microfinance. In the early years of the project, internet and mobile phone connectivity were sparse. Additionally, in the early years few people who were not participating in microcredit programs even knew the programs existed, much less knew where the offices were. To find the institutional personnel, I went to the offices. Sometimes the staff people were eager to talk and other times they stressed how busy they were, asking me to come back later. I was never really sure why those who were generous with their time were so generous, and I felt a little guilty for "taking" working hours. Of those who were eager to participate, several took me on tours of their offices and their field visits. Most of these tours were on foot, walking from vendor to vendor. Once I was driven around on the back of a motorcycle, and watched the loan officer's daily activities, such as trying to get a payment from a tardy borrower. Typically, a loan officer was my tour guide, and he would introduce me to vendors who explained that the business was doing well because of microcredit. Sometimes, depending on the language, the officer would translate, while other times the officer would debrief afterward. The tours occasionally seemed superfluous, as if the field officer was employed that day more as a tour guide than a collection agent.

Clients of microfinance were the hardest subset to reach independently of the MFIs. I could not identify which market vendors were microloan borrowers without asking, and attempts at learning this information were sometimes met with skepticism, and refusals to be interviewed. Because of this, in my first round of fieldwork, I had MFI personnel join me and identify clients.

I never heard a negative experience in the visits with an MFI escort. It is possible, if not likely, that these testimonials were colored by the staff presence. Additionally, there might have been a selection bias on the part of the connecting field officer, choosing to showcase only successful clients. Such showcase tours provided little information and grew tiresome, but thankfully they were not in vain. However selective, the guided tours helped me to know what kinds of businesses and, moreover, which markets were populated by microcredit-targeted prospects. Then I set out to make connections in the field outside these channels to find members of the target populations.

I went about this in two ways. First, I got familiar with the types of markets potential micro-enterprise borrowers operated. I began making daily laps through the outdoor markets, where the mainstay of targeted microcredit clients tended to run enterprises. The open-air markets normally lined the corridors between the larger enterprises with more permanent structures. Sometimes there was shade from overhead coverings.

I sought to establish trusting relationships, as someone who was connected to this community to some degree. It was rare for a person who looks like me (white skinned and not uniformed) to shop at, much less hang out at the outdoor markets which patched through the city center and around various nodes of town. Normally, people who look like me—*Khawaja* we are called colloquially—shop in the permanent supermarket in town. I stuck out.

I normally began by asking where their goods came from, and I would ask salespeople where they were coming from, too. I could banter in Kiswahili, Luganda, or Lwo (languages common in the neighboring countries they had lived in during the war) as appropriate. Responses to these simple introductory questions helped me to see just how far the market goods had traveled to be sold in Juba as well as the importance of language networks in accessing all kinds of resources.

SECURING AND CARRYING OUT INTERVIEWS

Once I developed friendly relationships with MFI personnel and individual market vendors, I began asking for interviews. I always carried with me a one-page Study Information Sheet (SIS), approved by my university's Institutional Review Board. The SIS contained an overview of what I was requesting: 15–60 minutes of their time, an explanation that respondents have the right to terminate participation at any time, that all responses would be kept anonymous, and that there would be no trace of subject identifiers in future transmissions of the interviews.[9]

Some people obliged interviews right away, and others preferred to schedule for another day and time. Of course, there were many who were reticent to participate altogether. Counting each willing participant a small victory, I was happy to work around their preferences. Unless otherwise noted, interviews were one-on-one in public places (lots done in the markets, naturally) but almost always out of earshot of others.

Each time, I reviewed the SIS with the participant, and then asked to either take handwritten notes or record audio. Most interviews were recorded digitally. Five of the participants asked me not to tape the proceedings but did permit me to take notes as we spoke. I transcribed their phrases verbatim.

During the interviews, I asked a set of questions that related to the issues relevant to the sub-sample. There were different sets of questions for the MFIs, the borrowers, the former borrowers, and for those who never borrowed. I asked questions but let people respond openly. I posed follow-up questions when something was unclear to me. In retrospect, reviewing transcripts, there were many follow-up questions I wish I had asked.

In 2013, I needed some help to capture time-sensitive information. People who had been borrowers but left the institution still had fresh memories, and I did not want to miss their stories. To that end, I trained two proctors, who were recruited through advertisements in the local newspaper. Proctors, sometimes called enumerators, were trained in accordance with the ethical protocol of the project and disclosed the same information to prospective participants. They were instructed to refrain from interviewing their acquaintances in order to avoid any response biases. Proctors took with them printouts of interview schedules, with ample room to take notes of the open-ended responses. I accompanied proctors on their first rounds of interviews (about half) to ensure the procedures were followed.

Most interviews were conducted in English, but translation was necessary for reaching the population who did not speak English. In these interviews, I asked questions in English, the translator relayed the questions to the clients in Juba Arabic, and then translated their responses back to me in English. This process was captured on an audio-recording device.

The audio recordings and transcripts of translator-present interviews were subsequently corroborated by a group of Southern Sudanese Juba Arabic speakers relocated in the United States, a two-hour drive from my university campus. They had no prior affiliation with the researcher, and were given no subject identifiers for the voices they heard and translated. During these translation sessions, the translators discovered only some marginal disagreement between the original respondents' statements and the translation executed by the on-site translator(s).

DEALING WITH BIASES AND POSITIONALITY

Each method of garnering participation, carrying out the interviews, and even my position as interviewer affected the participant responses. It is impossible to extricate the scientist from the data, and even more from the analysis. A social scientist who ignores this point disregards the simple reality that people's experiences and opinions are not created in a vacuum. That said, some specific dynamics at work in this project merit discussion as they relate to the quality of the data, and my role in interpreting them.

Participants I met in South Sudan had, more likely than not, been surveyed before due to a litany of non- and inter-governmental agencies surveying everything from demographic data to prices of food. The Juba residents of this postwar era saw aid and other assistance interventions abound, and auditors engaged community members about practically every program in one way or another. Even before the CPA, most participants had been living in places where they were exposed to such aid programs and their enumerators searching for data about their effects.

Agency self-evaluations also create promotional materials for the organizations. Interviews with borrowers are often filmed or recorded with obvious intent, and the clients were aware of this. The materials produced by such interviews are 100 percent positive. Criticisms are edited out of the final products.[10] Personnel who worked within the purveying organization normally conducted the surveys, and it was not strategic for program recipients, including loan clients, to speak against agents that supported them. Analysts from outside the purveying organization should help temper these concerns.

Easterly advocates for an approach that "aid agencies should each set aside a portion of their budgets (such as the part now wasted on self-evaluation) to contribute to an international independent evaluation group made up of staff trained in the scientific method from the rich and poor countries, who will evaluate [aid programs]."[11] Still, unaffiliated research teams evaluating studying organizations do not happen often enough. Very few people in Juba were familiar with non-partisan researchers in my position.

While my ethnic appearance, including my light "white" skin, differentiated me from the population, that difference generally produced inquiry about why I was there. Many market workers, for instance, queried about who sent me. Nobody went to Juba without a business affiliation or NGO acronym. I had to explain to prospective respondents that I did not belong to an organization, that I was impartial, and that their responses would not impact their ability to gain services ahead. I was just "the researcher," as several strangers called me over time. Reactions to this were generally positive and surprised.

I took extra care when introducing myself, to clarify that I was not attempting to learn exclusively positive stories that would be utilized or even heard by their lending institutions. I let the interviewees know that they could tell me frankly what they thought because I do not report to the organizations. We learn from the struggles as much as the successes—I would say often.

Still, my presence was complicit with not only the analysis I conducted but also the creation of the data. Failing to acknowledge the dynamics present when researchers interact with participants, misses some part of the contextual meaning available. Indeed, others before me have suggested "that researchers should systematically seek out their subjectivity."[12] Whereas social research that ignores researcher subjectivity perpetuates the fiction of objectivity, acknowledging and managing bias allows us to forge credibility by delineating the value and boundaries of their contributions.

I was talking about money with poor people. While not wealthy by any standard in my home country, I come from the United States, a country with a significant reputation for wealth. Unlike other visitors, I as a researcher had nothing to "offer" participants in the immediate sense. I had no NGO that was offering services, no company offering jobs, and no money to spend. I was never asked in the research context for charity, but I was asked occasionally, when the issue of currency exchange or purchasing items wholesale came up in interviews, to convert US dollars. This was a practical matter, and we both had much to gain financially from the interaction outside of South Sudan's fledgling foreign exchange market. I could have changed South Sudanese pounds for US dollars and won on the currency market compared to the formal bank rates, and so would the people who proposed the exchange. But I felt I could not in context, because such an exchange would have changed my role to a researcher who was enmeshed in local business dealings. I was asking to have some of their time and offering nothing but the hope of some distant day improving policies in return. Perhaps if I was donning an organization t-shirt, participants might have felt their responses would influence policy more immediately than what I could promise. My distance from being able to change their circumstance was both an advantage and a disadvantage. I feel confident about the merits of the data this process produced based on the choices made.

Similar can be said of my more fixed and apparent identity markers, in particular that I am a woman. This shaped many aspects of the data creation. I believe that my gender facilitated access to certain varieties of intimate information among the women borrowers and market vendors. It also informed the conversations I had with institutional personnel. I feel confident about the merits of the data analyzed through these factors.

DATA ANALYSIS

I used a variety of systematic methods to analyze the many stories told to me. I used narrative analysis[13] supposing that "each statement has to be related, in the whole of its movement, to the stage to which it belongs, and acquires its full meaning only if we take into account not only what it says explicitly, but also its place in the whole that constitutes its latent content."[14] In other words, the analyses in this book situate respondent storylines within the broader context in which they live. The goal of the analysis was to glean social dimensions of stories, not just the structural or literal components (as occurs in content analysis). The two main methods of analysis were narrative and semiotic cluster analyses.

Narrative analysis teases out elements that speakers emphasize as important. For those who told me stories, I used a semiotic storyline technique. Stories convey significance and change—either in characters or circumstanced faced by them. In this research, the stories that participants told about themselves and others in relation to microfinance were an obvious fit.

For those narratives that did not contain a clear story arc, I uncovered underlying logics through the interpretation of both denotative (or explicit) and connotative (or implied) meanings in their narratives. I used this process to uncover what classic rhetorical studies call the "enthymeme," which is such a vital part of everyday speech that Aristotle called it the "most effective means of communication."[15] A commonplace enthymeme is the unstated parts of a person's story because the speaker either assumes that the hearer already is attuned to them, omits them by accident, or intentionally omits them to pique the hearer's curiosity.[16] For example, a person might omit that he applied but was rejected for a loan when talking about his disdain for a creditor. For these types of narratives, I first drew out a "working story line," then identified the implicit and/or explicit oppositions within the storyline. I then performed the narrative analysis outlined above.

In all analyses, I relied heavily on semiotic—rather than structural–linguistic tools. Semiotics is concerned with the signification process. "Signification refers both to the processes by which events, words, behaviors and objects carry meaning for the members of a given community and to the content they convey."[17] In short, the implied meanings of particular words and objects of reference often point to other, profounder meanings than those that are literally heard. After several years working in the region, I developed a comfortable grasp of many non-literal meanings of sayings, and where not self-evident, I identify them here in footnotes when they occur in individual narratives or excerpts.

To uncover those processes by which members produce and replicate meaning about microfinance in each sample group, I then undertook a Semiotic Cluster Analysis[18] to analyze the competing meanings of what might literally be seen as a singular concept: microfinance. For example, Feldman (1995) analyzed that something as seemingly discrete as a building—in context of various significations for different people—could connote many things including physical infrastructure, home, or control. Just as the biscuit had meanings that were appropriated or shifted to take on new meanings that are local, this analysis helped inform a better view of microfinance through the various relationships people in Juba have to it.

Theories and themes created in the first couple of years helped me generate the questions I asked in the last two years. I developed interview schedules which provided time and space for open-ended responses as I did throughout the project. I used an axial coding method to interpret open-ended comments that were then counted and categorized to observe any trends. This coding method provided a way to systematically compare responses and ensure that the essence of the respondents' words was interpreted with context.

When summarizing major themes from the interview data, I highlighted the magnitude of frequencies—how many people felt similarly, based on the semiotic codes I devised to sort responses—to map and trace relationships between opinions and behaviors. Yet, the themes with high-frequency counts did not mean that the widespread views told the whole story. Given the fact that the borrowers were hailing from very different economies and economic value systems, I indicated where a pattern was made or broken by naming the participants' storylines and situating them with the participants' contextual markers. As Krane et al. said aptly, "Placing a frequency count after a category of experiences is tantamount to saying how important it is; thus value is derived by number. In many cases, rare experiences are no less meaningful, useful, or important than common ones. In some cases, the rare experience may be the most enlightening one."[19] Indeed, each story and contribution was valuable and worth relaying.

GROUNDED THEORY AMID REAL-TIME EVOLUTIONS

I took a Grounded Theory approach[20] to generate the theories presented in this book. Grounded Theory entails openness to unexpected possibilities emerging through an inductive approach. Because of this, it is seldom linear and tidy, but it can provide a wealth of robust information for analyzing.

Before Glaser and Strauss named Grounded Theory, they called it "the Constant Comparative Method." I happen to think the latter name remains more appropriate, given that frequently once data has been collected and theorists work to frame their contributions against what already exists, they discover new avenues for getting back to more data, or more "grounding" as it were. This study involved several iterations of analysis and data collection. For example, after collecting the first round of interview transcripts, original audio recordings and field notes, several analytical categories emerged. Analyses of the coded data informed a return to the literature to find my theoretical contributions regarding initial group loan access examined in *Cookie Cutters and Meeting People*, maintenance of solidarity groups I detail in *What's Trust Got To Do With It*, and diagnosing client independence, which we return to in *They Think Food Grows on Trucks*. In short, this process involved reading what others had found on the topics I was examining and elaborating on how the findings at hand either confirmed what was found elsewhere, or contradicted it. Sometimes I found parts of both. When what I found was unique, then theorizing entailed describing the nature and import of that contribution.

Early rounds of fieldwork and analysis yielded a new set of questions that could not be answered from within that same dataset. Respondents were not accessible and the audio transcripts were not changeable when I left Juba. Most of the analysis took place elsewhere, while working at my university in the United States. I could not rely on tracing borrowers from one visit to the next. Unanswered questions required that I return to the field. While subsequent interview schedules were always open-ended, the scope of new questions reflected the themes that emerged from previous rounds of fieldwork.

Doing Grounded Theory is not a tidy or controlled process. One ends their study with questions, sometimes more questions than they began with. I learned a lot about *how* microfinance functioned the way it did in South Sudan, but I also could not explain in-depth *why* each particular finding was what it was. I simply could not have known to ask the right follow-up questions in real time. It was sometimes not clear to me that a trend was developing until I was back home. And moreover, ground-level circumstances inevitably changed by my next return to the field.

In 2012, for instance, I returned to interview people in more detail about the findings that had emerged in previous rounds. During that visit, I was surprised to watch the two main providers of microcredit in Juba close shop. After some serious thought, I decided against publishing the original write up of this text, about lived experiences of postwar microcredit, and that the story must include an explanation for the Juba microcredit industry's closure. Though I knew of many problems, theorizing the decline could not be done with what I had learned up to that point.

During my effort to learn why it declined in the following year, I heard starkly different explanations, depending on with whom I spoke. It was not just that borrowers were responding to programming, but they were engaging a multifaceted system whose actors all had different aims. Just as this project set out to map borrower meaning making, it seemed important to understand the origins of the institutional narratives as influential to the decisions made. I opted to tell the story by triangulating the field knowledge with the narratives of the broader microfinance threads of thought, of the institutional personnel beyond the field site, and of official records.

Data about the MFIs were extremely challenging to piece together. Field staff was generally willing to comment on practices, but data supporting results claims were harder to come by. Failure to implement a management information system (MIS) was a fatal flaw for one MFI, and undercut what was possible for me to analyze. I asked all the local MFIs for their borrower databases and offered to protect borrower profiles and analyze them. I contacted all the donor agencies, and only one accepted a request for information. One MFI provided a summary report of their portfolios at risk for one year, and another furnished a glossy annual report for one year.

I turned to official records including program documents, grant and loan contracts, and agency press releases for a paper trail. The apparent lack of checks on the figures made the process of compiling data challenging and also illustrated the precarious evidence upon which many claims to success have been made. For example, figures reported in different versions of annual reports and to the MIX and Microcredit Summit Campaign—two different MFI data aggregators that are important to the tale at hand—were seldom the same. The data found in these reports were imperfect, and that is an important takeaway from the text.

The data presented cannot tell the whole story. However, I believe that between the participant observation, the narratives told to me in interviews, and the available information about the agency agendas, there is a convincing case to be made for the reasons the industry transformed as dramatically as it did.

Those involved with the mainstream aid and development sectors lack an appropriate methodology to gauge success for the beneficiaries themselves. Big ideas like peacebuilding and poverty alleviation cannot be realized unless complexities of lived reality are addressed and understood. Deductive, quantitative metrics and statistical experiments cannot accomplish this adequately. The methodology presented here takes an inductive look at what informed participant views and practices. Talking to people in-depth yielded findings about behavior and beliefs that were invisible in the literature, yet can inform future microfinance policy, not just in South Sudan, but elsewhere.

NOTES

1. David Lewis, "Anthropology and Development: The Uneasy Relationship." In *A Handbook of Economic Anthropology*, edited by James G. Carrier (Cheltenham and Northhampton: Edward Elgar, 2005), 480.

2. William Easterly, "Why Does Foreign Aid Fail?" *Big Think*, 2007.

3. Amartya Sen, *Development as Freedom* (New York: Knopf, 1999, 2000), 80.

4. Clifford Geertz, *Peddlers and Princes: Social Development and Economic Change in Two Indonesian Towns* (Chicago: University of Chicago Press, 1963), 5.

5. J. K. Gibson-Graham, *A Diverse Economy: Rethinking Economy and Economic Representation* (Community Economies, 2003), 2.

6. Paul Bohannan, "The Impact of Money on an African Subsistence Economy." *The Journal of Economic History* 19, no. 4 (1959). V. A. Zelizer, *The Social Meaning of Money: Pin Money, Paychecks, Poor Relief, and Other Currencies* (Princeton: Princeton University Press, 1994). Jane I. Guyer, *Marginal Gains: Monetary Transactions in Atlantic Africa* (Chicago: University of Chicago Press, 2004). Bill Maurer, *Mutual Life, Limited: Islamic Banking, Alternative Currencies, Lateral Reasoning* (Princeton: Princeton University Press, 2005). Bill Maurer, "The Anthropology of Money." *Annual Review of Anthropology*, 35 (2006).

7. Louis Cohen, Lawrence Manion and Keith Morrison, *Research Methods in Education* (London: Routledge, 2013).

8. Esther Duflo, et al., "The Miracle of Microfinance? Evidence from a Randomized Evaluation." *National Bureau of Economic Research* no. w 8950 (2013). Gwendolyn Alexander-Tedeschi and Dean Karlan, "Crosss Sectional Impact Analysis: Bias from Dropouts." *Perspectives on Global Development and Technology*, 9 (2007).

9. Research institutions and universities require reviews of prospective research that involves human subject. IRB reviews are intended to ensure that the process of doing research does not harm participants. The reviews give special protections and take extra care to make sure vulnerable populations are not made more vulnerable by the research process itself, whatever it may be. These reviews distinguish whether certain aspects of proposed project methods (i.e., to pay respondents for their time, and asking certain types of questions) are appropriate.

10. See Anke Schwittay, *New Media and International Development: Representation and Affect in Microfinance* (New York: Routledge, 2014) for an excellent analysis of one.

11. William Easterly, *The White Man's Burden: Why the West's Efforts to Aid the Rest Have Done So Much Ill and So Little Good* (New York, NY: Penguin Press, 2006), 370.

12. Alan Peshkin, "In Search of Subjectivity—One's Own." *Educational Researcher* 17, no. 15 (1998).

13. William Labov and Joshua Waletzky, "Narrative Analysis: Oral Versions of Personal Experience" *Journal of Narrative and Life Story* 7, no. 1–4 (1997).

14. Maurice Merleau-Ponty, *The Visible and the Invisible* (Evanston: Northwestern University Press, 1968).

15. Cited in Martha Feldman, *Strategies for Interpreting Qualitative Data* (Newbury Park: Sage, 1995).

16. Edward Corbett and Robert Connors, *Classical Rhetoric for the Modern Student* (New York: Oxford University Press, 1965).

17. Stephen Barley, "Semiotics and the Study of Occupational and Organizational Culture" *Administrative Science Quarterly*, 20 (1983) 394 as cited in Martha Feldman, *Strategies for Interpreting Qualitative Data.* Qualitative Research Methods Series, Vol. 33. (Sage, 1995), 21.

18. From William G. Manning, "Health Insurance and the Demand for Medical Care." *RAND Health Insurance Experiment Series* (1987). Martha Feldman, *Strategies for Interpreting Qualitative Data.* Qualitative Research Methods Series, Vol. 33. (Sage, 1995).

19. V. Krane, et al., "Issues of Qualitative Research Methods and Presentations." *Journal of Sport and Exercise Psychology* 19 (1997), 214.

20. Barney Glaser and Anselm Strauss, *The Discovery of Grounded Theory: Strategies for Qualitative Research* (New Brunswick: Adline Transaction, 1968).

Chapter 4

Blueprints and Architects

The beginnings of South Sudan microcredit

The dispersal of faraway ideas from DC and Dhaka to Juba played out like the childhood game of telephone. The message uttered by the first person was never precisely the same by the time it reached the last. There are, after all, numerous steps—ranging from formal documents to verbal communications—before a donation actually reaches the beneficiaries of a program or before an investment reaches its clients. What is important here is the extent to which the expectations of microcredit made their way to the field, and whether these expectations were met. This chapter introduces architects of the Juba microfinance sector, their particular visions for what was possible, and the scaffolding of support they put into place to achieve these visions.

At the time of my fieldwork, there were three main MFIs operating in South Sudan (although several small MFIs emerged by the end of the study period). These three, licensed by the Bank of Southern Sudan, were Sudan Microfinance Institution (SUMI), BRAC-SS, and Finance Sudan Limited (FSL). Together, the former two comprised over 90 percent of the microloan market. The third, FSL served most of the remainder. Each MFI on the ground was supported by donors and beholden to their policies, as well as those of the state. There were also two major organizations that collected, allocated, and oversaw donor funds: the South Sudan Microfinance Development Facility (SSMDF) and the World Bank. Each organization was comprised of individuals whose personal and professional viewpoints varied depending on their positions. To retreat to our telephone game metaphor, in the conversation between actors, borrowers, and prospective borrowers, certain voices received more airtime than others.

Loans in Juba ranged from US $75 to 3,000 and were usually issued for a period between four to eight months. Group and individual loans had weekly or biweekly repayment schedules, while salary loans had schedules defined by employer payday schedules. BRAC offered group and individual loans; SUMI offered group, individual, and salary loans; and in its first wave, Finance Sudan offered group and salary loans.

The funds and the ideas mobilized in Juba microcredit originated mostly in Washington, DC, and Dhaka, Bangladesh. The ideologies underlying their two models were different. The South Sudanese microcredit story illuminates this ideological war between the Washington and Bangladesh consensuses on poverty, and the debate on commercial versus community microcredit models. The Juba microfinance experiment was one of the many battlefields in that war.

So how did microcredit land in South Sudan? The logic that undergirds theorizing on how microcredit can solve the issue of poverty claims that it fills the void of capital—or assets available for investment in a given community—in the impoverished world. Indeed, the civil war in Sudan destroyed its economy, and there was scarce capital circulating in the southern region. Capital came in first through oil revenues, but such revenues did not get distributed to the public, as they did not circulate much beyond GOSS accounts for security and politician mansions.[1] Unlike many developing nations that underwent "shock therapy" to liberalize their markets, Southern Sudan had not yet built a strong central government whose public programs or industries could be privatized. In other words, there existed no state entities to privatize or social spending to make austere. Because of such nascent state and local governance, there was also external pressure for economic planning to occur outside the realm of the state. The South Sudan microcredit regime was but one complex web within the larger sophisticated aid architecture.

It did not originate in South Sudan, but rather ended up there. The debt capital came from outside the nation; it was not at all a homegrown or grassroots effort in South Sudan, and there was no local origination for the institutions or the ideas. The Sudan Microfinance Institution—whose name implied local origin—took pride as being a national microfinance pioneer with local stewardship: "a source of indigenous pride." SUMI was the only MFI run by Sudanese people. However, microcredit was an idea exported by other continents, cultures, and customs.

In the days before the Sudanese civil war ended, existing assistance projects were operated primarily by humanitarian organizations, largely through the UN and independent NGO channels. The United States was one of the only countries working directly with the nation,[2] and thus did not need to seek consensuses within the international community before selecting support vehicles and objectives. The United States was not restricted by the ongoing UN sanctions when the south was still part of Sudan either, but had crafted exemptions into its bilateral sanctions with Sudan such that they could employ and deploy contractors in what was then southern Sudan. The United States also happened to be the biggest provider of Official Development Assistance (ODA) to the south. Since the US government was the leading international donor to South Sudan in multiple sectors, from military to infrastructure to development, it had a special level of state influence and tremendous amount of autonomy as a bilateral actor in South Sudan.

That the United States chose to focus its efforts on South Sudan was not entirely a stroke of moral impulse; stability in the region was strategic for the United States. In 1989, human rights scholar John Prendergast wrote that "the people of Sudan are unlucky to have been born in a region the U.S. considers strategic."[3] The United States was supportive of Sudan through foreign aid when it was seen as a Cold War ally, but in 1989 when the Bashir regime came to power, the US position shifted. By 1993, the Clinton administration classified Sudan as a state sponsor of terrorism (including harboring Osama bin Laden), and subsequently downgraded diplomatic and trade relations.[4] After the civil war in Sudan resulted in a newly independent Southern Sudan, it became a smart ally of choice for the United States. The US assistance to Southern Sudan helped to strengthen the south against its northern adversary, and also gave the United States a friend in the Middle East and North Africa (MENA) region. Thus, it is not surprising that the United States helped the south through providing support of the Sudan People's Liberation Movement (SPLM) as well as through the many USAID projects aimed at rehabilitation in the post-conflict region.

Even once other foreign actors arose after the peace accords, the United States remained the dominant, independent player, acting mostly on its own accords. Contributing nearly half of the total support by all Organization for Economic Co-operation and Development (OECD) states to the South Sudan efforts,[5] the United States was the largest donor and exercised certain power on its own by its sheer magnitude of support. Other donors that coordinated funds had to satisfy the agendas of both northern and southern governments in compliance with the CPA's mandate to "make unity attractive." The United States, however, remained both staunchly against al Bashir, and staunchly bilateral, dealing separately with north and south. Its "determined bilateral approach outside the pooled funds" tended to go to NGOs (rather than its OECD counterparts) much more often through "a liberal use of contractor services."[6] The USAID independence contributed to setting the agenda for microfinance on the ground.

USAID was the first to introduce microcredit in South Sudan. Though the pioneering agency maintained a firm lead in aid investments through several sectors in the country, it did not initially set out to establish credit programs. During a field visit in 2009, when things were good enough within the MFI sector, one manager ruminated on his microfinance institution origin story.

> Historically, SUMI came in from a grant from USAID. The goal was to boost up agriculture. They came in and realized the infrastructure was not there. Nobody was doing agriculture. They realized everybody was like-minded. So, along the way it was changed to micro-enterprise so there would be micro-entrepreneurs.

Donors wanted to prioritize the agriculture sector in South Sudan as the optimal channel for growth and sustainability, not an uncommon narrative on those agriculture efforts: the land in the south is tremendously fertile and has not been over-cultivated for decades. In other words, this region could feed the whole continent and beyond with little to no government intervention; "we" outsiders just need to establish ways for local people to enter the sector.

The original mission of the USAID Southern Sudan Agriculture Revitalization Program (SSARP) was to jumpstart the agricultural sector. SSARP set out to be a four-pronged development assistance program that would include agriculture skill-training centers, a data collection and analysis center, and vehicles to strengthen supply-chain networks. The early observation that agricultural enterprises required capital led to SSARP's fourth activity: a US $10 million budget to "provide access to capital to agricultural enterprises through a microfinance institution through an autonomous Agricultural Enterprise Finance Program (AEFP)."[7] AEFP was "a key part," totaling just shy of half the US $22.5 million SSARP budget.[8]

USAID maintained unyielding confidence regarding credit in tenuous environments, and policy makers were determined in leading its microfinance program to become the beacon of liberal peacebuilding: "an integral part of the USAID effort to provide further stability in a fragile state and foster economic recovery through support of small business growth."[9] USAID substantiated its approach by following the industry's "best practices," while also promoting the ideas of those who wrote the "best practices."[10]

Karen Doyle's 1998 *Microfinance in the Wake of Conflict: Microenterprise Best Practice brief*, sponsored by USAID, is a central guide piece. Her rationale for the start-up approach was that "[a]lthough this strategy can take more time and investment, it can be a blessing if prewar organizations are associated with a former regime, or with a certain ethnic or political group."[11] In light of this, it was seen as positive for a new credit provider to instead be (presumably) free of reputation and able to lead without prior allegiances. Their *modus operandi* thus supported start-ups with the anticipation that they become "'market leaders' and demonstrate the viability of microfinance."[12]

Despite the USAID formulation that the Sudanese MFI would be a "start-up," they did not have enough field staff to establish a USAID-branded MFI on the ground. To my knowledge and research, USAID never staffed or branded a public-facing MFI. And it rarely displayed its support of microcredit openly on the ground as it did with other aid efforts such as by displaying its logos on sorghum bags distributed by World Food Program, or on signs alongside the roads it paved. In any case, there was no microfinance institution anywhere in Southern Sudan with which USAID could partner with. Accordingly, USAID therefore founded the SUMI in 2002.

USAID designed SUMI to be administered solely by the Sudanese. In need of an implementation partner, however, USAID established SUMI via collaboration with Chemonics International, a forty-year-old American international development company founded in Washington, DC, to coordinate the implementation of development projects all over the world. Chemonics is an employee-owned firm that had already partnered with USAID in other broad-based efforts in South Sudan, including a famine early warning systems network. The USAID thereon after birthed its new microcredit project, contractually set to last five years in the first step of a two-phase effort.

So, while SUMI was cast as "the all-Sudanese MFI" it was uniquely bilateral—operated by both American and Sudanese staff. Beyond that, because USAID was the sole investor behind SUMI microcredit, USAID had the exclusive voice in shaping the ideology of its trained bankers, and in the formulation of policy. This voice came to be an extension of the American fervor for neoliberal market-based projects over government-led growth projects.

Yet the debate about what the standard American method for microlending should be was far from settled when SUMI was established. Between USAID and various US lawmakers, dissent among the architects of American microfinance has lasted decades.[13] Thus, despite its history of providing credit to the poor abroad, USAID constantly navigated competing views in the United States on exactly how to do this.

SUMI was ambitious, but it was not the first time that USAID had attempted long-term development efforts. The agency had implemented humanitarian and development projects around the world, especially in new countries, since its creation by the Foreign Assistant Act in 1961 under President Kennedy. In fact, USAID had even tried its hand at distributing loans earlier than many ODA givers, too. As early as 1974, the agency began lending to developing countries and local agencies that served small entrepreneurs.[14]

But key to this is where exactly the loans were being distributed. The early years of USAID sponsored microcredit provided credit by channeling it to foreign governments, but by 1985, "nearly every USAID Mission ha[d] developed projects for assisting small and micro-enterprises" implemented through grants "to local or international nonprofit organizations, or through bilateral projects with public and private sector entities" in other words bypassing the national governments themselves.[15] Similarly, when microfinance came into fashion, the global sector immediately privileged the NGO and private finance sectors to be providers rather than the state governments.

Blayney and Otero (1985) observed that those loans ended up favoring larger enterprises over small ones overall, due to the costliness of the programs created by complex factors inherent to developing economies in general.[16] This observation was the beginning of the conceptualization of the Washington diagnosis—people were noticing that the danger was within the channels through which microcredit was being provided.

It was around this time that a distinct fork in the road appeared regarding the approach to official American microfinance exports. Blaney and Otero found that there was a great costliness inherent to reaching the *very poor*, and this rhetoric began cropping up in the global microfinance conversation. The costliness, some later argued, was inhibiting outreach.[17] What was the solution? In broad strokes, the mainstay of USAID administrators at the time set out to do what was least risky and seemed most natural to them—leave their financial services to market forces. In other words, they gathered they could reduce risks and costs by serving the slightly poor, but not the *very poor*. This became the Washington Consensus' propensity for efficiency over social protection.

As Ananya Roy said, "at the very center of D.C." was a citizen group that challenged that hegemonic ideal.[18] The Self-Sufficiency for the Poor Act of 1987 bill for microfinance can largely be credited to the lobbying of an organization called "Results" founded by Sam Daley-Harris in 1980. Results wanted to ensure that the wonder of US-sponsored microfinance did not skirt the very poor. USAID personnel reacted to new lobbying pressures from Results and sent letters to every member of Congress that asked them to oppose legislating a small maximum loan size ($300). The letters asserted that "loans to the very poor were not feasible, not cost effective, and not mandated."[19] Despite opposition, Daley-Harris credits the success of the 1987 Act to those who framed poverty as one with tremendous bipartisan appeal, especially attentive to the Reagan administration's neoliberal economic ideology.[20] Both ideas—that the poorest people needed to enter the responsible market, and that the efficiency of the market could prevail—were adopted by Congressional policymakers.

It was some time before the implementers practiced both the text and the spirit of the laws. USAID had escaped less than rigorous reporting on its outreach. The Results team again went to Congress to ensure the poorest would receive financial services. The lobby group sought laws in place to ensure USAID programming would address their concern that the credit needs of the poorest were met. Through the debate, a new criterion for inclusion of the poorest was created, as well as impact measurement requirements.

The 2000 Microenterprise for Self-Reliance Act (HR1143) contained several important features that would eventually prove mutually exclusive in practice, or create room for practitioner cherry-picking. The law established that the United States Microfinance Loan Facility would "provide credit and other financial services to entrepreneurs who are very poor," with loans in Africa of US $300 or less, and "can cover their costs in a reasonable time period." The loan size criteria acted as a proxy indicator for client poverty for a number of years.[21] The "very poor" clause appealed to the Results lobbyists and the poverty-outreach camp, and the cost recovery appealed to the commercially minded USAID administrators. Administrators could spend on the financial services under the conditions above, or alternatively offer "demand-driven business development programs that achieve reasonable cost recovery" for clients holding "poverty loans." It legally authorized wiggle room on the occasion that borrowers did not, as one of the MFI managers in Juba used to say, "get in the system" right away. The bill also required monitoring (also costly) so as to ensure social targets be met, or be adjusted "to enhance the sustainable development impact of such assistance, particularly the impact of such assistance on the very poor, particularly poor women."[22]

As with the 1980s debate, USAID administrators renounced the 2000 bill, implicitly maintaining their position that it was better to serve not the very poorest, but instead those slightly above. The consensus across agencies in Washington, DC, was that microcredit should serve the slightly better-off poor, allowing for a trickle-down effect to occur. They ventured that relief activities should be reserved for the absolute poorest yet did not point to practical ways this need would be filled.[23] Despite these preferences gaining momentum, Congress required USAID to shift the scope of its activities to be more inclusive of the very poor.

SUMI was emblematic of the constant debates between its parent agency, USAID, and Congress. Though microcredit was not the biggest USAID expenditure in South Sudan, it was undertaken during the same period in which microfinance was becoming a bigger part of the USAID budget through legislation. Thus, SUMI, a slice of 175 million US foreign-aid dollars earmarked for microcredit, was beholden to these new policies. The trade-off between attempting a high loan cost recovery and serving the "very poor" became a real issue felt by those on the ground in Juba.

The USAID vision of what would be possible in the first five-year phase of SUMI was ambitious and, as you will learn shortly, adamant. The original USAID vision was that by providing access to working capital for micro-entrepreneurs, SUMI would be a self-sustaining microfinance institution. USAID administrators expected that the end of Phase One would establish a headquarters office and "several branches." SUMI was expected to have a US $3 million loan portfolio, half of which would be directed toward women and a tenth of which would be reintegrated internally displaced persons (IDPs) and returned refugees, as characterizing the region's post-conflict displacement of individuals.[24] In order to be fully sustainable, with a scheduled expansion in five years, SUMI was expected to charge "adequate cost-recovering interest and fees" by 2008.[25]

The new legislation backing the USAID microcredit provision was ambitious. Would it even be possible to carry out in an average economy, much less one with the post-conflict complications of South Sudan including demographic disruption, nascent state and local governance, and a deteriorated physical infrastructure? The vision that created SUMI was likewise ambitious. How costly could it be to start an MFI from scratch, and how would this brand-new MFI manage brand-new borrowers so as to meet the demands mandated by law? Leaders behind SUMI would soon confront these tensions.

INSTITUTIONAL POLICY FINDS A PLACE ON THE GROUND

Despite the complications behind the scenes, I had a great deal of respect for the staff I met in Juba, who were all to my knowledge Sudanese passport holders. Most had spent the wartime outside the country, and some had even secured asylum in the West, but they still chose to be in South Sudan and work in that sector. In between meetings, I learned their backstories. As goes the modern South Sudanese, no two shared even remotely similar pasts.

I came to know a loan officer in his late twenties who was raised in a refugee camp in neighboring Uganda. He refused that I audio record fieldwork business but was glad to oblige his personal story. He relayed to me how while growing up, the refugees had to stay in the camp.

> There was no money there, only food which was delivered. People did not want to hire refugees because of rules and because they preferred to use their own people. We could harvest a little around the camp and sell it. That way they could have a little cash. But for the rest of us it was impossible to be hired for a job. But in Juba, it's easy to get a job if you were a refugee and have an education.

He did not plan to stay in finance forever, but felt glad that he could come to this place he had heard about his whole upbringing, for the comfort of a middle-class job. He told me that if I "come back and don't see [him]" it is because he had aspirations to return for studies in Uganda "or anywhere I can go. I am a degree holder. I just want to continue to a master or Ph.D. in business accounting, to continue in what I have."

I also met a middle-aged manager who was an amazing storyteller. He entertained me and several others over evening meals, sharing the cliffhangers that led him by foot to the Middle East, by train to Europe, and to his then-dream of being resettled in Canada. Although he had met this goal, he soon felt a sense of duty to help rebuild his native country, which is why he returned for the job at SUMI. He greatly missed his wife and children who he only saw for one month per year. In the early years, "next year" he would bring them when the schools were good enough, but over time that idea faded from conversation. He was one of the most committed advocates to ensuring that microfinance benefitted the very poor that I met in Juba.

SUMI opened its doors in Yei in 2003 and had more than 2,100 clients in its first year of operation. It then expanded with apparent ease. Branches opened in Yambio in June 2004, Maridi in June 2004, Rumbek in February 2005, and then Juba in February 2006. SUMI had started with the group loan offering, and then rolled out salary loans to employees of organizations in the five towns. Thereafter, SUMI offered individual loans for group-loan clients who had already repaid five group-guaranteed loans and for new individuals with collateral and a business that had operated for over a year.

With this snapshot of growth in mind, SUMI may have appeared ready to be weaned from USAID, and become independent.

DONOR HARMONIZATION

Flash forward to 2005. The Comprehensive Peace Agreement was signed in Nairobi, and donors from around the world set out to strategize on how to help Sudan recover from the war, as donors do. The head of the Japanese delegation saw a strategic geographic position and "pushed his country 'to do something' to help for its stability." The chief of the German delegation likewise "likened aid to Sudan to the Marshall Plan that helped rebuild her own country after World War II."[26]

The Oslo International Donors' Conference in April 2005 was a key event in the current case. Pledges at Oslo created two trust funds—one for each the north and the south—to be administered by the World Bank, "working together with UN partners, donors, civil society, and the respective governments." The Sudan Multi-Donor Trust Funds (MDTF) came from the Netherlands, Norway, United Kingdom, European Commission, Sweden, Germany, Denmark, Finland, Italy, Iceland, Greece, Canada, Spain, and Egypt, adding to a "historic" US $10 million contribution from the World Bank's net income.[27] The trust fund of US $344 million was specifically designated to Southern Sudan as the MDTF-S.[28]

The 2005 *Sudan: Framework for Sustained Peace, Development and Poverty Eradication* report, written by the Joint Assessment Mission (JAM) comprised of the World Bank, the UN, and International Monetary Fund

(IMF), presented "the reconstruction and development requirements for the consolidation of peace, and for attaining broad-based growth, poverty reduction and sustained human development towards the Millennium Development Goals (MDG), firmly grounded in the historic Comprehensive Peace Agreement (CPA)."[29] Compared to UN annual work plans, the JAM evaluation looked to plan years ahead, through the interim period, and thus was "an opportunity to 'think big' in terms of long-term development planning for Southern Sudan."[30]

The JAM report was an important record of agency values to be emulated by the donor community. A year later, the GOSS drafted an Aid Strategy for Southern Sudan[31] based on the JAM assessment, to become the basis for managing aid and development activities. Importantly, it outlined basic donor coordination mechanisms, specifically, "aid coordination and harmonisation became the key principles for the international engagement in Southern Sudan."[32] In the earliest years of peace, the harmonizing vehicles were UN-based and pooled funds—such pooled funds marked an important moment in the recovery period as they aligned with a liberal peacebuilding approach. They offered a way to be efficient, as well as to align with priorities within the international finance provider regarding the superiority of the private sector (over the government). Pooled funds also represented the negotiation and melding of donor ideas in the microcredit sector, which received such funds.

The JAM's first follow-up assessment in 2006 revealed IMF/WB established preferences for aid programs that incorporated liberal peacebuilding goals. The "short note [was] analogous to the Joint Staff Assessments that Bank and IMF staff routinely prepare for consideration alongside national poverty reduction strategies." The initial report had hundreds of directives within its hundreds of pages, but this seventeen-page report contained fewer, and had substantially more pointed action items in such that it might be seen as a microcosm. One thing was certain: it obtusely called for a limited role of the state in matters pertaining to markets. It was a World Bank boilerplate, as Graham Harrison has said of similar documents,[33] which emphasized the role of the private sector. So advised the report, "There is a temptation when planning for a new era for the nascent GoSS agencies to evolve towards a system with too much government involvement in the economy and in service provision. This, however, needs to be avoided, as the private sector is, in many cases, a more efficient agent to deliver on service provision." To those ends, JAM recommended a four-pronged approach to private sector development, and encouraging microcredit schemes was chief among them.[34]

The extensive JAM report and the MDTF-S made economic growth a priority, and proposed that microfinance was a key strategy for achieving and sustaining this growth. As the first of five stated economic goals, JAM advised a diversification in income sectors from oil (its largest by far, upon which the south was seen as too reliant) to other sectors including mining, manufacturing, and agriculture. To accomplish this, the assessment suggested key policy interventions and "developing mechanisms for increasing access to seasonal credit for small-scale farmers, and to micro-finance in general for rural residents." This forecasting was reminiscent of the USAID vision a few years prior.

A senior World Bank staffer in Juba described in an interview how the microfinance effort "started right from the beginning" in 2004 and 2005 when there was a joint assessment mission.

> Now, we looked at this situation and said fine the MDTF has come in under the administration of the World Bank and there were quite a lot of things that they wanted to do. Some of them were relegated to second stage, but others had to be fast tracked. One of them was the support to microfinance lending to micro enterprises. *Yes!* That one had to be fast tracked because we didn't have to wait for the policy and the bill and all that to be prepared. That would have been a blessing before we started the microfinance on the ground. We needed a law on the ground to guide us, but we couldn't wait for that law because people had to recover. And one of the characteristics of a post-conflict environment is always setting up these petty cash kind of home-based businesses, which are for recovery purposes. And we say "no," let's allow the people to recover in a better way, in an easier way, by unleashing to them this possibility of getting financial support.

The MDTF funds administered by the World Bank created the opportunity to leverage its vision. In 2007 the World Bank Fund launched the microfinance support plan and began laying out disbursements by 2008. In 2009, the leadership realized it was becoming too much of a burden on the central bank and subsequently created a new apex organization on the ground called the South Sudan Microfinance Development Facility (SSMDF).

The SSMDF was established by the interim Government of Southern Sudan as a private company to coordinate donor funding for microfinance. The SSMDF was an apex institution, a conduit bringing together the prior mentioned donors and investors in efforts to promote loans and microcredit support in the South. Formalized as a company limited by guarantee,[35] the SSMDF received funds from stakeholders such as the MDTF, the Central Bank of Sudan, and GOSS, with expectation that the technical assistance (TA) funds were grants (not to be paid back), but that their zero to very low interest loans to the MFIs would be paid back. The SSMDF furthermore organized TA, wholesale loan funds, and supported policy advocacy for the sector.

Many major state and multilateral agencies put their money and faith in the SSMDF to allocate funds to the MFIs. The MDTF-S and Bank of South

Sudan each contributed US $1 million—a seventh of all private-sector funds available for microfinance in South Sudan at that time. This also amounted to a fifth of the Southern Sudanese microcredit pie as a whole. Other pooled funds added to the microfinance sector through the SSMDF fund, too. The World Bank's Gender Action Plan and the United Nations Capital Development Fund (UNCDF) would also put US $4 million of debt into the pot, and the United Nations Development Programme (UNDP) was a sort of gap-filling funder, offering its funding as grants toward training and TA through the SSMDF.

The World Bank consultants selected the MFIs that would receive support. One told me that this was done quite competitively. Accordingly, twelve or thirteen companies showed interest in receiving such support, yet decision makers only selected the three that were "doing a really good job and could be groomed." They reasoned that "the best way is to have homegrown microfinance because this is the one that understands the people and the people understand it." While none were genuinely homegrown, the idea that certain MFIs were most plugged into what people in Juba needed was the basis for the World Bank choosing to support BRAC and SUMI with loan funds during the pilot period. SUMI received US $344,000 (and $56,000 in TA grants) while BRAC received US $200,000.[36]

Besides the monetary support, the SSMDF pushed its will through a good deal of advisory work and training. "We also have the bold business plans," the director told me proudly. "Some of the new institutions are small and they have the vision, but how to fill that vision in the home of strategy, they can't. So you have to dissolve their vision and turn it into actionable strategy. We have them do that." Future funding was contingent on planning according to *their* vision. This also explained why Finance Sudan, a small MFI in Juba town, was not among the first round recipients.

SSMDF considered Finance Sudan during the pilot period, but held off for a couple years. A director explained their decision-making process to me:

> ARC was an NGO, but it had a window, a microfinance window, that was Finance Sudan. We thought it was not going to be the best model, because [the clients] were already used to donations so whatever they received they were just using for consumption and therefore not paying back. That's why some of our banks, then, were collapsing. We didn't want that to happen again with the new microfinance paradigm. So we advised ARC to legally register that window as a microfinance body because that was the only way to impart the knowledge on the entrepreneurs and teach them whatever they borrow, they have to pay back.

The World Bank's vision for microlending precluded a large amount of blending with charitable services. Loans that proved too costly to beneficiaries were adjusted. For this reason, The World Bank also rescinded support for MFIs that went too far off course. Citing a local MFI that formed a cooperative structure beginning in 2008, a senior World Bank field staffer described the reason the MFI was overspending.

> We thought the microfinance could help in supporting the farming community by giving them services. Basically what these farmers needed was just the services to do their businesses. But later on we found out that the model was too expensive, even for they themselves to survive, let alone the enterprises they were going to support. They were outgrowing such that they were going to tap into the resources. So we thought that was not going to be the best way and we canceled them off.

SSMDF was a lifeblood donor and gatekeeper for the MFIs. Donors deferred to their vision and in the process, tacitly supported the World Bank model for microfinance. In an expected World Bank style, not just any kind of microfinance would be encouraged, but only those that were "establishing commercially viable microfinance service providers." The Washington market-style microfinance ideal was soon adopted as a calculated maneuver to achieve the desired sustainability outcomes. World Bank staff managed monies earmarked for loans and grants needed to support capacity building, which equated to training and inculcating local staff. Staff members also gave advice to those working in MFIs, much like a wise grandmother who tells you what you should think—and if you want the loan, you have to follow the "wisdom." Meanwhile, another up-and-coming Juba NGO began to offer microloans.

INSIDE THE BANGLADESH RURAL ADVANCEMENT COMMITTEE

BRAC arrived on the scene with its own support base. BRAC South Sudan is a subsidiary of the large parent NGO Bangladesh Rural Advancement Committee. BRAC was founded in 1972 by Sir Fazle Hasan Abed and is the largest purveyor of microfinance in Bangladesh, the so-called birthplace of microcredit. Bangladesh is also where Nobel Prize winning Grameen Bank was born a decade later. BRAC has done more than microlenders anywhere to equip microcredit with a broader landscape of financial tools, like savings, that can be mobilized in the event of a crisis. BRAC includes so much assistance alongside its credit programs, that Roy's major thesis analyzing the competing lending paradigms places its practices more within the realm of "social protection" (i.e., relief) more so than just lending, in contrast with how BRAC emphasizes its credit programs in its branding and marketing approach.

"Unlike Grameen, which is mainly a microfinance and savings operation, BRAC does practically everything," praised *The Economist* in 2012.[37] Between BRAC's long history of community-focused microcredit provision, alongside activities in sanitation, agriculture, and education, it is the largest development NGO in the world, "measured by the number of employees and the number of people it has helped." BRAC is commended around the world, even by the likes of Nobel Economist Amartya Sen, former US president Bill Clinton, billionaire George Soros, and Economist Paul Collier, all of whom are quoted on the BRAC website homepage, which also proclaims, "BRAC is the most outstanding social enterprise in the world." Such endorsements correlate with a strong donor base that secures its funding and allows it to expand beyond its origin Bangladesh borders.

Birthed out of its own conflict in Bangladesh, BRAC seemed particularly well prepared to engage the complexities of the postwar economy in South Sudan. "Just after the independence of Bangladesh, BRAC started as a relief organization to rehabilitate the war affected country," the BRAC-SS director reflected in an interview. "And later from our experience, after some days, we conducted some studies through our research unit in BRAC to know the impact of the relief program. And from this study, we learned that relief is not the right approach for sustainable development. That's why BRAC become a development organization and, like BRAC did in Bangladesh, we changed many things." As early as 2002, BRAC was expanding franchises abroad, "because every community invited us from other countries," the director told me. Given that the paradigm of flexibility was built into the organizational fabric from its mission statement to its integrated research, BRAC management believed the organization was well positioned to adapt to a range of particularities in South Sudan that it had not encountered in its hometown experience.

From the start, BRAC-SS conducted in-house research and monitoring that was far more robust than everyone else's. Before knowing that this strength was part of their global reputation, I was struck by the attention their staff paid to what was going on in their programs. Field workers were keenly aware of the challenges faced by their members. Initially establishing itself as an MFI in 2006 in South Sudan, by 2009 BRAC-SS wrote their new master plan for microfinance.

The BRAC master plan differed greatly from the other two cornerstone MFIs in Juba. On the chasm between Washington and Bangladeshi MFIs, the other two (SUMI and FSL) had in their mandates a priority for sustainability that was less urgent for BRAC. One important distinction in the BRAC mission from much of the microcredit industry is the established commitment to "hearing from the poor;" over the years, a variety of programs were deployed that were shaped to fit local needs. Hence, in BRAC, lending is typically coupled with several types of programs. The BRAC master plan in South Sudan experimented with outreach to women and adolescent girls (all their borrowers were women, compared to more or less half at the other MFIs), as well as skills training. "For the microfinance operation, we are following the group closely," one of their top directors told me.

BRAC also had a unique support system. Its capital came from multiple sources, but most came from the support of its parent organization. The BRAC African Loan Fund, a US $62 million socially minded fund for debt financing, was raised to expand microfinance services in Uganda, Tanzania, and South Sudan. "Committed to principled prosperity," writes the fundraising agency on its website, "to improve the livelihoods of all in ways that over the long-term are equitable, effective, and preserve the earth's resources as opposed to short-term gains that require unacceptable trade-offs between economic, social and environmental objectives."[38] BRAC also accessed funds through the SSMDF and the UNCDF, both of which were channeled by the World Bank. According to their in-house researcher-historians,

> The programs started in 2007, and concentrating in Juba first, then it went to four other areas, extending to Yei, then Jonglei, and other two places. And all these ones from 2007 up to 2009, we were having some African Loan Fund, and coupled with support from Stromme Foundation and another network of organizations. And we also got some support from UNCDF.[39]

By the spring of 2008, Kiva, the American nonprofit that channels individual contributions for loans to MFIs, joined in the support for BRAC. Kiva cited an appreciation of its targeting returning war refugees and widows, "most of whom lack confidence, capital, skills in income-earning activities, and opportunities for financial access." Kiva seemed sensitive to the idea that the very poor need and can use credit. While Kiva finances only zero-interest capital eligible MFIs, choosing BRAC was a tacit endorsement of the subsidy-requiring model. *As long as their donors receive full repayment.* Kiva therefore furnished BRAC its standard capital offering. While subsidized projects would still have to be supported by other means, Kiva nonetheless became a significant contributor to the South Sudanese microcredit sector, providing over US $1.7 million to BRAC in just three years. Notably, once BRAC rescinded its loan operations, Kiva moved their its support to another MFI open to funding; repayment had been the conditional factor for Kiva.

My experience at the BRAC offices felt as warm as the organization's reputation. I was referred to Mr. Siddique, who had a reputation preceding him that even non-industry Juba dwellers said he had been working for BRAC for thirty years and would "know everything." I emailed him and did not hear back; so I later showed up without appointment to attempt a meeting. After signing a visitor's sheet, I was taken directly to his office. He was jovial right away and told me he did not reply to my email requesting an appointment because he did not think it was appropriate to write to a woman late at night. I had never paid attention to the timestamp on emails, but I found his apology to be a kind effort to be respectful. He was so aware of courtesy, yet unaware that this norm in his culture had little salience in mine.

I told him I wanted to hear what BRAC does and that I wanted to know about the differences between working here and working in Bangladesh. He told me this work should be very interesting for my research. He indicated that he would tell me more about how they had at least three iterations of the lending program. They would try one plan and then change it according to the circumstances, so it would require some time to discuss the Juba microcredit program trajectory.

INSIDE FINANCE SUDAN LIMITED

Tied for second place with BRAC-SS in terms of setting up shop in South Sudan, Finance Sudan was the first MFI that I visited in South Sudan. I discovered Finance Sudan while investigating systems that received Sudanese microcredit clients who were headed home from refugee life in the northernmost parts of Uganda. In November 2006, The American Refugee Committee (ARC) founded Finance Sudan to facilitate microloans for returnees establishing their livelihoods back home in Juba. The connection between ARC and the Uganda MFI that sent their borrowers to pursue loans at Finance Sudan in Juba was apparent immediately. I realized that FSL bore the same logo and color scheme as Uganda Microfinance Limited (UML)—a blue diamond with rounded edges and a red shadow. This was not by coincidence. It was a visual brand, transmitting familiarity to borrowers coming to Juba who had previously borrowed from UML while living in Uganda during the war.

ARC is a relief NGO focused on displaced people around the world. Its webpage states, "ARC works with its partners and constituencies to provide opportunities and expertise to refugees, displaced people and host communities. We help people survive conflict and crisis and rebuild lives of dignity, health, security and self-sufficiency. ARC is committed to the delivery of programs that ensure measurable quality and lasting impact for the people we serve."[40] ARC had been operating in South Sudan since 1994, focused on capacity building, health care, and protection. They knew the population well and of course, the organization was familiar with displacement-scenario dynamics.

ARC had a deep history with relief and settlement for displaced populations, but far less with purveying credit. Returnees within its system remained the focus of ARC's small credit Juba operations for the first year or so. Finance Sudan instead offered group and salary loans for the first couple years, and even by its third year in operation, it still had not expanded outreach in any way comparable to BRAC who came at the same time.

Unlike the SUMI directive to hire only Sudanese people, Finance Sudan had no such restriction. This was evident in its staff composition, who came from various East African countries. And though its target clients were Sudanese, most were in a position to borrow (i.e., familiar enough with either ARC or microcredit), had been living in East African countries during the war, and were therefore familiar with this composition of providers.

Despite a long history serving displaced populations, the ARC microfinance model focused on the poor more than the profits. Though its commitment to supporting refugees might have been costly, Finance Sudan established a practice of business training and "close follow-up mentoring" of clients.[41] Under ARC's umbrella, the MFI was not particularly solvent,[42] but it met its community impact mission standards. As an MFI, the outreach of Finance Sudan was paltry in comparison to SUMI or BRAC; Finance Sudan had just two branches in two states by 2008, compared with SUMI's and BRAC's combined dominance, covering 93 percent of the market at that time.[43] Still, the infrastructure Finance Sudan built physically and technically was enough to gain the attention of business people looking for a new endeavor.

By the end of 2008, two years after its founding, ARC sold its shares of Finance Sudan to Micro Africa Ltd, a privately held East African company, and Finance Sudan became Finance Sudan Limited (FSL). In 2008, the owners of FSL were bought out of Uganda Microfinance Limited—a profitable multi-branch MFI—by Equity Bank, a large institution originating in Kenya. By January 2009, the new owners transformed FSL from an NGO into a company limited by guarantee, with new market-based standards to uphold. This transition brought FSL out of charity and into the culture of East African microcredit.

Against a plexiglass window at the FSL offices was a handwritten sign that read: "trust no one." I assumed the sign was a reminder to staff about the clientele. Still, the message felt like it applied to me too. My requests for an interview were put-aside, leaving me to assume that a meeting would be a burden. After all, their staff were busy running a business. This was a contrast with my experience at other MFI offices. I was not given much sit-down interview time in the early years of fieldwork, but FSL managers sent me on a tour with their loan officer who also translated. Everyone we met loved the services.

Microcredit can be a lucrative industry. Much like the East African business people, "cowboy capitalists" came to seize this opportunity in Juba. Finance Sudan's owners, who had profited greatly from sales of MFI chains in neighboring countries, saw the ARC infrastructure in place. One of them, James Mugabi, had his success reported as an impressive innovator in an article entitled "Serial Entrepreneur Finds Success in Microlending." In it, he praised less what microfinance offered the poor, and more for what it offered him professionally.[44]

When I was finally able to get a lunchtime meeting with a manager, he verbalized his appreciation that I arrived on time. Notes were okay but audio recording was not. As we began, he made a point of saying that he was brought in with a corporate perspective, not an NGO one. He emphasized his expertise. He emphasized his knowledge of the work. In the moment, I remember that it felt cold and arrogant. Then I realized he wanted me, a foreigner from another continent, to know that he felt clear about the needs of East Africans. He stressed that we—both his staff and my curious self—should stay out of personal reasons why borrowers struggle and stressed with the same to his officers.

Purchasing FSL was a venture that sought profit. Though the smallest in the first years of a South Sudanese microcredit history, Finance Sudan was the MFI in town with the most unabashed profit orientation. In fact, it was so business-minded that I was told more than once by various informants that the Bank of South Sudan hired its CEO regularly for policy advice.

During my time in the field that summer, challenges were mounting for Juba residents, including some in the microcredit industry. Transportation of goods remained difficult because of poor roadways and lack of security. According to the only circulating report of the industry, there were problems, but none too severe by 2009. "Overall," it stated, "the MFI's experience a low default rate in Southern Sudan."[45] The report continued,

> An exception to the rule is FSL, which has been suffering escalating defaults (74.3 percent 30 day PAR) recently due to (a) poor management and controls, and (b) a high concentration of clients in the recently destroyed market place in Juba. FSL has dealt with issue (a) by hiring new management and introducing relevant monitoring and control systems for staff performance and financial management. It is currently in the process of modifying its strategy for future expansion to resolve.[46]

At that time, Finance Sudan was the one with the most to overcome. By 2010, Finance Sudan managed only 7 percent of the Juba microfinance market and was its poorest performing MFI. Nevertheless, within just a few short years it would be the last of these MFIs standing in town.

NOTES

1. For example, in 2012 headlines were made with President Salva Kiir's letter reprimanding government officials for robbing the country of some US $4 billion. See Smith 2012.

2. Apart from Germany after the peace accords, the United States was the only OECD state to avoid pooled funds. Other non-OECD states like China, India, and some Arab states aided bilaterally as well, but to lesser extents.

3. John Prendergast, "Blood Money for Sudan World Bank and IMF to the 'Rescue.'" *Africa Today* (1989).

4. Lauren Ploch Blanchard, "Sudan and South Sudan: Current Issues for Congress and US Policy." (2012).

5. US $1.7 billion or 42 percent of all OECD funds to South Sudan combined, 2005–2009.

6. Jon Bennett, et al., "Aiding the Peace: A Multi-donor Evaluation of Support to Conflict Prevention and Peacebuilding Activities in Southern Sudan 2005–2010." *Ministry of Foreign Affairs of Denmark,* U. K. (2010), 65.

7. Chemonics International, "A Component of the: Southern Sudan Agricultural Revitalization Program (SSARP) Second Annual Workplan." (2004).

8. USAID, *Sudan Agricultural Enterprise Finance Program (AEFP) Tenth Quarterly Report,* (2005).

9. Chemonics International, *Sudan Agricultural Enterprise Finance Program Final Report* (2008).

10. See Warren Feek, "Best of practices?" In *Deconstructing Development Discourse,* 2010 for a commentary on "best practices" being unscientific and impeding diversity or context sensitivity.

11. Karen Doyle, *Microfinance in the Wake of Conflict: Challenges and Opportunities* (Washington, DC: USAID, 1998), 33.

12. Oxfam, "Smart Development in Practice. Field report from Southern Sudan." *Smart Development in Practice Field Reports* (Oxfam Publishing, 2009), 5.

13. Ananya Roy, *Poverty Capital: Microfinance and the Making of Development* (New York and London: Routledge, 2011).

14. USAID, *Spring Review of Small Farmer Credit.* vol. 1–20 (Washington, DC, 1973).

15. Robert G. Blayney and Maria Otero, Maria, *Small and Micro-enterprises: Contributions to Development and Future Directions for Aid's Support.* Report for the Employment and Enterprise Development Division (Washington, DC: USAID, 1985), 7.

16. Robert G. Blayney and Maria Otero, Maria. *Small and Micro-enterprises: Contributions to Development and Future Directions for Aid's Support.* Report for the Employment and Enterprise Development Division (Washington, DC: USAID, 1985).

17. Marguerite S. Robinson, *The Microfinance Revolution: Sustainable Finance for the Poor* (Washington, DC: The World Bank, 2001).

18. Ananya Roy, *Poverty Capital: Microfinance and the Making of Development* (New York and London: Routledge, 2011), 94.

19. Bob Sample, *How RESULTS Activists Collaborated With Microcredit Leaders and High Government Officials to Build the Microfinance Movement* (Washington, DC: Results Education Fund, 2006).

20. Sam Daley-Harris, *Reclaiming Our Democracy: Healing the Break between People and Government* (Philadelphia, PA: Camino Books, 1994).

21. Anicca Jansen, *USAID's contribution to Microfinance: From Microfinance to Financial Inclusion* (Washington, DC: USAID, 2014).

22. H. R. 1143 (106th): Microenterprise for Self-Reliance and International Anti-Corruption Act of 2000.

23. Bob Sample, *How RESULTS Activists Collaborated With Microcredit Leaders and High Government Officials to Build the Microfinance Movement*, (Washington, DC: Results Education Fund, 2006).

24. Chemonics International, "A Component of the: Southern Sudan Agricultural Revitalization Program (SSARP) Second Annual Workplan." (2004).

25. Chemonics International, "A Component of the: Southern Sudan Agricultural Revitalization Program (SSARP) Second Annual Workplan." (2004).

26. Sudan Tribune, "East Africans Drive Business in 'Boom Town' Juba," 2006.

27. World Bank, "How Social Capital is Measured?" n.d.

28. ITAD, *Mid-Term Evaluation of the Joint Donor Team in Juba, Sudan* (Oslo, Norway: Norwegian Agency for Development Cooperation, 2009).

29. JAM, *The Report of the Sudan Joint Assessment Mission (JAM): Framework for Sustained Peace, Development and Poverty Eradication.* Vol. 1. Prepared by the UN and World Bank JAM team in collaboration with the GoS and the SPLM, (2005).

30. ITAD, *Mid-Term Evaluation of the Joint Donor Team in Juba, Sudan* (Oslo, Norway: Norwegian Agency for Development Cooperation, 2009), 46.

31. Ministry of Finance and Economic Planning, *GoSS Aid Strategy 2006–2011.* Government of Southern Sudan, (2007).

32. Jon Bennett, et al., "Aiding the Peace: A Multi-donor Evaluation of Support to Conflict Prevention and Peacebuilding Activities in Southern Sudan 2005–2010." *Ministry of Foreign Affairs of Denmark* (U.K. 2010), 1–5.

33. Graham Harrison, "Financing Peace?" In *Peacebuilding, Power, and Politics in Africa*, edited by Devon Curtis and Gwinyayi A. Dzinesa (Athens: Ohio University Press, 2012).

34. JAM, *The Report of the Sudan Joint Assessment Mission (JAM): Framework for Sustained Peace, Development and Poverty Eradication.* Vol. 1. Prepared by the UN and World Bank JAM team in collaboration with the GoS and the SPLM, (2005), 11.

35. According to The Companies Act of 2012 by the Ministry of Justice in South Sudan, a company limited by guarantee is characterized by "having the liability of its members limited by the memorandum to the amount that the members undertake in the memorandum to contribute to the assets of the company if it is being wound up." Companies limited by guarantee may have share capital.

36. The Frankfurt School of Management. *Southern Sudan Microfinance Development Facility (SSMDF) – Final Report* (Juba: South Sudan Microfinance Development Facility, 2011).

37. The Economist, "The Path through the Fields; Bangladesh and Development." *The Economist* (2012) Bangladesh and development: The path through the fields.

38. Enclude, Principles: "The Principles that Inform our Work and World-view", n.d.

39. United Nations Capital Development Fund.

40. ARC, "About Us." Arcrelief, About Us, n.d.

41. ARC, "About Us." Arcrelief, About Us, n.d.

42. Return on investment was rated at 67 percent in 2009, according to Mix Market 2013.

43. According to unaudited figures published by Melody Atil 2009.

44. Simon Cirri, "Serial Entrepreneur Finds Success in Microlending." *Business Daily* (2015).

45. Melody Atil, *Expanding the Provision and Impact of Microfinance in Southern Sudan* (Juba: World Bank Southern Sudan Office, 2009).

46. Melody Atil, *Expanding the Provision and Impact of Microfinance in Southern Sudan* (Juba: World Bank Southern Sudan Office, 2009), 6.

Chapter 5

Cookie Cutters and Meeting People

The role of postwar social ties in acquiring microcredit

In the summer of 2013, I was invited to screening of films by young South Sudanese filmmakers at a consular meeting hall in central Juba. There were several short films about life in Juba—all very interesting. One showed a ceremonial cattle exchange up in a Lakes State. A more controversial one was about a wife cheating on her husband. Each film was an aspirational conversation—the creators' effort to show the audience some part of home, or their depictions of the many cultures that comprise South Sudan in the modern era.

The film that I found to be the most intriguing, however, actually appeared the least "exotic" to me. It was shot in venues I had frequented in Juba, and its cast was women in their early twenties, a demographic with which I was familiar as I was most regularly in contact with them. The film began with two groups of women exchanging skeptical looks with one another. The audience and I did not know why, until the scene let us overhear one group conversation: they were criticizing the other group's skirt lengths.

Throughout the film, Juba women were regularly coming into contact with people from different places and were navigating new ways of vetting who and what was worth their trust. Although the cast included all young South Sudanese women, their wartime residences had them wearing different styles of clothing from each other, which led to an initial stream of judgment. By the end of the film, the women eventually bonded over common interests, which then shifted the prior meaning of the clothing from wrong to fine. The point of the young filmmakers' story was to reflect how, even through division, common interests and values have the power to unify the South Sudanese.

South Sudan is often referred to as a *returnee state*. Following its 2005 Comprehensive Peace Agreement (CPA) with northern Sudan, an influx of more than two million Southern Sudanese returned to their homeland, after decades in exile due to the Second Sudanese Civil War.[1] Many development programs were introduced to stimulate South Sudan's economy and social ties among people whose lives had been affected. While activities aiming to stimulate recovery were vast, ranging from reintegration of ex-combatants, to rebuilding damaged infrastructure, little was known about how such programs might impact a tense postwar society.

Optimistic observers hoped that the prosperity of group loan format would create much-needed social solidarity in the wake of conflict, but they were largely blindsided by the role that postwar social networks played in shaping borrower access to the loans. This chapter shows the way in which the mutual guarantee group loan model worked as a sorting mechanism, but not one that accurately assessed risk. Social prerequisites that were built into the loan process ended up governing borrower access unevenly, fostering an unfair system.

GROUP LOANS AND MICROCREDIT

For new clients, the group liability contract is a necessary requirement in order to obtain loans.[2] With group loans or "solidarity loans," members guarantee for one another in lieu of material collateral. This joint liability system benefits the lending institution because it transfers the risk from itself to the co-borrowers.[3] Because the individual members in the groups know more about one another than the banks do, and can impose pressure on one another to pay, group loans are thus viewed as a solution to problems of adverse selection, moral hazard, auditing costs, and enforcement.[4]

Much of the research on group lending builds upon the idea that microfinance uses preexisting social capital in place of material capital in order for people to attain loans. This is thought to produce higher repayment rates. As a result, much of the work written on group lending has examined the social ties that happen within peer borrowing as a potential predictor of repayment rates. Studies have looked at the role of borrower willingness to repay loans,[5] personal trust between group members and social homogeneity,[6] and strong in social capital[7] has been able to affect repayment rates.

Broadly speaking, the co-borrowing arrangement also receives praise for *creating* social capital. "The solidarity group, because of its basis in mutual support, frees borrowers from . . . dependent relationships. Further, the peer group itself, becomes the building block to a broader social network."[8] Ideas like these allow for the intervention to be dubbed socially beneficial in a postwar society "because it helps to reconstitute assets, it repairs or mobilizes social capital and it gives a kick-start to income-generating activities."[9]

Yet many others surfaced with different viewpoints, arguing that group lending transforms social ties in ways that are less than beneficial for participants. Since joint liability programs create pressure on and among borrowers, for instance, sometimes borrowers see the reliance spawned from these relationships as burdensome.[10] Many scholars have noted the ways credit as capital has exacerbated social tensions between borrowers, their families, and their communities.[11]

Whether microfinance makes use of social capital, produces it, or both, it elicits distinct empirical questions. Supporting evidence for such claims may be found in the group composition itself. In past studies on group lending, analysts assumed membership is self-evident or automatically gained. However, while peer groups are central to microlending, little is known about *how* client groups have formed, and whether or not different kinds of group formation processes have been significant in determining the borrowing, investing, repaying, and social restoration that the literature anticipated.

All the microfinance institutions operating in Juba practiced standardized group lending, regardless of whether institutions prioritized commercial viability or poverty relief. It was used in virtually the same way, too. The logic was that groups that self-selected their members could better monitor each other than people who were not already tied to other members.[12] As a result, all MFIs tended to loan to self-selected groups, a norm that solidified itself within microcredit practice by the dusk of the twentieth century. The MFIs observed in Juba practiced the hands-off approach, whereby borrowers selected their peers. What follows is an analysis of the process by which groups formed in the early years of the Juba microcredit experiment.

HOW TO GET A MICROLOAN IN JUBA

In early 2009, I sat down with a top manager at the largest MFI in Juba. I asked him about the nature of his clientele, and whether any specific demographics were targeted for services. Targeting women[13] and ex-combatants,[14] for example, are methods often used in post-conflict microfinance strategy, and I wondered whether they might be used in Juba. Instead, he offered a description of the clientele based on identifiers I had not seen before in microfinance literature or in the field. He estimated that of those receiving microloans, more than 80 percent were formerly internally displaced persons (IDPs).[15] The returnees[16] began coming back to Juba just after the IDPs did, he told me, starting around 2006. No non-Sudanese nationals were receiving loans.

His response to my question surprised me in many ways. While I was caught off guard by how he characterized the demographics, I was taken aback by this figure. My first thought was that 80 percent of customers were Sudanese IDPs was very high, as the group was one of the proportionally smallest demographic factions in the city. Unfortunately this was before the First Census in 2009, so hard facts were hard to find. I suspected that those percentages were not representative of the city's demographic profile. At that time, people were coming back to Juba from all over the region, and many from even far beyond. In fact, most of the people I met after the peace agreement were repatriating from Kenya, Ethiopia, Uganda, and elsewhere. In any case, I did expect borrower demographics would to be representative of the state or national demographics because of my association with "financial inclusion"—a term used to describe the purpose of microfinance activities within the scholarly community.

Juba was uniquely cosmopolitan compared to other states in South Sudan. Within a couple of years from that initial interview, data was published that confirmed my suspicions that there was a significantly higher amount of returnees who had crossed international borders, than the amount of IDPs returning from other states of Sudan. In fact, the vast majority of the population in Central Equatoria, the South Sudan state that houses the capitol city, was repatriates. Eighty-seven percent of the near 40,000 individuals returning to that state had been outside the country—refugees—during the war.[17] Only 13 percent of the Central Equatorial population were IDPs, that is, people displaced somewhere within greater Sudan during the war. This unique makeup of the Juba population contrasted with the rates of returnees across the whole country.[18]

In a place with such demographics, why did the micro-lenders disproportionately service IDPs? Was there something about IDPs that made them more desirable clients?

I was curious about this, but carried on. At this point in my research, I remained on my original course, asking the MFI staff broad open-ended questions. I continued to ask about the institutional process from the same interview schedule. It was not until several months later that I was able to situate these lingering questions into the broader story at hand.

I continued the conversation about institutional practice with Michael, the manager mentioned above. I asked him about the types of loan products his MFI offered, and he told me the standard offerings: group loans for new borrowers, individual loans, or advanced loans for those already operating medium-scale businesses. The mainstay of their service was group loans, as they could target small-scale entrepreneurs. Then, I asked about the maximum loan size available to first-time group loan members. (I wanted to know these figures, as they would help indicate the scope of the projects that clients were able to undertake with such loans. It would also have helped me understand whether or not the bank was targeting the very poor.)

He delayed and then said, "It depends but, but I'd rather, first of all you have to—to be at least five people. Yeah, and not more than nine because we realize it becomes tedious for the group members if the group is big, so managing it and following up is a bit difficult."

I had asked him about first-time loans amounts, yet he responded with information regarding group formation, specifically the preferred size of the groups. While group size was an interesting organizational concept, his response was tangential to my question.

At first, I surmised that his changing the subject meant that either he did not know his institution's predetermined loan amounts, or there was no specific rubric for him to reference in the conversation. However, both of these theories seemed highly unlikely since he had worked in the industry for fifteen years and knew it intimately. Instead, his assertion of what he would rather discuss suggested that group size was a higher priority to him than loan amount. If group size and the process of group formation were of greater importance to the institution than assessing the amount of capital disbursed to any member, then perhaps the manager was pointing toward something significant. The question was how this emphasis might influence creditor practice or client experience, which became clearer through other statements, relayed below.

The manager's response also carried another point relevant to the nature of group formation. He reported that his targeted population was inclined to form groups that were too large for the institution to manage successfully. In his experience, there had been too many recruits per group, such that the size eventually had to be limited. But this shows that the problem was not group formation itself, as it had to have occurred with relative ease considering the problem of large group size.

Several narratives repeatedly emerged regarding group formation, all of them casting it as a pivotal moment in the microfinance process. It soon became clear that the ways borrowers joined groups were nuanced; the different layers of it were important to consider. Group formation was, in part, socially based and, in part, institutionally designed. Descriptions of the microlending process by various MFI personnel demonstrate what each perceived to be the central activities.

I sat down with Thomas, a young loan officer who had come back home to South Sudan the year prior, and asked him about the process of loan acquisition. Thomas explained that after a microloan prospect first learns what microfinance is, the next step for them was to form a group.

> When a client comes in like this, he contacts you, you explain to him the products of the institution. You have to explain to him the product of the institution. You tell the clients to go and form a group. But that the group she's forming should not be of the same relative. Should be from different tribes. The reason behind is because if you know that this is a group formed by what? By the same

> relatives. Then they can connive; all of them will run away. Then where will you get the what? The clients. So that loan will be a bad loan. The reason is if they come from different families they cannot organize, they have different ideas. One may attempt to influence others, "let's do this," but others would say "no."

Thomas's description of the process implied that group formation was the primary task of a prospective borrower. A new client might have only heard about available services before he or she was then immediately encouraged to form a group. Unlike most strategic investors, here there was no assessment of their prospective businesses, nor how they might suit the market of their region. Instead, they received a simple directive to go and form a group. In other words, although he did not explain what made a good business, he elaborated in detail about what made a group function in the microfinance process.

For Thomas, groups were not only central to acquiring a loan; they were social machines that informed policy at the local level. It was in the institution's policymakers' interest that groups formed in ways that ensured solvency, and the Juba management was tasked with translating what would accomplish the aim locally. The policy that was thus crafted to govern group membership, he explained, was that borrowers could not join group loans with their relatives. His description suggested that the kinship network was the primary heuristic through which loyalty was practiced, and the policy assumed that its uniformity could be applied across time and space to improve the group loan application process. These family criteria could sort the good from the bad as, according to the logic, too much familiarity could breed troubles in the payment process.

A branch manager, Joshua, explained the process as follows:

> So we take them through the induction training, and along the way—it's 30 minutes every day, but we do it for about two weeks. They come in just about three times, so basically just about one or two hours training to take them through the loans and a little bit about record keeping. And along the way they also have to now select their office bearers; they have to get a chairperson and then to select a secretary. They have to get somebody they trust who can collect their payments and bring them into the institution. So, along that time we are also assessing them and they know that they can tell whether they can meet the conditions or not. So by the end of the training, that is when we start the disbursements.

Not unlike the MFI literature and advertisement campaigns, Joshua's description suggested that groups were formed *before* the lender process began. At Joshua's MFI, the entire prospective group underwent induction training to learn about record keeping and, during this process, the members undertook selecting trustworthy group leadership. It was during this process, he said, that borrowers in the already formed group would have the capacity to determine whether they could "meet the conditions or not."

Sharon, a seasoned MFI staff person responsible for outreach events, described the membership process in a strikingly similar way to Joshua. Her emphasis on the formation of groups at the beginning of the process highlighted the primacy of group formation.

> We normally go out for marketing. We just tell them what we have, with what we are dealing, either they like to join the company; they like to become a member of a group, and come and get money from us. We just tell them the date and then they just come. We give them training. So they come after training, then we pay—give them the loan.

Like the others, she pointed out that once a potential client hears about microfinance products at a marketing event, their next step was to become a member of a group. After forming groups, and undergoing the required training sessions, they were finally able to "come and get money from us." Group joining had occurred immediately after learning about the new service. It sounded very easy to do.

The passage below comes from Tony, a branch manager, and it similarly outlines the process of loan acquisition for working capital group loans. He specifically accentuated the ease with which clients became official group clients, while obscuring the details required for other loan options.

> Most of our loans, with the exception of the consumer loan and the salary loan, are the working capital loans.[19] So that when they take the loan we really want to say, "It has to get into the business" that's why we make . . . an analysis of basically your cash flow and then if it satisfies us, that's how we go about giving the loan. The individual loan is a bit detailed because we need collateral and you need documents for those collateral. But for working capital it's just basically a membership card, which you have to fill in and you sign and attach your photos, and then we just go to the assessment in the field, because the application form also includes the guarantee of the groups.

Tony's summary of the membership sequence once again placed group formation at the initial and pivotal position for group loans. The group guarantee was included on the application to borrow. Prospective group clients evaluated one another's businesses according to the institution's standards, by verifying that each member's business was indeed operating.[20] In the case of Tony's branch, unlike in other branches, there was an additional step: a cash-flow analysis between the contract and loan disbursal.[21] However, just like the other MFIs in town, a group had to be formed first, in order for such peer evaluation (of one another's businesses) to occur. Yet, there was a flaw in these evaluations. As I will further unpack in the next chapter, instead of choosing people based on their business capability, borrowers more often vetted one another informally through other observations such as feelings of closeness.

From the perspective of practitioners in Juba, decisions to offer microloans were determined by whether members came as a group or not. There was otherwise no systematic framework substantiating viability or market demand across the surveyed institutions; only one of the three suggested they conducted any analysis of the businesses, and even then, it was not done regularly for the group loans. Collectively, the multiple MFI staff and administrators that I interviewed in Juba were mainly satisfied with knowing that potential clients had businesses already in operation, but were not nearly as interested in what those businesses were, or what they needed to grow and succeed. Instead, institutions focused on other indicators for success of their loan disbursements.

Why would so much weight be placed on group formation, and so little placed on the soundness of businesses?[22] The reason is actually quite simple. Group making, for the MFIs, offset the cost and responsibility to "monitor" and "enforce" a host of details. While there was a spectrum of institutional involvement with group affairs once they were formed, most MFIs around the world deliberately chose to put the responsibility of business verification onto the group participants themselves. They explicitly argued that those who work in the markets knew each other and their businesses better than a loan officer who only occasionally visited ever could. Those in favor of this approach championed its cost-effectiveness as well, even if the "bank remains as ignorant as ever about who is safe and who is risky."[23] It made good business sense.

However, the procedures implemented by the Juba MFIs were not particular to Juba; they were standardized to almost everywhere in which group loans are offered. Furthermore, although institutions emphasized the primacy of group formation, what was almost never discussed was how groups were actually formed. Since groups formed by themselves, one might expect that the membership composition would reflect the overall demographic. Yet, as I mentioned earlier, returnees were substantially underrepresented in comparison to IDPs, indicating that the sorting had to have been occurring at some point within the process.

I returned to resolve this with another round of interviews.

HOW TO JOIN A GROUP IN JUBA

I asked Thomas, the branch manager I have mentioned above, about what information his institution has collected about incoming clients, for instance, if applications asked any specific questions about their background, or if there was anything unspoken that practitioners were attentive to. He responded,

> No no no. We don't assume. Like, for the education level, we always ask, "Did you go to school? Up to what level?" Primary, secondary, and so on. And also we ask them where their original places were, so from there we are able to determine where this person is an internally displaced person or a returnee or an indigenous person of the area. So we always ask those questions.

Of all the personal identifiers his institution might collect about its borrowers, the only two that the manager listed were educational level and "where their original places were," as in, where they lived before and during the war. These data were collected for identification purposes rather than eligibility. Nevertheless, prospective clients noted the latter and would determine if and how they would apply the frame when selecting their group mates.

This was the second time that this dichotomy, contrasting IDPs and refugees, had been presented to me in a conversation regarding microfinance procedure. There was a theme, one that extended beyond the microfinance policymaker emphasis on group processes and delved into the realm of social ties. MFI policy appraised certain social relations that allowed for the group process to be beneficial to loan performance, expecting the formulation to correspond to higher repayment rates. Unlike the rule prohibiting family co-borrowing, the MFI field staff did not use the wartime location metric as a policy to determine eligibility. And yet again, it had become worth noting.

My interview respondents continuously mentioned the places potential beneficiaries had been during the war. This mirrored what I frequently heard elsewhere around town. In a city comprised of more than sixty ethnic groups, vast income disparities, as well as geographical knowledge, one can imagine that citizens would be inclined to generalize groups of "others" according to various taxonomies; but this taxonomy was unexpected in this context. While mainstream international media narratives about the conflict characterized the regional social divisions around issues of race and religion (Dinka versus Nuer, Arab versus Christian versus Animist, North versus South), people in Juba were instead referencing groups according to where they had been—their place of exile during the war. They were adapting labels for groups during the war, for use "after" the war. This was the predominant distinction. This occurred in various contexts, and of important relevance here, it emerged in conversations pertaining to capabilities, work ethics, and even in regards to microfinance feasibility.

Past or present tense, this wartime location distinction was spoken often by Juba locals and was appropriated by outsider MFI personnel that were working there. For example, in the following excerpts from interviews, industry respondents referred to people in the present tense as what they were classified as (by international norms of refugee nomenclature, and by social constructs) in the past. Repatriates were thus commonly called "refugees" as if they had not yet returned already. Eventually, the MFI staff began noticing the language use, and applying it to their analyses. They even sorted the data that was collected accordingly, if only informally. By applying this language, the MFI staff appropriated the semantics, shifting to the form of newly understood local connotations. The fact that this labeling was arising consistently in interviews about microfinance signaled its significance. The question was, how was this location dichotomy affecting the process of borrowing?

It took time for the field level MFI staff to theorize the connection between this location distinction and repayment. What follows are excerpts from follow-up interviews with the same MFI personnel, organized in an effort to understand this relationship between wartime residence patterns and group loan access. These interviews suggest that locals-at-large, clients, and high-level microfinance personnel all perceived that microfinance functioned differently for the different demographics.

I asked Michael during his second interview, "Have you noticed trends between those groups [IDPs and returnees]? How do their behaviors compare?" He replied,

> Well, to a small extent, a few of our clients have an idea of microfinance. Yeah, they know that MFIs give loans, that they are repaid, with interest, or a service charge (he laughed),[24] but the majority of them don't know about microfinance. And the reason why—even those that went out into exile and came back with a little knowledge of microfinance—is that they did not even have access to those services, so they are unable to move free about microfinance.

The main contrast Michael pointed out between the two groups was their level of understanding about microfinance. People who were in Sudan (and what is now South Sudan) during the war did not know much about microfinance services, while those who were outside the country were more familiar with them. Michael later described the challenge of operations given that, as he said, for many borrowers the "aspect of loan [was] still foreign." Although those who were outside the country were aware of microfinance projects by reputation, they had not been able to access the services. They were, as he put it, unable to "move free about," or make use of microfinance.

Geoffrey, a loan officer, noted how little the average Juba local knew of microfinance in the early days of peace.

> By then—it was a situation, which anything can happen beyond five kilometers. It wasn't secure. So we were limited, but right now we remove that one,[25] so we give them induction training because in most cases nobody really knows what microfinance is all about, from at least now they know.

There was little exposure to the programs, further limited by security protocol that prohibited outreach to distant regions. When the MFIs were able to expand and set up branches in neighboring areas, they initiated conversations about their programs. He told me that once they were able to explain and expose their activities to community members, that "at least now they know what microfinance is: money . . . which is intended to boost up your business." As told by many MFI staff, these were mostly new concepts for those who had not left the country boundaries.

The majority of people who lived in South Sudan camps and towns had never heard of microfinance before it came to Juba, but those who were coming from large cities outside the country had been exposed not only to microfinance but also to many different forms of banking including formal banking, saving, lending, and money-sending services. Later in our conversation, Geoffrey returned to the different ways new and old clients related to microfinance. He affirmed the finance knowledge that the returnees had gained abroad and summarized the differences between the groups as follows:

> Comparing the IDPs and the returnees, well, the best we could say about the returnees, they came with the knowledge. Uganda, for example, they have over, I think 500 MFIs altogether. Almost everywhere you go you'll find an MFI. And most of those people know what an MFI is like.

Microfinance was very popular in Uganda, and the other countries that the South Sudanese were returning from. Those who had lived outside of Sudan therefore gained a clear understanding of microfinance institutions. It was virtually impossible for them not to be, as MFI offices were public fixtures and so many people in those communities utilized their services. This exposure fostered familiarity with the services and sometimes even an interest in participating.

The experience of IDPs and the few that remained in Juba contrasted with those of the repatriates. A branch manager, James, described internally displaced locals' views of his program. Leaning back in his desk chair, he retold the first impressions of those in Juba toward microcredit. He spoke of the era immediately after the CPA was signed. This was a period when NGOs, including his own MFI, began to establish themselves in the region, and locals and former IDPs were still the majority of the population because the returnees had not returned yet.

"Here, when we started, nobody understood exactly what we were doing," he explained. "Actually, we were considered to be fleecing the community. In one way or another, people wanted us out rather than in." In short, most people within the region considered the program a scam; microfinance did not fit with South Sudanese preconceptions about what is beneficial to their community. Aid, on the other hand, was common. So were local rotating savings circles, which were in many places around South Sudan called *thanduk*.[26] People within greater Sudan during the war were skeptical of microfinance institutions, however, not only because they had not been exposed to it but because the Sudanese state was governed under Islam, which had explicit sanctions against lending with interest. The community in Juba at the dawn of peace understandably saw credit services as so detrimental that they even wanted purveyors to be barred. But skepticism did not get in their way of joining shortly. It was easy for them to join.

A critical challenge existed between the folds of the members' self-selection. Those who were receiving microfinance services were those who knew the least about it. How could this be? Geoffrey, the same loan officer mentioned above, reported that repatriates had not broken into the microcredit group-lending system due to the difficulty of group formation.

> When these people [returnees that were abroad] came in, they got the system immediately. Instead the challenge they had was meeting the conditions. Because with the group loans, they really have to find somebody to allow you to the groups. Because they didn't know anybody. So if you're still new and nobody knows you it's a bit difficult. So what happens they had the good knowledge, they are well versed about the microfinance and they had that good impact with the others. Because in most cases we do advertise ourselves but the word of the mouth is so important about the microfinance. They suit in so fast.

The problem for returnees, who already understood microfinance well, was that they could not begin the process until they were able to meet the recruitment requirement of having a group to apply with. Returnees did not have clearly delineated peer circles, were locally unknown, and often not invited into groups.

Jubans were—and still are—frequently typified by their place of residence during the war. IDPs and camp dwellers were considered alike because they, for the most part, lived in communities together and had continuity into post-conflict Juba. They also remained in contact with one another and maintained social bonds. For instance, it was common for registered displaced people living together in camps to move back to Juba together through organized returns. Meanwhile, on the other side, almost ten times as many South Sudanese were traveling back "independently" from cities they had lived in outside Sudan—especially urban capital cities like Nairobi and Kampala—where they mostly also lived alone.[27] Though they had often lived in heterogeneous communities with their own trusted social networks while abroad, these people had weaker social networks within Juba. Their social networks were thus semantically invisible to the group forming to acquire microloans. Because having a group was necessary in order to participate in the credit service, one's place of residence during war—in country or out of country exile—could single-handedly determine their access to microcredit.

Under typical microfinance operating procedures, joining a group is one of many steps that legitimate a potential member to the lenders. But in the case of Juba, it seems to have been the most critical barrier to entry. This language typology—this categorization of people—had thus effectively shifted meaning within Juba microcredit. For this reason, we can see why the IDPs were the smallest segment, but represented the majority of microloan recipients in those first years of the rollout in Juba.

It is in this context that we find that microfinance in postwar Southern Sudan was built upon specific preexisting social capital. Returnees were not invited to participate, at least in part, because implementation of the group model presupposed a specific type of bond between members. Access to credit was only granted to prospective borrowers who were willing to trust others based on previous social networks. While IDPs had microfinance knowledge, they also had less salient social formulations; this meant they had little to no access. Whereas much research anticipates the impacts of social trust on repayments, this research was important in tracking the role of social capital leading up to loan disbursal (Figure 5.1).

Sometimes hands-off approaches to group self-selection work but it was harmful in this case due to the failure to incorporate the social history of the war. Each post-conflict region contains unique contextual factors that pose operational problems and opportunities to the clientele. Here, the competing factors surrounding wartime diaspora were of critical importance the process of acquiring loans.

There is furthermore difference between recognizing diversity on principle compared to in practice; though the local meanings of wartime residency were functional in some ways, they were far from "bridging diversity"

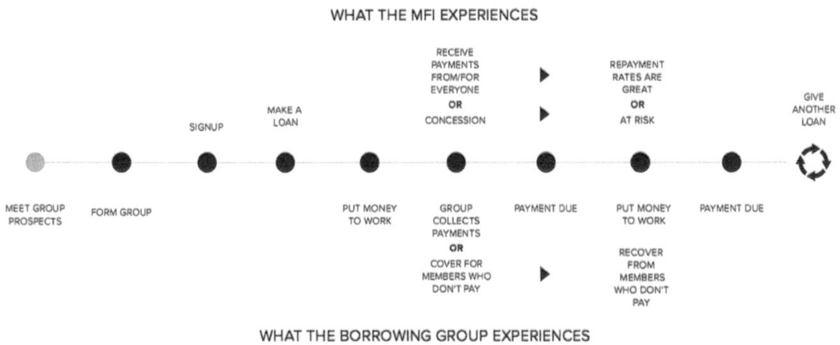

Figure 5.1 Comparing Lender and Borrower Experience. *Source:* Author.

enough so that the borrowers or the institutions could thrive long-term. To put it simply, by applying the standard, hands-off, group self-selection procedure, the Juba MFIs ended up giving access to some people over others. I call this "de facto preferential lending".

A FAILED MICROFINANCE INDUSTRY: DE FACTO PREFERENTIAL LENDING TO BLAME?

Several important effects of de facto preferential lending can be seen by looking back on what happened to the Juba microcredit sector during the period following its introduction. I had the privilege of returning to the field after these initial findings were made to see what, if any, the impacts of preferential lending were in Juba. Much had evolved between my visits. The public had grown less skeptical of MFIs as more of them had cropped up around town, and borrowing had become much more common. In this new period, I was also able to identify some outgrowths of the de facto preferential lending. Specifically, the groups that initially formed around displacement networks faltered in carrying out the MFI procedures and business practices.

The nature of the postwar economy was one of several challenges that threatened the Juba microcredit industry. The economy itself presented several hurdles, and borrowers put the loans to use in many different kinds of businesses. Some bought charcoal in bulk, and others bought and sold various foods: dry beans, fish, and cooking oil, to name a few. Others sold fresh foods like tomatoes and cabbage. Some did a mixture of many of these practices. Almost every item that borrowers bought and sold was imported from abroad.

The postwar market structure provided plenty of challenges in its own right, and the borrowers that had been abroad wielded strategies to overcome them. Repatriates had the social networks they had created as expatriates to exploit and maintain. However, that capital was not local, and thus it was invisible to the MFI policymakers and to many potential co-borrowers.

There is good reason to suspect that the de facto preferential lending also influenced the sector's demise. Reasons not specifically tied to the economy, as identified by those who participated in the sector, included the financial skill deficit among those who received loans combined with scant business opportunities. One manager with intimate knowledge of South Sudanese borrowers reflected:

> they have gone through a long war, you'll find that the number of income generating activities in South Sudan is very low. That is the people, most of the people here, they lack skills. So, when we provide them loan, as they do not have skills, they do not know how to utilize that fund using their skills.

His commentary suggested that those who were actually receiving the first wave of loans were not prepared for the business undertaking. I elaborate upon the hazards of field staff diagnoses of borrower ailments in chapter 8, but for now I simply draw attention to one assessment within a complex web of challenges I believe he was right about. In fact, staff remarks about borrower unfamiliarity with running businesses with credit in many ways forecasted aspects of the eventual demise of the microcredit system in South Sudan. A couple of results from surveys of 100 borrowers past and present from 2012 to 2013 illustrate the lasting wartime dichotomy relayed to me by MFI staff.[28] I was able to ask borrowers where they were during war, if they had been somewhere with microcredit services offered, among many other questions about their experiences. Did familiarity with microcredit yield better results? Not necessarily. Being familiar with microfinance prior to Juba did not predict whether or not borrowers had a good experience in the eyes of clients, or the difference between quitting and being kicked out. But it did influence how these borrowers used their loans. Even though fewer repatriates received loans in the early years, these borrowers who had been exposed to MFIs abroad demonstrated a couple of advantages in their business strategies. For one, people who had borrowed prior to Juba were twice as likely to have businesses that combined food and non-food items. This meant a diverse portfolio, which spread those borrowers' risk across their spectrum of commodities, including things that could not rot. One the other hand, people who had not borrowed or never saw microfinance during the war were about 30 percent likelier than their counterparts to have sold food only.[29] Relatedly, people who had seen and used MFIs in the past were far likelier to earmark or set aside a loan payment at the beginning of their loan period, than those who had not. Though again, not a perfect proxy for success in the eyes of the borrowers or the MFIs, this suggested that they might generally have been better at making timely loan payments.[30] These results did not predict whether or not borrowers resultantly attained higher incomes or better quality of life, and neither do they show the extent to which even well-prepared borrowers struggled to meet their achromous social and market demands, which are discussed at length in chapter 7. However, they do show that the de facto sorting put those with better business and borrowing strategies at a disadvantage.

But the nascent Juba microfinance industry did not reach those who were better suited for the services. The policies that MFI staff enacted in South Sudan precluded many poor returnees who already understood commerce and microcredit methodologies, at least to some degree. Many seasoned entrepreneurs and seasoned borrowers did not receive services due to limited or undervalued local social bonds. Instead, the institutions' portfolios skewed toward beginners, with the majority of those receiving loans being comparatively inexperienced in the marketplace and also in borrowing practice. Many were so unfamiliar with the premise of borrowing that they were even skeptical of the program at first and needed to learn about its basic components. Lending to individuals without skills was negligent and more needed to be done to bridge the divide responsibly. They required education about the payment schedule and marketing education for altogether new entrepreneurs. But I heard time and again that they received too little, if any at all. It was not enough for the borrowers to succeed. The people who became clients ultimately failed—and were failed by—the standardized hands-off microfinance procedures.

The solidarity group loan replication in Juba set the microcredit sector in South Sudan on shaky foundations. It overestimated the predictive value of social cohesion during the loan cycle and underestimated the role of wartime social networks in attaining the loans in the first place. The self-selection model worked as a sorting mechanism along the wrong lines.

While practice of group self-selection offset lenders' institutional overhead and was efficient in getting the loans out, it did not result in positive balance sheets. And, although the strength of social ties among borrowers despite hardships was remarkable, what came after group formation was much more challenging for the borrowers to navigate based on that trust alone. The loan parameters proved exceedingly difficult to navigate in Juba's post-conflict market. And, as chapter 6 will show, the supposed levels of social capital that got borrowers into groups did not function to garner satisfactory repayment rates.

The cut-and-paste model of de facto recruitment set in motion a sequence of haphazard circumstances that were felt throughout the borrowing process. It was a problem for those who easily gained access to loans and a problem for those who were left out. In a short time, it became apparent at the MFI unit of analysis, too, when the disbursed loans showed signed of souring.

NOTES

1. South Sudan National Bureau of Statistics 2010.

2. Jonathan Morduch, "The Microfinance Promise." *Journal of Economic Literature*, no. 37 (1999).

Beatriz Armendariz de Aghion and Jonathan Morduch, *The Economics of Microfinance* (Cambridge: Massachusetts Institute of Technology Press, 2005).

3. Richard Montgomery, "Disciplining or Protecting the Poor? Avoiding the Social Costs of Peer Pressure in Micro-credit Schemes.'"*Journal of International Development, Special Issue, Sustainable Banking with the Poor* (1996).

4. Maitreesh Ghatak and Guinnane, "Group Lending, Local Information and Peer Selection." *Journal of Development Economics* (1999).

5. Timothy Besley and Stephen Coate, "Group Lending, Repayment Incentives and Social Collateral," *Journal of Development Economics*, 46, no. 1 (1995).

6. Alessandra Cassar, Luke Crowley and Bruce Wydick, "The Effect of Social Capital on Group Loan Repayment: Evidence from Field Experiments." *The Economic Journal*, no. 517 (2007).

7. Dean S. Karlan and Javier Gine, "Group versus Individual Liability: A Field Experiment in the Philippines." *Center for Global Development Working Paper* (2009).

8. Shari Berenbach and Diego Guzman, "The Solidarity Group Experience. Growth and Equity through Microenterprise Investments and Institutions Project." *Action International* (1992), 4 as cited in Montgomery 1996.

9. Joan Parker, *Microfinance in Post-Conflict Countries: Towards a Framework for Action* (Geneva: Enterprise and Cooperative Development Department, ILO, 1999), 1.

10. See Richard Montgomery, "Disciplining or Protecting the Poor? Avoiding the Social Costs of Peer Pressure in Micro-credit Schemes." *Journal of International Development, Special Issue, Sustainable Banking with the Poor*, 8, no. 2 (1996).

11. Sidney Schuler, et al., "Men's Violence Against Women in Rural Bangladesh: Underdetermined or Exacerbated by Microcredit Programmes?" *Development in Practice*, 8, no. 2 (1998).

12. Joseph Stiglitz (1990) suggested that self-selected groups (as opposed to individual loans, or group assigned by the MFI) could curb risk-taking among borrowers. See also Giné, Jakiela, Karlan, and Morduch, "Microfinance Games." *American Economic Journal: Applied Economics*, 2, no. 3 (2010) for a more recent analysis of the virtues of self-selected groups.

13. Susanne Alldén, "Microfinance and Post-conflict Development in Cambodia and Timor-Leste." *Sojourn: Journal of Social Issues in Southeast Asia* (2009).

14. Karen Doyle, *Microfinance in the Wake of Conflict: Challenges and Opportunities,* (Washington, DC: USAID, 1998); Nagarajan 1999.

15. The United Nations Secretary-General defined IDPs as "*persons or groups of persons who have been forced or obliged to flee or to leave their homes or places of habitual residence, in particular as a result of or in order to avoid the effects of armed conflict, situations of generalized violence, violations of human rights or natural or human-made disasters, and who have not crossed an internationally recognized State border*" (1999). (Guiding Principles on Internal Displacement, UN Doc E/CN.4/1998/53/Add.2.). Here, when referencing IDPs, it is generally understood to be in the past tense. That is to say, the IDPs are no longer displaced because they are now in Juba town.

16. "Returnee" is a term used to describe those who were refugees during the war—displaced outside international borders. This term used colloquially distinguishes between the past and present tense (unlike the IDP usage). A formal definition of refugee is a person who, "*owing to a well-founded fear of persecution for reasons of race, religion, nationality, membership of a particular social group or political opinions, is outside the country of his nationality and is unable or, owing to such fear, is unwilling to avail himself of the protection of that country.*" (Art. 1(A)(2), Convention relating to the Status of Refugees, Art. 1A(2), 1951 as modified by the 1967 Protocol).

17. Between January 2007 and May 2009, 39,329 tracked with IOM. IOM/SSRRC "Sudan Spontaneous Return Tracking Report" 2009.

18. Nationally, only 19 percent of returnees to all South Sudan states were refugees from outside Sudan. IOM/ SSRRC 2009, p. 8.

19. Working Capital Loan is another name for a group or solidarity loan.

20. The MFIs required between three and six months of consistent business operation.

21. Institutional policy varies depending on the kind of business, which qualifies for microloan services. The types of businesses are in general unconstrained. Institutions seldom require data explaining what kinds of businesses the loans will be used for. The only explicitly forbidden businesses are brick laying and charcoal farming, although I met clients who were doing those very enterprises.

22. This occurs elsewhere, too. See Isabelle Agier and Ariane Szafarz, "Subjectivity in Credit Allocation to Micro-entrepreneurs: Evidence from Brazil" *Small Business Economics*, 41, no. 1 (2013) for an analysis of how gender was more likely to predict loan approvals than profession types in by a Brazilian MFI.

23. Beatriz Armendariz de Aghion and Jonathan Morduch, *The Economics of Microfinance* (Cambridge: Massachusetts Institute of Technology Press, 2005), 90.

24. Earlier we had a conversation about how his institution was trained to use the phrase "service charge" instead of "interest" for Muslim clients, because "interest" was illegal under Islam. His laughter was a nod to that conversation.

25. By "remove that one" he referred to the boundary on operations due to insecurity, which had since been lifted.

26. Referred to in the financial inclusion literature as Rotating Savings and Credit Associations (ROSCAs). In them, members pool money and disburse to a member or selected members, so as to speed up savings for all members except the last to draw their disbursement.

27. IOM/SSRRC, "Sudan Spontaneous Return Tracking Report" 2009.

28. These surveys were developed based on responses to open-ended questions, which were subsequently categorized by type. An explanation of this procedure is in chapter 3. No questions asked directly about repayment or income rises as the outcomes.

29. Significant at 0.008.

30. Significant at 0.002.

Chapter 6

What's Trust Got to Do with It?

The value of postwar social ties within the group borrowing procedure

After they had closed up shop in 2012, those in charge of the sector blamed the dearth of social capital among the populace as a key culprit for microcredit's failure in South Sudan. It was a surprising analysis to hear because, as mentioned in earlier chapters, it was easy for certain groups of returnees to find trusted friends with whom to join group loan contracts. As time passed, after the 2005 CPA aperture, MFI branches appeared all over Juba. Microfinance grew more commonplace, concerns about microcredit "fleecing the community" had subsided, and adoption flourished. By 2010, there were 45,000 borrowers counted by the MFIs. Some borrowers became interested because they had friends relay how it worked. Compelling marketing events near their shops convinced others. As time went on and people resettled into Juba town, more joined the lending programs. The people interviewed in this chapter borrowed during this period, when borrowers were no longer just the IDPs who came into Juba with friends. In fact, by that time, I seldom met any borrowing group that had met within Sudan prior to the CPA. The fact that borrowers joined joint liability groups indicated some level of comfort not just with the programs, but with each other. Nevertheless, many industry observers believed the social solidarity was too low for microcredit.

SUPPOSING THAT WAR DESTROYED TRUST

One manager reflected in 2013 to me, after his MFI had closed shop, on the industry shutdown in South Sudan. He spoke directly to the significance of social capital in ordinary microfinance, and how he saw it in postwar Juba. In particular, he indicated that Juba borrowers had weak social bonds among them, which compromised their ability to enter joint-liability contracts. "The situation of South Sudan," he told me,

> the social bondage is not really there. That means you have to make sure that the people, in order for them to co-guarantee each other, should be friends first and get to know each other. But in other places we use the same model, and we find that it's easier because you find that people have settled for so many years. They know each other and more details, and you ask, "can you co-guarantee this person?" They say "yes" because the kind of social cohesion is very close.

The manager went on to explain how social cohesion influenced not only group joining but also the procedures of covering for a defaulting peer.

> The group approach was not appropriate for South Sudan because these people, the social bonding of the people here in South Sudan, especially in the town areas, the urban areas, is not as strong as it is in Asia or even in Uganda. Because in Uganda from our experience, we found that if a member of a group failed to repay their loans, other members pay on behalf of the defaulter.

By stressing the importance of the cohesion found in communities that had been settled for long periods of time, he underscored the notion that such bonds are prerequisite for group loans to function. By describing what made the group loans work in non–post-conflict regions, he inferred that the absence of those features would result in failure. Indeed, he concluded by juxtaposing his experience elsewhere with what he saw in South Sudan, "But this thing is totally missing here. This is because of lack of social bonding here, because these people have been affected by long war of almost 40 or 45 years."

This manager asserted the expectation in microfinance practice that social trust gets people into groups, and that once in, the social trust would engender the proper functioning of the group guarantee. His comments made plain that the two most important things he believed the social bonds were supposed to do were to get people comfortable enough with each other to cosign debts and to motivate borrowers to follow through on their commitments. By contrasting Juba with Ugandan and Asian experiences, his retrospective highlighted why he believed the social ties in an area ravaged by war were inadequate for either part required by the model. While there is little doubt that wars create social fissures, the manager's postmortem begs the question: Was social capital scarce in Juba?

The very foundation of microfinance group lending presumes that social capital enhances the economic process. A standard-issue group loan (aka. solidarity loan or working capital loan) is received after the whole group—however you find them—signs up. Signing up means guaranteeing for others, should they fail to make a (weekly or biweekly) payment. Each person receives his or her own loan. All three Juba MFIs had borrowers collect the group members' payments, and a chairperson delivered the total sum to the MFI. This was supposed to incentivize repayment: borrowers cannot apply for another loan if payments are not made. How borrowers dealt with the payments within their group was up to them, and little has been written about how people manage what happens within the groups to make the payments to the MFI happen.

A peaceful Juba meant new social ties had to be formed and put to use. Because it is so central to the microcredit arrangement, it is important to ask how social capital is made and managed anywhere loans are given, and especially after four-plus decades of violence and diaspora. This chapter details how participants navigated the social and economic dilemmas present when co-borrowing. It shows how borrowers determined trustworthiness, how they carried on when things went well and everyone could pay, and also what happened when not everyone could. There were surprising flashpoints of tension and, sometimes, resolution.

SOCIAL CAPITAL WITHIN SOLIDARITY GROUPS

Social capital can be either the bond among people with shared qualities or can bridge diverse others. To Robert Putnam, who is often credited with propelling the term into popular theorizing, both were valuable for civic life.[1] "By analogy," he wrote, "with notions of physical capital and human capital—tools and training that enhance individual productivity—'social capital' refers to features of social organization such as networks, norms, and social trust that facilitate coordination and cooperation for mutual benefit."[2]

Social capital has taken root as a tremendously powerful idea in the development world, yet its popularity has also led to the vocabulary being used indiscriminately.[3] Despite this wide valence, social capital is most frequently described as an enhancer of money—an external force that can solve the market failure of imperfect information.[4] Imperfect information is, in simple terms, when either the producer or consumer of a commodity does not know something important about its worth. A common example is an unwitting person buying from a shady used-car dealer who is selling a lemon. Social ties allow a consumer to buy with confidence. People are less likely to exploit someone they know, because there is an assumed degree of built-in accountability. Consequently, when more social ties are present in a society, more transactions become more efficient.[5]

As for its application to microcredit, social capital is supposed to allow people to get into peer groups and convert their relationships into economic assets. Microcredit peer lending is also, as Michael Woolcock (1999) pointed out, a perfect terrain to observe the capacity for intragroup social ties confront external economic cultures. Traditional lenders had an imperfect information problem: they could not bear the costs associated with studying risk of individual prospective borrowers. The group lending strategy offset this risk by transferring the work of collecting information to the group and put group members in charge of selecting and monitoring each other.[6] In theory, familiarity among group members would lead them to perform well; social sanctions should deter or rectify bad behavior. The positive side of this is reflected in the industry language, "solidarity groups." Most theorizing on the social dimensions of microfinance follows such logic. For instance, Besley and Coate (1995) argued that social sanctions actually give group lending an advantage over individual lending, whereby peer pressure enhances loan repayment. Strong social sanctions inhibit the moral hazard that people will shirk paying back their loans.

Similar to the MFI manager's analysis above, most research on social capital in microcredit revolves around two main questions: Can we identify social capital when we observe it? And what good does it do the lending process? Too often, as readers will notice in the literature summary that follows, the questions are blended together. To better understand, we must understand the nature of the social ties and their application in practice.

The effects of social connection have been measured in many ways. One common belief is that trusting behavior is helped by similarity within a group. For example, Karlan (2005) observed connection as ethnic homogeneity in Peru, where he found that ethnically homogeneous groups were more trusting in microcredit experiments.[7] In observation of actual borrowing practice from a Peruvian MFI, he found that borrowers living closer to one another or who were "more culturally similar" also did better at repaying and saving. Cassar, Crowley, and Wydick (2007) also tested "social homogeneity" but through clan names shared within the groups they experimented upon in South Africa. As with Karlan, and despite deploying different observational metrics, they found that homogeneity "is a good thing for group loan repayment." Notice in all these cases however, social capital was presumed to exist when researchers observed the predicted consequence on borrowing. In other words, they only identified social relations as "social capital" when behaviors fit their economic theories.

Others looked at whether the depth of bonds among borrowers enhanced loan performance. Wydick (1999) found that groups comprised of acquaintances showed no significant difference from total strangers' repayment rates in Guatemalan microfinance.[8] Cassar et al. (2007) found that "the strength of acquaintanceship between members and the distance between their homes to be insignificantly (and in some specifications negatively) related to group performance." They suggested the finding could imply that "the most important component of relational capital may be interpersonal trust between members rather than the underlying threat of social sanctions for non-contribution."[9] Godquin (2004) reinterpreted the depth of intragroup social ties as a function of the length of time groups had been together, thusly the researchers expected that an older group would be better able to monitor and sanction members. Homogeneity among group members, measured in terms of age and education level, had no impact on repayment performance. They, like Wydick, found that "group homogeneity and social ties among group members are not always associated with a better repayment performance" in Bangladesh.[10] Social ties proved to have a negligible impact on rates of loan repayment; older groups were no more likely to repay than newer ones.

Abbink, Irlenbusch, and Renner took a different approach in 2006. In a university student lab experiment they simulated microfinance and used participants' self-reported perception of interaction frequency to measure social closeness. They found that social ties in this construction hardly affected repayment rates, and that repayments among close participants dwindled over time in the experiment.[11] Despite the widespread championing of social capital's effects on microloan repayment, these findings suggest that it plays quite a small role. Part of the problem is that the constructs used to measure social capital varied so greatly, as did the populations they studied. Most studies reflected the drive to predict what social factors influence repayment, not necessarily to find "social capital." Such research was designed to help MFIs and policy makers strategize and fine-tune their services so as to hedge risk and turn profits. Clearly, the literature is conflicted as to which "independent variables" matter most for garnering loan installments. Ethnic and age homogeneity, time spent in a group, and many other indicators fell short in predicting whether borrowers would repay the MFIs.

Not only do the above researchers measure social capital as an influencer of repayment, most presumed that it is good for business. Social bonds, though, can work both ways. The positive effects of association are what one World Bank summary referred to as "Putnam effects," whereby relationships facilitate economic gain by increasing trust. Yet, when testing propositions on the effects of social capital on economic growth, another trajectory is also possible. This is what the Bank report dubbed as the "Olson effects," whereby "associations stifle growth."[12] In other words, associations can be just as disposed to corrupt behavior as they are to motivate good behavior. Strong bonds among borrowers might result in "positive" outcomes to the institution (in this case, loan repayment) or they may result in "negative" outcomes (coup de shirk, if you will). For example,

Sharma and Zeller's analysis of several Bangladeshi MFI solidarity groups found social ties and group homogeneity (defined as enterprise and asset similarity) negatively associated with repayment. In that case, group intimacy was counterproductive for repayments. They issued an important call to action: "the important thing for financial institutions is to tailor services such that it becomes worthwhile for the poor to establish a profitable long-term association."[13]

The question of what social capital does—beyond the repayment as dependent variable formula—is woefully understudied. I emphasized in the first chapter that loan repayment may not reflect the ways a borrower would consider a microloan a success. It is possible, for instance, that perfect repayment results can exacerbate poverty, as when borrowers recycled their debts, eventually piling them up to an unmanageable debt. And several researchers have uncovered serious social tensions when looking beyond economic-focused outcomes. Indeed, solidarity lending can shroud pernicious effects happening outside the banks, including inciting increased violence in borrower groups and households.[14] Richard Montgomery observed "forced acquisition" of personal items from defaulting members.[15] Lamia Karim observed public shaming and "house breaking," or selling off defaulting members' homes in Bangladesh, such that she situated microcredit within a "political economy of shame."[16] Outcomes such as these are unseen, or at least unreported by MFI staff, and call into question what good social capital might do within the multifaceted social systems in which microcredit is delivered.

Though the group-lending model is applied all over the world, its functioning relies on social networks, norms, and obligatory customs. In its implementation however, the group loan relationship is new to the participants and should not be collapsed wholly into the social systems that predate it. These are not simple economic or cultural processes. They cannot be understood as singular events, and they certainly are not universal.

Determining whether social capital exists in any society requires knowing how participants construct ideas about their bonds, before we can know if they mobilized them as assets in borrowing communities. The complexity is further complicated in a postwar community that is receiving returnees from exile on an ongoing basis. But time in local residency was not the only problematic variable when studying the Juba case. Community norms around pricing, and market demeanor, and negotiation were established and negotiated along numerous social networks for people with multiple language and exchange traditions—there were eighteen tribes represented among the hundred people interviewed. There were also presumably class, age, gender, and other norms at work. No collection of ethnic anthropologies would reveal the underlying metaphorical conversation about what might drive and nurture social bonds.

In an effort to map the domains that mattered to participants, I asked borrowers a series of open-ended questions regarding how they selected their groups, how they determined trust for each other, and what that meant during the borrowing process. This information about group processes was somewhat shrouded from the institutional personnel, as one manager stated: "We only know when individuals get the loans; we don't know anything beyond that. After that point, we only know them as a group." What follows are brief interview vignettes that paint a picture of the social lives of loans. The borrower testimonies noticeably disagree with the antisocial analysis of MFI managers.

VIGNETTE 1: JUST HERE FOR BUSINESS

Irene's story exemplifies the concern of many post-conflict microcredit observers, given that it speaks to the consequences of postwar mobility and low social cohesion. I met with this thirty-three-year-old Juba resident at *Souq* Melisa, an area that offers everyday foodstuffs. She was seated in a booth in a row of lively women. She had her own table, made of one-inch-diameter sticks and covered with a tablecloth. Upon it sat perfectly piled pyramids of lemons and tomatoes. Underneath the table were clear, plastic gallon-size tubs full of lentils and red beans. Hanging from the shady overhang above her head were rows of seasoning packets. She seemed happy, with a bright demeanor.

At that point in time, Irene was no longer borrowing. I asked her why. She immediately launched into a story that was wrought with frustration, though her tone remained positive throughout the telling.

> I just left the group because they were some members, two members, who did not pay the loan when we were paying back. So they met and knew it, but I just moved out of the group and left. But the group is still there. But for me, I just left because the others are not contributing and it made me annoyed. I contributed to pay for the other ones who missed, because they refused to pay.

This woman did not have the leverage needed to enforce payments from all group members. Whatever group consensus existed, it operated irrespective of her. This may have been a case of the "Olson effect," where the other members' social ties ignited a maladaptive behavior. Whatever sanctions Irene could enact, if any, were insufficient to persuade the rest of the group to make their payments. Irene was unable to control the group, but she could control her participation.

Without sanctions to make the delinquents pay, Irene grew perturbed. I wondered what was lacking for Irene to enforce complicity from her co-borrowers. Suspecting that social capital played a part in the ability to enforce sanctions, I wondered how she had become acquainted with her group. I asked where she met them. She replied:

> We just organized for the loan. We met in the market for just one month, we took to get used to the members in the market. We all had shops in different markets, at Customs and the market where we meet currently, but we met as the group in Customs Market.

In order to give a loan, the main concern of the MFIs was that the co-borrowers guarantee each other. Business verification was not done by the MFI, but by the group. The MFI instructed borrowers that they should know the businesses and suggested that they observe them operating for some months. Ultimately observation was confirmed with a binary "yes" or "no" by members when enrolling in microcredit solidarity loans.

Irene cleared the observation confirmation with one month of monitoring. At the time when she was entering the group contract, Irene felt that one month with the others was satisfactory, even though it was a task suggested by the MFI. Saying "just" one month, in retrospect, emphasized her feeling it had not been sufficient to judge the merits of her peers' companies, or their trustworthiness after all. In her analysis, time was a central component of confidence building.

Another central point Irene drew attention to was distance. She and her group members' shops were in different markets. Implicit in her telling was that having shops in the same market allows borrowers to observe one another. The opposite was true in her experience. Vending in different markets prevented regular observation, and that was detrimental.

I asked, "Are you friends now?" She giggled and shook her head. "Since 2008, that time, up to this time now we are not friends. I have not met with them. So I am no longer with them."

Did the lack of an enduring relationship mark limited social capital in practice? Weak social ties might explain why she was unable to sanction group behavior, as predicted by the literature. Irene's group knew each other for only a short period of time and was not nearby in the market, and monitoring was costly. But, these were not the only things she would stress before trusting another group.

I asked her, "Imagine you could go back in time and choose your group differently, what would you do?" She replied:

> If I'm to form a new group, I'm going to consider one: the business the person is carrying. Whether it's a good business, if it's going on well. And the second one I want to know is the home of that group member. I'll want to know whether she or he is renting or owning his own land. That's what I will consider.

Irene recognized the inadequacy of the MFI staff's suggested binary checking whether or not the businesses existed. She wanted to see for herself not just whether the businesses were running, but running well and more. I asked if she knew those details of the people in her former group. She replied with a tone of consternation.

> I did not know their homes; that is why things did not work out well. Those ones came from Uganda. They just came for business, to make it here. They were not here. They are Ugandans. So they are not here with us; they organized in the market.

People who came to Juba for business opportunities were not trustworthy, on her telling. She explained they were "not here with us," to evoke that they were not genuinely part of the community. Here in the telling, the "they"—"not us," must be read as part of the newly independent South Sudan post-conflict story. Entrepreneurial hustlers undermined the procedure when they were not "with us." Irene's experience taught her that a deeper knowledge of cosigners was necessary.

Specifically, she described knowing homes as a way of knowing whether or not people were just there for business. Hence her reasoning that she should distinguish between home renters and owners. She believed home-ownership would better indicate a lasting investment in the community, if not also personal wealth, and therefore merit her trust.

Most of Irene's analysis of her experience affirms the importance of social cohesion in co-borrowing. Though strong business acumen was desirable, being in Juba solely to conduct business was not. One month for her group "to get used to" each other was insufficient too, because acquaintance and comfort were not equivalent to more the necessary social knowledge, or the consequent possibilities for monitoring on an ongoing basis.

VIGNETTE 2: A CLASSIFIABLY POSITIVE EXPERIENCE

The next vignette is the kind of "success story" that an organization would print on a brochure. It is also a story that departs slightly from the previously researched predictors of why that would happen. Joyce's story shows us that the value of time was particular to the nature(s) of social relations in postwar Juba.

Joyce was an active borrower when we met, in a small group comprised of five women in total. I began our chat asking how her group organized.

> You know we were suffering sometimes. We sat [came to work], but we didn't bring enough goods. So we talked, and by now there were people who were moving and telling us about the loans. So we decided to join, and we went to [the MFI] there, and they agreed, so they start giving us loan. We met here in the market. Before the market, we didn't know each other. But here in the market we have been working together for long, for like three years. Now, in the group together, it's almost to one year. I know them. I know their homes. Some are here in Munuki; others are outside.

I asked for clarification on whether she knew them as well as she described before joining the group, to which she replied, "Yeah, we are all friends. Like family friends." The time spent in the market had blossomed into real friendships for Joyce, and knowing her peers' homes was a genuine outgrowth of the friendship that preceded the borrowing procedures.

Though Irene and Joyce had different experiences—the former did not know where her co-borrowers lived but this one did—both saw familiarity with residences as an important marker of knowing others well. Notably, both ladies had the same three preliminary reference points for trust: time, regular business observation, and a sense of intimacy through knowing homes.

I wondered if any other prior association could explain the depth of their familiarity. I asked, "Did you all come from the same place?"

> *No, no*! We are not coming from the same places; we even come from different tribes. We just met in the market here, then we saw each other, then we decided to join ourselves.

Place of origin and tribe, according to Joyce, had little bearing on how this happy group formed bonds. She went out of her way to stress that tribe was unimportant to her. Seeing each other regularly at business was more important. Confidence bred first in the market was unifying. While some element of homogeneity was important (daily place, goal and latently, gender), the ones used previously by other researchers (ethnicity and provenance) were irrelevant.

When I asked what she was looking for when deciding which kind of people to join with, she replied,

> You know, when you stay with somebody you can know her according to her behavior: how she behaves, how she does work in the market, if she is hardworking. We know each other after one year like this: I know what kind of person you are. When I am working with you I will know if you are lazy, if you are hardworking, probably true. That is how we came to sort each other anyway.

She laughed a hardy chuckle and continued with specific, observable scenarios:

> Ah, you see the way somebody work. You can see another person the table is empty. Maybe there is money, but she doesn't want to go and bring goods. Others, they quarrel with their customers. Those people who bring goods to them, they don't want to pay; they start quarreling. After selling, they misuse the money. You can see them! When the walkers are passing with clothes [for sale], you bring [or buy the clothes]. When everything is passing, you bring. And that is the money for business. You can know that this woman is not good in business if she is shopping. Yeah, that is how we study each other. We know, but mostly for those ladies who are single, they are serious with their work. Because they are mother, father, they have not to joke around.

As with the last respondent, time allowed for observation was integral, a point Joyce brought home by stating that all the required behaviors could be judged within one year. Good business virtue, to her, was marked by professional courtesy and chaste personal consumption. The observations she was making for vetting included some based on business acumen (like keeping supplies in stock), others on business etiquette (like avoiding when bartering turns to bickering, which signified appropriate conduct), and other more personal situations (like being a single mother, which signified motivation). Each of these observations required eyes in the market.

How we interpret her constructs of daily life though might not explain her successful group borrowing experience. No one in Joyce's group exhibited deviant behaviors. Trust was observed before and affirmed throughout the borrowing term. Was the vigilance effective in dissuading delinquency? "The way now they are behaving, how they are behaving for those three years, nobody has missed [payment]. So we know we trust each other," she emphasized. I wondered what it might be like to be under such constant scrutiny for her cosigners. "Have there ever been any problems or tension within the group?" I asked.

> No, it's not difficult to work with the group. Yeah, they're there, other people who have a problem. You know, when you want to join as a group, you don't start each other. There are other people who aren't good; they have bad characters. Others they just get the money like that and they run away. They leave the burden to the other people. They are difficult. But in our group, we have never made that one.

"No one has ever skipped a payment?"

"No no no," she laughed. "We trust ourselves. Before we start going for loans, we sat down and we see which kind of people can join with us together."

Joyce's group had no problems and their long-standing social ties remained intact. In this woman's view, her group's front-loaded observation strategy served them well. Saying "you don't start each other," denoted her belief that one cannot champion others to improve. At the same time, she emphasized that trust had developed as an effect of seeing each other repay. So, while the nature of how they related within the borrowing context changed, the social ties continued without anything to do with the group.

Joyce's analysis centered on individualized agency, where each is responsible for her own fate. In contrast to the first vignette, Joyce's story emphasized that business acumen and personal situations were more instrumental than the friendship depth or the business legitimacy. The stability of these categories during her observation enabled her to move her frame of analysis to the individual. Though her group was good friends, she made it clear they would not have joined the group on the basis of friendship alone.

In all, it is remarkable how much people learned in a short period when they had the opportunity to monitor each other's behavior ahead of contract. This might be good news, suggesting that post-conflict demographic transitions might not be such a terrible impediment to microcredit once people are able to observe each other in the new context. It challenges the presumption that recently created social trust is of no value and sheds light on the ways that borrowers vet each other. "But we are going even asking for big loan, now they were telling us after fifth round, they are going to give each person her own loan. And we are happy; we are now waiting for that [individual loan]," Joyce concluded. However, not everyone has these rosy experiences.

VIGNETTE 3: OLD FRIENDS MIGHT NEED NEW WATCHING

Next is a story of longtime friends. It is a story about a group that had been internally displaced together during the war, and because of that fact had gained access to loans rather easily, as described in chapter 5. It is a story that upsets the theory that familiarity over a long time generates better financial outcomes for the group. This story probes the limits of solidarity under duress and illustrates what goes on behind the perfectly reported payments to the MFI when microloans are declared successful.

Helen had her son on her lap in the shaded side of the resale area of Konyo Konyo market. She was a dedicated group borrower despite small complications. Upon our introduction, when asked whether she had participated in a group loan, she launched into her story. Pointing to a vendor in the adjacent stall, but out of earshot, she spoke with a comfortable poise.

> We are just neighbors in the market. Before, we were 14. We were 14 in number when we started borrowing the loan, and there are seven left because we are not

trusting. Sometimes they don't pay; they use the money in their own way, they don't make a good profit maybe, like in time for payment, sometimes they are not willing to pay. So that's why we just decided to remain seven; the seven are the ones who are cooperating. The seven who are not cooperating, they are out now. They are no longer in the market. They are not here. It is us who are cooperating, so we are still continuing with our business.

Failures to cooperate resulted in diminished trust that broke up the group. Half of the original group, Helen judged, did not cooperate for reasons that included not being able to pay due to business struggles and unwillingness to pay, which were qualitatively different. For Helen, cooperation was a term that encompassed multiple reasons for peer non-compliance. She had little sympathy for failures either due to both personal and impersonal market forces. She continued.

The seven who left are selling greens outside there at the greens tables outside. They were at first selling in the shop when we started borrowing in the loan. These other group members who were not contributing sometimes, sometimes they didn't pay in time. Those people [from the MFI], if they come, they give the pressure on us. So the burden was mostly on us, which is why we had to chase them. I contributed, because I'm the leader. So did other group members. So, we are contributing to the other members who are willing to pay on behalf of the others who are refusing to pay. So that's why we decided to remove those people out.

The group devised a strategy for evaluating how to proceed as guarantors for each other based on a criterion of cooperation. If and when the MFI enforced payments (note this was not uniform), group officers pressured the others to do what was necessary to make payments. This was unpleasant and costly to the cooperating members, some of whom covered for the delinquent ones, so they deliberated and imposed a sanction on the less cooperative borrowers. Willingness to cover for others was the most important feature that distinguished those who the continuing group allowed to remain. Even if borrowers were failing to pay because of their business struggles, what mattered, in her telling, was less about their preparedness to pay and more about their intention to do so. And the group honored those willing to cooperate.

Together they resolved to remove the uncooperative people from the group altogether, and then devised a system to deal with it after the fact. The struggling seven were pushed outside to a cheaper, less desirable rent-free area of the market without stalls.[17] Their sanction entailed not only removing them from the loan group, but its costs removed them from the "formal" area of the market. The significance of the market outskirts was multifaceted. The greens tables outside were smaller and less permanent than the market stalls that these women were renting. This was a visible demarcation of class, on the periphery, separated from the interior social world they had previously enjoyed. The ejected members lost prospects for their business afforded by being within the market proper, where customers headed to make bulkier buys. The MFI simply marked this event as a loan clearance and a loss of customers at the office level.

I struggled to make sense of how Helen found herself in that position, of evicting her longtime friends. I wondered why the successful women could not convince the others to repay in the first place. "So before, you trusted those seven who aren't in the group anymore?" I asked. It was then when it became clear that she had learned to distinguish between notions of trust.

> I know them. We stayed for 15 years together so we know about each other very well. I know how I feel about the type of work they are in because we have stayed for long. Over 15 years.

Helen's experience borrowing taught her that knowing peers over a long period during the war did not, however, result in co-borrowing success. It turned out that she was too optimistic and could not have predicted capacity to make timely repayments or the willingness to guarantee for others when the need arose. Given that the long-standing relationships proved to have limited value for this kind of business relationship, I asked what she might look for next time. She relayed new criteria based on this experience.

> I know some people if they take the money, if they start their business, sometimes they are not regularly in the market, sometimes some I cannot trust them. I'll know that some people are lazy. Sometimes they eat too much (laughs) so they don't think of the business. So those people I will not trust.

Co-guaranteeing reshaped her criterion. Helen's story located why the greens ladies failed in both their own businesses and in cooperating to make full group payments. Her conclusion linked non-cooperative attitudes with the work ethic of borrowers. She looked for discipline in a way that she did not notice over many years of friendship prior to borrowing. Ahead, thus, she would monitor that colleagues were not eating too much while working (or perhaps being fat in general, a comment I heard from several others) and pay attention to how often they showed up to work at the market. Co-borrowing transformed the quotidian relationship.

Deep friendship and shared wartime experiences were not wholly useful predictors for borrowing success. Inside the group, business trust was broken: not enough remained for the original members to continue together.

At the same time, the intimate trust served to facilitate the necessary sanctions within their market culture and leave the microcredit event there as but memory. The still-necessary intimate bonds were thusly kept in-kind. While Helen's group is a testament to the informal remediation techniques made possible by friendship, the true test of the convertibility of social capital was a willingness to see the entire group through. After all, while the MFI got its payment to meet its short-term repayment rate reporting requirements, it ultimately lost some clients.

The kind of trust developed over fifteen years of friendship was not convertible to a continued payment, and yet, it was indispensable. She continued describing her forward-looking criteria, by emphasizing that the role of friendship was not irreplaceable, even if it failed to be fully functional last time. "I may be determining things like maybe if the person is trustworthy," she said. "The person is within—maybe the person's home—I have to know the home where the person comes from." I could not help but ask, given how prominently housing was a theme. "Before, when your group was 14, did you know each of their homes?" She said yes. I asked if she remained friends with those who were ejected from the group. "We are still friends," she laughed, as if my question were absurd. "No problems. We stay together even chatting with those ones. We are still friends; we have not separated forever."

VIGNETTE 4: TINY TOMATO TABLES

Albert had a stall on the perimeter of the market. It was much larger and sturdier than the average. It was built of solid wood, out in the sunshine apart from the main covering of the market, with its own roof built overhead. Albert sold many imported small items, most of which were durable: soaps, combs, plastic goods, tea, plastic bags, mirrors, and more. His wares were things that everyone needed, but not every day. Some goods, like the bags, were bought by other market vendors who divided batches of things like groundnut paste, the small dried fish, or greens for unit sale. Scanning the market from his place at the edge, I noticed he had a strong comparative advantage on these particular goods.

He spoke English with a British accent, which was rare, and an indication that he had spent some time farther abroad than most. Compared to most with whom I spoke, Albert was less chatty. He was also a man in a program that largely targeted women. I consider his story worth sharing because it brings home poignantly the learned predilection to vet potential partners not by social trust but by market-based metrics. His story also reveals the lengths to which he went to avoid drama.

Albert was a former borrower. He had been in a group of five people. He knew them from the same market where I met him. "We knew ourselves *very* well," he accentuated, when I asked how they knew one another. Like many, he used a measure of how long they had been working in the market to establish his knowledge of others. "We have been working in the market for so long—I think two years—so we knew each other very well."

I asked how he selected the people in his group. "There are many people in the market, but you should choose the one you trust. Knowing that you will go away and pay the money on time. And, let me say, somebody you trust." "How do you define trust?" I asked. He burst into laughter at the silly question of this foreigner he had been seeing strolling through his market, and then finally replied, "Trust is when you know someone very well. And you'll know anything that . . . maybe you will do it together, you'll do it in the way you wanted it to be." I interpreted his words as a desire for a shared entrepreneurial vision among his partners.

Albert had high confidence in his group members, yet he was no longer borrowing. Something had happened. A series of breakdowns had occurred in his group. The first breakdown was declining business, such that some members were unable to make their payments. He blamed that crisis partly on the local market problems, and partly on the microcredit terms not suiting the market flow. The problem of repayment scheduling was a common concern. Payments were expected at equal and regular intervals, but profits were secured last in the sale of purchased inventory, and larger purchases at reduced prices would mean the longest delays in realizing profits. I asked what happened next, when people were unable to get the money required.

> We could just explain to the person, to the loan officers, that we have a problem like this and they'll sort. Others could understand and the rest could not understand. If they fail to understand, then we in the group have to contribute something to fix up the other amount. So when she finally gets the money, she would return it to us. That is what we were doing.

At first blush, their back-end intragroup repayment system sounded functional, if not smooth. Encounters with unsympathetic loan officers forced higher performing cosigners to devise a back-end repayment schedule for those whose businesses were not turning a profit at the pace required by the loan contract. Better-off members covered. Their system ensured the MFI received its payment on time, and then the group would see the borrower repaid those who covered her obligation "when she finally gets the money." I was struck by Albert's empathy for defaulters. In his telling, their failures were related to the market and understandable, and therefore merited grace;

he reacted much like other respondents who understood illness or similar exogenous shocks. Besides, trust was earned through having seen them "sometimes" pay already. He hardly batted an eye when he had to pay for others. If his large stall was any indication of his wealth, he was in a position to do so.

Yet this did not explain why Albert quit the microcredit program. I could not resist asking this former borrower directly: "Did you ever miss a payment and need others to contribute for you?" He laughed again. It was here that the final breakdown to have occurred: "it occurred when complaints arose."

> No, no I didn't. I don't do microfinance anymore because the group—our group—other members. Now, they were complaining a lot of those failing to pay the money, so I decided to leave. Leave the group. So, I think that when I get a good group that I trust, that I can we can go up with them well, then I will. I'm interested in doing that.

This man trusted his prior group, but by saying what he looks for in a future "good group" that he could trust, he pointed to what did not work for him last time. Tracking down those missed payments was easier said than done, and he measured the difficulty by one metric alone: complaints.

Here was the friction: not everyone in the group shared Albert's application of the MFI principle in practice. I was amused at his matter-of-fact tone, as if to say, "covering a payment was not that big of a deal." But other group members complained when they were required to pay for delinquent cosigners. For whatever reason, covering for others was not as smooth for all members as it was for him. It got sticky for a spell. Though they bounced back as friends, their MFI would not know or care that the drama created inside the group was untenable. The MFI received its investment back, but they lost another relatively stable microcredit customer.

In light of the nagging complaints, he acknowledged that the trust he had from familiarity with his co-borrowers was not enough to make the group loans work as planned. He would need to trust his next group in different ways than his last group. He had to reconsider what constituted as trust. I asked him if he were to do it again, how would he choose the next group?

> I think, for our first group, they were giving . . . they were giving even to people having a small, small table. And with those people, you know, people selling these things like onions and tomatoes. Sometimes there will be no tomatoes even in the market, and then they will not be working. So it is really, if at all, a group will be having people who are at least selling at bit of mixed, mixed things, then I will trust the group. If they have mixed things it would be better for the group.

Albert used the example of a tomato vendor's vulnerability to market constraints to illustrate his desire to find partners less dependent on a single small product. This would be, it seemed, the shared vision that he described at the beginning of this story. His next move would be more practical. He would move upstream to partner with people who carried less risk, whose businesses had scale and diversity equal to his.

The tiny tomato retailers also bring out his awareness of external market dependencies. He never spoke about frustration with the borrowers who were not successful enough to make their payments. He was compassionate and implied the loan officers should be sympathetic of the very real challenges micro-entrepreneurs face, too. But, he did recognize that the group loans put others in a position to be frustrated and complain. Selecting new, less risky co-guarantors, he forecasted, would help. He would seek peers with diverse portfolios because payments, for Albert, had more to do with business scale and product diversification than with individual habits other borrowers had found important.

In the end, Albert was not the only lost microcredit client in this story. None of his group mates continued taking loans or went back to borrowing from MFIs. "But, we are friends here in the market," he added. "They are all here." And they still hang out together on weekends, he said.

Preserving social relations was more important than what the loan offered his business. If anything, social cohesion was an impediment to enforcing sanctions in this case. Albert believed his only choice was to quit the group so as to spare him the awkwardness of drama in his daily market life. According to Albert's logic, friendship remained necessary but not strategic. Instead, he developed a view that one can buy their way out of problems by assortative matching: like him, his next peers would be better able to shoulder the costs of covering for each other. And critically, he hoped, they would do this without complaining.

VIGNETTE 5: MAKING THE ROUNDS

The atmosphere was happy, and music was playing loudly when I met a woman who giggled at my poor Juba Arabic skills. I giggled too. Sharon and her group initially met and continue working in the market where we met. As with the others, I asked how she determined they should join together. I asked how she vetted the fitness of her cosigners. She had been among her group's leaders, with a responsibility for selecting participants.

> So we are determining the group members by looking at how their business is going on, how they are working on their business. After we joined the group

> in the market, we gathered; we moved from one family to another to various homes to know where they are staying, where they are living. So, we were introducing ourselves to know where each other lives. We were like, meeting them in our various homes; this is how we met and trust each other.

"And how is it going?" I asked.

> We were somehow good, according to the payment. Three of us are okay, but there are two, that sometimes they don't pay in time because of the market. Sometimes their market is totally down. Sometimes they put in paying in time, so sometimes we understand their situation. But the other two, there's no problem. So there's nothing bad, we are all okay in the group.

What differentiated those who were okay versus not? "Do they do something else, those two?"

> So three of us are selling fish, then the two are selling paste only—G[round] nut paste. And then the other is selling things like beans and some other small, small things like red pepper and lemons.

Sharon described the value of visiting member homes, as had others, but with a different meaning. The group members met in the market, and then officers instructed them to visit the homes. This created a different type of knowing than many others, who saw home knowledge as a way of establishing intentions to place roots in Juba—to be part of the new South Sudan. In this context, though, the MFI personnel devised the practice of seeing member homes so as to haunt borrowers, and to envision potential recourse should a payment be missed. Still, it created a feeling of trust, she said.

Although the market for commodities was ever in flux, there was no shortage of empathy in town even for fresher friends. Following many stories of discomfort with carrying out the group procedure amid business struggles, understanding was easy in this group that was not so acquainted that they even knew each others' homes before borrowing. Here again, though the particulars varied, social currency expenditure was predicated on understanding what ailed the borrowers. Where this appeared, the market challenges were understood to be beyond the scope of what a borrower can predict and buttressed by earned confidence in the person. And it was affirmed by seeing that peers had paid at other times, when they were able. The latter, of course, could only have been learned through co-borrowing experience.

The inability to make regular profits was not interpreted as a personal failure or insufficient risk-taking. Sharon, like Albert, deduced that the smallness of their shops made it difficult for those co-borrowers to repay consistently. Because the better-off fish-selling women understood the market troubles, they were gracious about recovering repayments for others. Unlike Albert's group, Sharon's did not complain about doing so.

It worked for them. There were, in Sharon's estimation, no problems. Members covered for one another, and none minded. And the group performed as the MFI wanted, too: the MFI saw its payouts recovered. And though it lost customers, the customers lost were poor ones. The various markers of trust meant this group functioned per global solidarity lending design. It was remarkable given the newness of their association. But in others, the quick-made friendships managed to threaten the MFI's desired outcomes.

VIGNETTE 6: HOME VISITS AND THE SHARED MEANING OF PAYMENTS

I spoke with a man in the shady central part of market. He looked to be over fifty years, much older than the average market vendor. When getting acquainted, I learned that Stephen was a former borrower. His group of five had met and eventually disbanded in that same market. His group seemed to me like a hustle to get in the program. They gathered friends, but friends that certainly were not so close prior to borrowing that they knew where one another lived. The MFI coaxed them to become aware of that.

> At first we were two so we went to the person in charge, the personnel. That person said, "you have to at least be five in number." And so, we came back to look for the other three. So we got our other friends now around us to join. The person who gives the loan was interested in knowing one person's home. We all had to know their homes after we had already joined the group. We had to introduce each other to where he lives so that in case anything happens, we have to reach them.

I asked Stephen if, during the time he and the friends he had made in the market were co-borrowing, anyone missed a payment. "We were all paying," he said, definitively. "Maybe sometimes a delay, it may be when the member is having some problems like funeral, maybe sickness. Maybe that one will cause delay, but all of us were paying."

When I asked why he was no longer doing microcredit he said, "We left at once, all of us as a group, because sometimes if one of the members had problems and delayed the payment with the money. So that when they collected the money, they are charging us for delaying them."

Although Stephen's group members knew each other only as professional acquaintances (having met in the market rather than as neighbors or friends), they did have a shared understanding of payment decorum that was not aligned with that of the MFI rules. When Stephen said his group never missed a payment, what he meant was that payments were made, if sometimes delayed. From his telling, neither Stephen nor his group members saw tardiness as a problematic or antithetical to proper repayment. Of course, the MFI had another view.

A reader might wonder if the MFI, whose policy was that peers had to fulfill delinquent members' obligations, had failed to properly explain the loan requirements. A reader might suggest that the group's failure to cover for behind members was emblematic of their weak social bonds. Instead, I suggest that their shared idea about the nature of payments superseded the will to appease the MFI's idea about the nature of payments. In this perspective of the delay situations, covering for each other simply was not necessary. By sharing the market world, the group saw one another's challenges and was able to interpret the failures to make payments as reasonable results of market forces. They saw each other rebound eventually. The group was willing to probe the consequences levied by the MFI—namely until they were charged late fees—but was unwilling to test the consequences of covering and whatever could mean thereafter within the group. Thus, preserving even relatively new social ties was a more currency than getting into the messy work of covering "tardy" members' payments. But MFIs do not count sympathetic feelings in their logbooks.

FINDING AND USING TRUST IN A NEW PLACE

In South Sudan, peace brought about rebuilding in both visible and invisible forms. By design, microfinance implementers place a great deal of faith that social ties will facilitate its processes. As such, those who design interventions requiring social relations have inquired about the nature of how bonds are made. It made sense why postwar researchers wondered about those bonds being damaged.[18] It also made sense why the Juba MFI observers questioned the adequacy of the social cohesion in its new communities after a long, long war. Indeed, the higher ups both in Juba and abroad argued that a shortage of social capital was one of the most detrimental pitfalls of Juba microcredit.

As evident within these few vignettes, not all groups covered their colleagues' defaults. Some felt it unnecessary. Some did cover their peers' debts, begrudgingly. But others disliked even the semblance of complaints from them. And still others did not mind covering, but were exceedingly reluctant to recover what had been covered. How do we make sense of such occurrences? First, we must step back and look at the metrics used for trust in their terms. Both the inputs, or how they determined trust, and then the outputs, or how they made sense of what trust did for them.

There was actually remarkable social bonding, solidarity, and trust forged rather quickly among Juba borrowers. There was no doubt that there was enough trust in circulation to form groups by the height of microcredit provision in Juba. People found ways to participate when it seemed profitable. Borrower indices for trust were sorted through a filter. Trust was a dual process within the group loan recovery process; two fields of trust operated simultaneously. There were different kinds of trust: social trust and economic trust. But trust as a referent for business confidence did not correlate with preexisting social trust.

One sense of trust was framed in the economic sphere. Economic trust took shape through exposure in the markets, seeing how others went about their businesses. While time knowing one another was not inherently helpful during the entirety of the borrowing procedures, time spent in the market was instructive here. As far as it concerned the groups—both in terms of feeling comfortable with the contract and once in—time with the lens to what people did in the markets did become an important currency. Many borrowers felt satisfied with how close they could become in a year or less. Borrowers developed and deployed the economic variety of trust more and more as they went through the borrowing experience.

We also saw how people put friendships to use in the business sphere. Take, for instance, the theme of "knowing homes" that emerged the most. Home-knowing had a place on the plane social trust. For a great number of borrowers I met, home knowledge was a signifier of genuine friendship and solidarity. The category also became relevant for co-borrowing inasmuch as it was a signal that others were rooted in the community. To have and maintain a home was interpreted as the intention "to be here with us," to be a part of the new South Sudan long-term, together. This became seen in the microcredit context as insurance against the worst case scenario of flight.

Yet visiting homes came up as significant to this process in another, business-minded way. The other was done specifically for the lending procedure so as to create a practical, economic worth. MFI staff encouraged borrowers who did not already know each other that well to become more familiar by visiting one another's homes. As respondents noted, such home visits were encouraged as a way of ensuring its group could find any borrower in case there was a missed payment. In that sense, home-knowing produced value that could, in theory, be drawn upon at a future date.

It was another issue altogether about what either form of trust achieved during the group loan cycle. Neither variety of trust—economic or social—was on its own a sure bet for repayment. Both built confidence, but they did not streamline the microloan socioeconomic processes. The agency-orchestrated home visits did not ensure loan payments. Instead, it

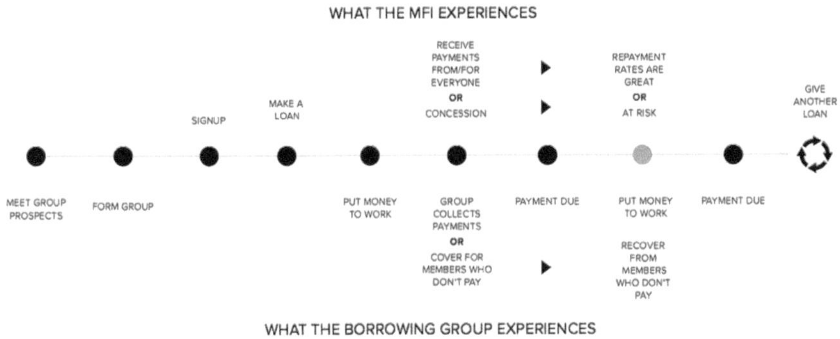

Figure 6.1 Varied Outcomes. *Source:* Author.

functioned more for prospects to get comfortable with the group procedure in practice. In reality though, visiting homes was almost never used in the recovery effort. Anyone I spoke with who had this variety of home knowledge was remiss to convert those visits into peer pressure so as to get payments thereafter. Though past research had elucidated the nefarious side of intragroup loan repayment seizures,[19] I never heard of this economic capital being cashed out in that socially embedded way in Juba. In fact, the more time I spent with borrowers, the more I realized how often they acted prosocially toward each other when the loan process got tough. Even among those whom knew each other relatively more briefly via the market. Meanwhile, participants who knew the homes of their co-borrowers in personal ways long prior to borrowing, not just as a way to chase down defaulting peers, had no better payment covering or recovery outcomes either. The same dynamic was true of the other localized metrics of trust, including how long they had known each other, ethnicity, or provenance: no patterns appeared regarding repayments.

Repayment was not the only possible outcome in the minds of the borrowers. Economic and social trusts generally remained in separate accounts. More specifically, the nature of social value deployed during the loan process was a kind that the Juba borrowers I met did not want to convert consistently to the economic demands of completing the loans at the MFI together. The social trust that drove these was not generally used as a convertible currency into economic deliverables—as "social capital" (Figure 6.1).

CHOOSING NOT TO SPEND SOCIAL CAPITAL

When social trust is converted to economic value it is called "social capital." However, among Juba microloan borrowers, some varieties of social trust and business trust were inconvertible. Social ties were plentiful despite their freshness, but they were spent or converted into economic value that was relevant to the institution, sparingly.

For instance, some groups had strategies to receive delinquent payments from friends, like the women who chased the defaulting greens-selling members out of the market proper. Together they created a sanction beyond the MFI lens. That sanction was economically costly for the evicted members but functioned so as to maintain their long-running friendships. The vast majority however, lacked such a system of recourse or quit in favor of keeping the peace among members.

Some clients felt the trust currency needed to be protected to the detriment of the loan requirements. In these cases, the social trust served to upkeep or solidify already existing social bonds on a plane independent of the economic outcome. Many, as described above, thus opted to remove themselves from the situation altogether. Commonly, empathizing with and even covering for each other was easy, and even those who complained about the delayed participants were described as problematic. Yet chasing friends down for payments was hard. Everyone knew the market was tough. Even where borrowers identified others as irresponsible, there was a sense that money would come back eventually. Social reciprocity had its own timetable.

Trusting was an ongoing and evolving process while borrowing. Some Juba borrowers knew what they looked for in colleagues and got it right. Others learned from misplaced confidence. Frequently, and especially after being burned, borrowers did not seek out greater social bonds to enhance their borrowing experience. Instead, they typically wanted to see markers of economic capital (i.e., well-stocked businesses, large business sizes, individual business acumen). For example, there was Albert, who said he would love for others to sell more items and wanted to partner with those who had less vulnerable businesses. There was also Helen, who blamed poor performing group members for laziness and wanted to see in future peers specific markers of a disciplined businessperson. These new, observable currencies, according to borrowers past and present, had value ascertained by time shared in the market and even more acutely through the experience of borrowing in this context. Nevertheless, while functioning on the plane of economic trust, and although borrowers learned this was not the exhaustive claim to success, this social trust was never seen as replaceable. The markers of friendship remained non-negotiable for too many to ignore, even if future peers will be subject to greater scrutiny while at work.

Social trust was valuable. The fact that no one was willing to forego friendship in future group selection affirms this point. The confusion between the borrowers and the MFI analysts was overstated confidence in what the trust could perform. Once in, and once challenges arose, the borrowers wanted to spend social trust wisely, to maintain what semblance of solidarity there was, and to remain together. And it was not often spent on economic ends; this capital remained social through and through. Social relations endured even after the loan contracts concluded.

Like in many other contexts, Juba borrowers were navigating the overlapping social and economic tradeoffs connected to the benefits of the loyalty offered by the MFIs and by their communities. MFIs were new institutions for many people, as discussed in chapter 5. And, as that chapter showed, trust was not confined only to what borrowers think of each other. While there was a set of intertwined social networks privileged, it really did matter whether they trusted microfinance institutions prior, too.

Sharma and Zeller (1997) argued that Bangladeshi borrower social capital expenditure was a function of the institutions proving their financial payoff. They suggested that in order to have borrowing communities willing to expend their social capital, that lenders must demonstrate that "these innovations and institutions were not transitory phenomena, that they addressed their financial concerns, and that it was worthwhile for them to invest in a profitable long-term association."[20] I suggest a refinement to extend their prescription to the case of Juba microcredit: Juba MFIs, and perhaps other post-conflict MFIs, must establish that the debts will be socially profitable as well.

Sometimes after war, like anywhere else or whenever else, people will do what it takes to protect each other over being loyal to a foreign bank.[21] Participants did not characterize these experiences in conflict language, even if their experiences inevitably colored their decisions. The fact that ethnicity was protected from borrowers' analytical scrutiny, keeping with a common one-nation-building narrative during that time, is an example that speaks to the care with which individuals wanted to maintain and privilege certain categories. Indeed, the postwar context may indeed have driven the predilection for social tranquility over the costs seen as necessary for recovering debts within the credit paradigm and procedures.

Several factors led to the Juba MFIs failing to receive their desired payment outcomes. However, of the social dilemmas that played a role, it was more often than not because of borrower's desires to preserve and maintain social bonds, however new they were. As C. S. Lewis said, "the mark of Friendship is not that help will be given when the pinch comes (of course it will) but that, having been given, it makes no difference at all."[22]

The MFI analyses did not recognize the social capital that did exist among borrowers, partly because it was not plain to observe, and partly because it was not often exchanged for an economic capital that was salient to the MFI aims: payments. The MFIs appraising poor social capital after the fall had a partial view: some borrowers did not have long-standing social ties that could leverage optimal payments, but the vast majority created strong ties, among other things, and nurtured those ties quickly along a couple of specific, but inconvertible metrics.

Borrower social customs did not readily fit the hands-off, cut-and-paste MFI policies. Their social norms around reciprocity, sympathy, and penalty had their own currencies and their own time timetables. Many groups broke down because the systems were out of sync. Social trust both helped and hindered microfinance aims in Juba.

These were costly mistakes. MFIs could learn from these less visible but robust social fabrics, and learn more about how they evolve, so as to put those bonds to use. Thus, based on the experiences of those I met in Juba, rather than suggesting friendship will be key to successful borrowing: practitioners can consider instead what is required to support the specific trust indices of post-conflict borrowers. If people share views on what constitutes timely payment, and are willing to risk institutional standing for it, there exists a dilemma for the banks. Can the lenders accommodate client norms of temporality? Can MFI payment schedules accommodate their reciprocity and business calendars? If the clientele shares views on locally appropriate ways of recouping payments from each other, can the bank nurture deliberation among them? Supporting borrowers in ways that supports maintenance of their social worlds rather than threatens them in the process is key. Until borrowers see the payoffs from loyalty to the bank over each other, the quotidian will reign.

NOTES

1. See John Harriss and Paulo de Renzio, "'Missing Link' or Analytically Missing?: The Concept of Social Capital, An Introductory Bibliographic Essay." *Journal of International Development*, 9, no. 7 (1997) and Michael Woolcock, "Learning from Failures in Microfinance: What Unsuccessful Cases Tell Us About How Group-Based Programs Work." *American Journal of Economics and Sociology*, 58, no. 1 (1999) for summaries of the term's intellectual and practical history.

2. Robert D. Putnam, "Bowling Alone: America's Declining Social Capital." *Journal of Democracy* (1995).

3. Michael Woolcock, "Learning from Failures in Microfinance: What Unsuccessful Cases Tell Us About How Group-Based Programs Work." *American Journal of Economics and Sociology*, 58, no. 1 (1999).

4. Michael Woolcock, "Social Capital and Economic Development: Toward a Theoretical Synthesis and Policy Framework," *Theory and Society*, 27, no. 2 (1998). See Ben Fine, "The Developmental State Is Dead-Long Live Social Capital?" *Development and Change Development & Change*, 303, no. 1 (1999) for critiques of this common analysis.

5. See, for example, Christopher Udry, "Risk and Insurance in a Rural Credit Market: An Empirical Investigation in Northern Nigeria." *The Review of Economic Studies*, 61, no. 3 (1994).

6. Joseph E. Stiglitz, "Peer Monitoring and Credit Markets." *The World Bank Economic Review*, 4, no. 3 (1990) found, through economic modeling, that the transfer of risk from bank to cosigner actually improved client welfare.

7. Dean S. Karlan, "Using Experimental Economics to Measure Social Capital and Predict Financial Decisions." *American Economic Review*, 95, no. 5 (2005).

8. Bruce Wydick, "Can Social Cohesion Be Harnessed to Repair Market Failures? Evidence from Group Lending in Guatemala." *Economic Journal*, 109, no. 467 (1999).

9. Alessandra Cassar, Luke Crowley, and Bruce Wydick, "The Effect of Social Capital on Group Loan Repayment: Evidence from Field Experiments." *The Economic Journal*, 117, no. 517 (2007), F103.

10. Marie Godquin, "Microfinance Repayment Performance in Bangladesh: How to Improve the Allocation of Loans by MFIs." *World Development*, 32, no. 11 (2004).

11. Klaus Abbink, Bernd Irlenbusch, and Elke Renner, "Group Size and Social Ties in Microfinance Institutions." *Paper presented at the annual meeting for the Royal Economic Society* (Coventry, England, 2003).

12. World Bank, "What is Social Capital." (2015); see Mancur Olson, *The Rise and Decline of Nations: Economic Growth, Stagflation, and Social Rigidities* (New Haven: Yale University Press, 1982).

13. Manohar Sharma and Manfred Zeller, "Repayment Performance in Group-based Credit Programs in Bangladesh: An Empirical Analysis." *World Development*, 25, no. 10 (1997), 1731.

14. See Sidney Schuler, et al., "Men's Violence Against Women in Rural Bangladesh: Underdetermined or Exacerbated by Microcredit Programmes?" *Development in Practice*, 8, no. 2 (1998).

15. Richard Montgomery, "Disciplining or Protecting the Poor? Avoiding the Social Costs of Peer Pressure in Micro-credit Schemes.'" *Journal of International Development, Special Issue, Sustainable Banking with the Poor*, 8, no. 2 (1996).

16. Lamia Karim, "Demystifying Microcredit: The Grameen Bank, NGOs, and Neoliberalism in Bangladesh." *Cultural Dynamics*, 20, no. 1 (2008), 15.

17. They only had to pay "market dues," which were 1 SSP per day.

18. See, for example, Tasmin Wilson, "Microfinance During and After Armed Conflict: Lessons From Angola, Cambodia, Mozambique And Rwanda" (Concern Worldwide & The Springfield Centre For Business In Development March), 2002.

19. N. Khan and E. Stewart, "Institution Building and Development in Three Women's Village Organisations: Participation, Ownership and Autonomy." *Research and Evaluation Division* (Dhaka: BRAC, 1992).Lamia Karim, *Microfinance and its Discontents: Women in Debt in Bangladesh*, (Minneapolis: University of Minnesota Press, 2011).

20. Manohar Sharma and Manfred Zeller, "Repayment Performance in Group-based Credit Programs in Bangladesh: An Empirical Analysis." *World Development*, 25, no. 10 (1997), 40.

21. See Hussan-Ban Burki, *Unraveling The Delinquency Problem (2008/2009) In Punjab – Pakistan,* MicroNote no: 10 (2009) for an account of client resistance practices and movements elsewhere.

22. C. K. Lewis, *The Four Loves* (New York: Harcourt, 1960/1991), 70.

Chapter 7

Borrower Breakdowns

Diagnosing postwar ailments

There were a myriad of factors that made Juba an irregular region to learn from in regard to experiencing the pillars of microfinance practice. Yet it is in this true story that social scientists, and even the public, can probe the boundaries of those pillars. This chapter contains good news and bad news—both are instructive. What follows are findings from a series of one hundred interviews of Juba microfinance borrowers, ranging from those who stayed in programs to those who stopped well before MFIs began closing their doors. There was especially a lot to learn from people who left and took another path. Many were struggling; some chose to walk away, while others wanted to continue, but were kicked out. The disparity between their personal needs and abilities, and what the microcredit agencies had to offer them, is significant. I asked each interviewee many questions, but the responses I note here focus more on the challenges that the borrowers faced, before and at the time of interviews. Some of South Sudan's particular complexities and some of the microcredit procedures were challenging for borrowers, but surmountable. Other challenges and opportunities, on the other hand, the participants deemed too much to withstand.

WHAT'S NOT WORKING?

South Sudanese people have a reputation for being tough despite the many serious trials. They are typically not the ones to complain. What makes our critical analysis harder is that program evaluators rarely asked about challenges. Agencies that were seeking to exemplify the benefits of their programming seldom published the woes experienced by the beneficiaries. This failure to interrogate the difficulties masked opportunities for the agencies to improve. Now, however, we can look at borrowers' complaints, and the reasons that so many departed, in order to get a more comprehensive picture of the situation.

Even when given the opportunity to give feedback without the risk of offending the service provider,[1] the majority of respondents I met had no initial complaint about microcredit whatsoever. When asked what they considered the most challenging aspect of microfinance, over half of the borrowers stated factors that had nothing to do with microcredit provision per se, and were instead exogenous to the program composition itself. For most, the biggest difficulties surrounding microloans correlated to the complicated economy in South Sudan, or their specific business challenges.

Some participants—in fact, a fifth of those I surveyed—simply had positive experiences. Half of those with no complaints clarified that it was because they were new, and had not participated long enough to form an opinion, or have any issues thus far. Still, all those who had no complaints conceded that it was because microcredit outright improved their business. Indeed, a fifth of more than one hundred borrowers I interviewed—even some who quit—felt that on the whole that microfinance was worthwhile. It is reasonable to surmise that for this share of the clients, the closures of the microcredit programs would be disappointing news.

Still, the vast majority had frustrating experiences. Business problems were felt by a fifth of former borrowers, but much more rarely (only 2 percent) by ongoing participants, signifying that many who experienced business problems ended up leaving the programs. These individuals framed their borrowing difficulties in ways that centered on factors such as the viability of their own businesses, and finding ways to turn profits. Sometimes this was expressed in a depersonalized fashion, like "sometimes the business is not running on well" or, "borrowing is hard when your business failed." One respondent inserted herself a bit more: "The most difficult aspect of microfinance is when I didn't use the money in good way, it affected [the loan payment]." Generally, such borrowers might likely have benefited from better training services to help them stay ahead of the grim market prospects.

The postwar economy proved an especially critical obstacle. Though there were tremendous benefits to peace—security, hope, and an opportunity to practice long-sighted development—there were also challenges that resulted. No one could deny the difficulties of operating a business after the 2005 Comprehensive Peace Agreement, as the economy was experiencing major changes. Microfinance itself did not, of course, create the inflation that made goods costly to acquire, or cause any of the other larger economic problems found in the complaints. Nevertheless, a good amount of borrowers referred to the issues within the post-conflict economy as the foremost problem with microfinance. In this light, microfinance institutions did not do enough to

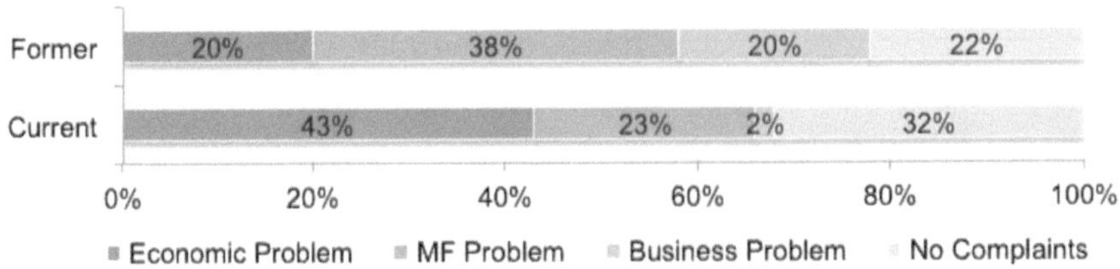

Figure 7.1 Borrower Chief Complaints. *Source:* Author.

account for the dynamics operating in such contexts. Increased competition, lowered profit margins, and varied wholesale prices were among the repercussions felt by businesspeople of all classes. Specific micro-entrepreneur responses that were coded under the umbrella of "economic problems" included the costs of wholesale goods, the lack of profits on sales, and the lack of customers (due to a bigger issue of market saturation for the particular items they sold) as well as the market demolitions described in Introduction. The current borrowers, who described market problems more than twice as often as former borrowers, felt this more acutely.

The microcredit supported businesses were naturally contingent on the available market options. The trends in enterprise type in South Sudan case are important to recognize because they were unlike trends reported in other, more stable microcredit operating contexts. Elsewhere, in more long-standing markets, micro-entrepreneurs had more options, so there was a greater distribution of enterprises across sectors. In Juba, long-distance trade was the driver. Almost all products were imported from faraway—not from nearby, and not grown within the region.[2]

IMPORT DEPENDENCY AND HIGH WHOLESALE PRICES

"The prices have gone up," a middle-aged woman I met in the market in 2009 told me, with her pointed finger moving from her waist up toward the sky. Borrowers stressed that the prices on wholesale goods from abroad continued to rise and rise. She went on to describe it as follows:

> So, those days when they used what? To buy bundles of the wild vegetables at maybe 35 Sudanese Pounds. But now prices have gone high in the market. At times a bundle you can get about 50 Sudanese Pound or about 70 Sudanese pound. The same is applied to okras. The rate is increased how much you could get it for.

Table 7.1 Sector of Borrower Businesses, BRAC 2008–2011

	Sector Name	*Percentage of Loans*
1	Agriculture	14
2	Handicraft and manufacturing	5
3	Household consumption	11
4	Trade and services grocery, hardware, bar/drink shops, food cooking and vending, local beer brewing, charcoal selling, raw fruits and vegetable selling, second-hand cloth and shoes selling, and beauty parlor	70

Source: Author.

Price surges were not uncommon. Another nearby microfinance client selling vegetables adjacent to our conversation chimed in, noting a 60 percent increase in the price of tomatoes, which were coming from Uganda that month. As Table 7.1 indicates, the vast majority of Juba borrowers were reliant on this complex import situation.

CURRENCY CURSES AND TRADER CIRCUITS

The currency was partially to blame for the high wholesale costs. Currency valuation in South Sudan was an ongoing struggle. During the study period, there were two state currencies in circulation. The Sudan Pound was introduced after the CPA, but after Independence in 2011 came the South Sudan Pound (SSP). The former's value relative to import currencies was erratic, but the SSP fluctuated less, and instead was in a consistent downward spiral. There is an entire book to be written on the currency challenges there, including a black currency market so pervasive that it was treated virtually as licit, except when the transnational agencies (including MFIs) were obligated to use the state money. Suffice it to say that currency exchange as a corollary of import dependency made it difficult for Jubans to pay for foreign goods in the early years, which only worsened with time.

Another major issue was the complications created by the physical shipment of goods. Retailers I met explained that wholesale costs were unpredictable due to port of entry, distance traveled to Juba, petroleum price shifts, and the rates levied by transporters. Certain social networks fostered during exile found opportunity during this transformation. During the first years of peace, friendly neighbors opened new border checkpoints, which opened new supply routes for traders, while others slowed down due to tensions and migration trends. For example, immediately following the peace agreement, goods came from Kampala and were primarily moved from Uganda via the

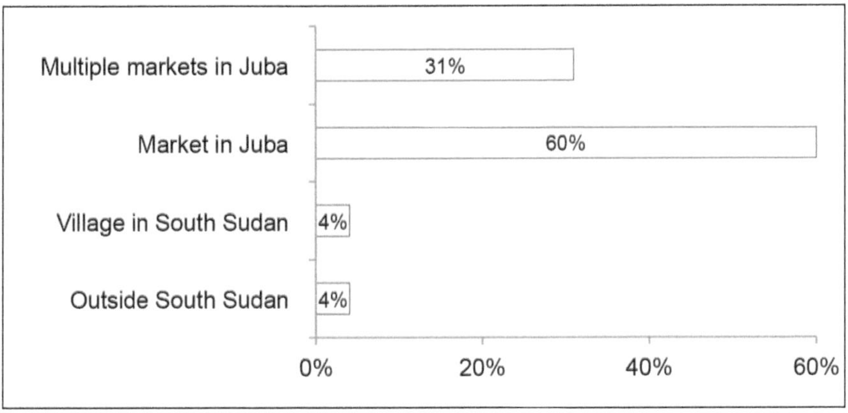

Figure 7.2 Client Supply Sources. *Source:* Author.

Nimule Road passage. As time passed, traders brought goods originating in Dubai and Nairobi, following that original lengthy route. Costs were higher due to the length of this route, but they were also more consistent than the less secure passages. More expedited routes directly through western Kenya opened, but they frequently suffered closures due to insecurity. Supply from Northern Sudan vacillated with border insecurity and political flashpoints, like the tense 2009 border arbitration. On the other hand, trade via the northern part of Sudan plunged during the observation period. In short, what came to the market depended on a host of people; when goods came during a given delivery, furthermore, the prices were rarely the same as they were in the last delivery. Borrowers knew about the unreliability of these circuits, yet had no leverage to deal with the individuals fomenting the problems that plagued what opportunities they had.

The transition to an open, competitive market created winners and losers. In this case, the micro-entrepreneurs did not stand to gain as much as the importers, wholesalers, and large-scale retailers. What little capital the microfinance borrowers had to invest was insufficient to persuade importers to bring more demanded items. What was delivered was what was delivered. Poor people's limited capital could not convince the traders, transporters, and the many individuals causing insecurity to bring more timely shipments. As they were from a totally different social class, microfinance clients also had limited leverage to negotiate prices down whenever there were larger traders, like those who ran air conditioned markets, who were willing to exhaust the supply with far greater purchasing power.

The majority of microfinance borrowers were retailers in Juba, and given the unpredictability of acquiring their required products, they were for the most part unable to influence import costs.

KEEPING UP WITH COMPETITION

The massive in-migration of returnees joining the market increased competition, while people from other countries came to capitalize on the high demand for imported goods, too. The latter group in particular had access to large amounts of investment capital, being well networked and operating from bases in their home countries, which served as gatekeepers to the supplies for basic goods sold by borrowers, as well as competed with them. Both groups ultimately made the businesses that microfinance aimed to serve less competitive.

In 2009 I met a borrower who was selling dried beans and grains. She had five nice gallon-sized containers full to the brim, and plastic bags for her customers hanging from the side of one. When I asked how business was going, she responded:

> Since the peace came after the signing of the peace agreement, there are still some challenges I am facing. Like right now in the market, you find there are many competitors. Once you take your products there you may find some steep competition from the other competitors, but still at the end of the road you have to strive among them so that you can also achieve what you want.

In light of the increased peacetime competition, small business owners experienced smaller profit margins than before the economy opened. This illustration of classical economics was no surprise; competition tends to result in lowered prices for consumers. But borrowers striving to meet the absurd pace of change had no guarantees on the profits needed for their livelihoods, much less loan installments.

One elderly dried fish vendor noted that, "When I sell it, sometimes I get a little bit of money. I get less even if I sell more." Like others, he emphasized that more effort was needed to make less money than before, thanks to the newfound competition. Sometimes he did not sell more, or did not turn a profit at all. In that way, the surge of incoming participants increased the market volatility as compared to the more consistent conditions through the war.

The borrowers' target market was in many ways their peers, who could not afford to pay satisfactory margins. One pointed out how, for instance, "[her] customers lack incomes." Micro-entrepreneurs primarily targeted other disadvantaged people who were inclined to buying marked-up small-portioned goods. Swells in the number of aid workers and hotel constructors did not improve their market. The development workers had little use for tiny bags of greens or flour; they would much sooner buy from the larger shopkeepers. Besides, Juba was so expensive that even their money was tight.

Micro-entrepreneurs found themselves selling whatever goods they got at unreasonably low prices. Whereas in more typical microfinance contexts, a client might anticipate a 20–32 percent profit margin,[3] in Juba they were seeing

5–11 percent.[4] This comparison does not take into account that personal reports of productivity were not as constant as when the market was relatively closed, and both supply and demand were much more static. In short, "working harder" could not surmount the new obstacles to business during peacetime competition. Microloan capital was not the solution to bridge the shortfall.

Almost all (90 percent) of Juba microfinance business owners toggled between three separate systems—the import system, the retail market system, and the loan system—each with its own temporal and cost intervals. The remaining 10 percent of borrowers replaced the import schedule with their own travel itinerary. The import schedules did not correlate with the timetables for loan repayments. The loan quantities available to borrowers also did not correlate with the exorbitant costs of wholesale supplies. As a result, borrowers had to navigate not only the wholesale supply and pricing situation, but their local markets too. Pricing their commodities competitively was their only hope at recouping any investment, yet even then they made very minimal profits if any. Borrowers switched between the registers demanded by each system regularly, and oftentimes they had to sacrifice optimizing in one domain for another. They could buy what was available but not set aside payment money, or negotiate prices bearable for their shoppers but not also negotiate with the delivering traders, but not all of the above.

How are we to read these complaints of MFI clients that were not levied at the microfinance industry itself, but actually obstacles particular to the postwar economy? The industry was satisfied to pin the failure of microcredit in South Sudan on the market challenges. Meanwhile borrowers negotiated the shifting landscape of the market, weighing risks beyond what they could control. Perhaps the market was not the sole problem, but also the limitations of the particular types of microcredit that were available to utilize in this economy. Juba's postwar economy was different from other economies, and that is a big reason why microcredit worked very differently there. Yet MFIs neglected to accommodate to this, and the same aspects of the cookie-cutter model were attempted in South Sudan—this deserves a share of the blame as well.

THE MICROCREDIT SPECIFIC CRITIQUES

Despite the majority of the overwhelming frustration related to the broader market problems, we must also listen to the borrower critiques of the programs as delivered. About one fourth of borrowing respondents and four in ten of those formerly borrowing described some element within MFI procedures as their foremost dissatisfaction with their experience. Of those, complaints focused the most on three aspects: the repayment regimen, the interest rate, and the features of their co-guaranteed group loans.

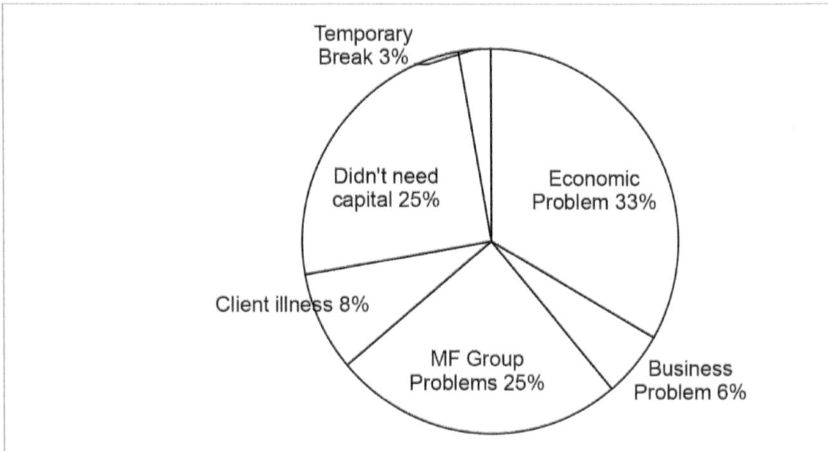

Figure 7.3 Reasons Former Borrowers Cited for Leaving. *Source:* Author.

Most complaints about the microcredit procedure were about the weekly repayment structure. While over a third of former borrowers thought it was too onerous, even more of the current borrowers struggled with weekly repayments. They felt that a week was too little time to invest in goods, sell them, and have enough (or any) profit to use toward their first repayment. The early and very frequent payments required having capital on hand to service such microloans. One borrower told me, how "few customers are buying the commodities, so it becomes difficult to pay back loan in the time." Turning a profit depended on getting customers as soon as borrowers got their supplies. As another said, "The most difficult aspect of microfinance for me was when I got microfinance I would buy products. The product would not be finished (sold) very quickly, and it can affect microfinance because I am paying every week." And of course, the payment schedule did not accommodate to when business was slow (which was a recurring reality

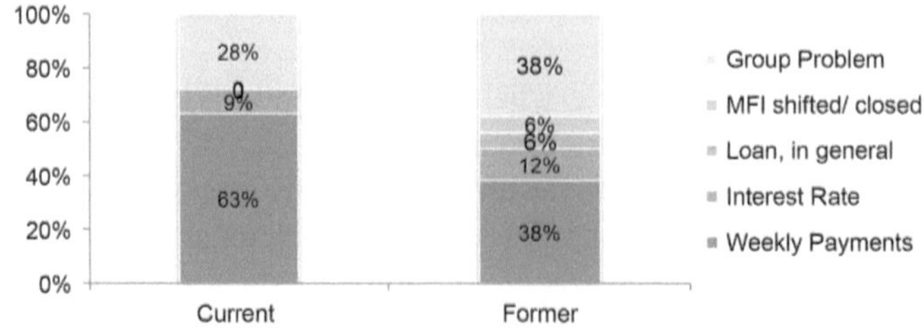

Figure 7.4 Most Difficult Aspect of Microfinance Procedure. *Source:* Author.

such that there were high levels of competition for micro-entrepreneurs). To generate funds for the first loan payment, borrowers had to turn a quick profit, or else forego investing their entire loan into business inputs. If their products did not sell before the next payment was due, a new problem was created in the group response to hiccups.

On the second most common microfinance complaint, solidarity groups were not always simple for participants to form, and cooperate in. About a third of overall microfinance-specific complaints were by borrowers who were frustrated by their peers not fulfilling their duties within the intra-group contract. Group problems were not just functions of business cycle struggles, but of the complicated interpersonal dynamics brought forth by the group guarantee model. For example, one borrower did not sell enough tomatoes because a shipment flooded her market that week, so she hoped to make up for it the next week. But when she did not make the numbers, the failure impacted her entire group. What happened next was up to her members. In some cases, groups were unwilling or unable to cover for such a delinquent member. One ongoing borrower complained that "sometimes some members misuse capital or delay paying back, which causes charges for group members." Her particular group had to cover the payment for an irresponsible member, which penalized and frustrated the rest of them.

As described in greater detail in Chapter 6, navigating the subsequent intragroup repayment was easy for some groups, but flustered others. Some groups, for instance, had no trouble covering for members when such situations arose over the short term. Many even devised intragroup payment techniques to recoup the personal debts among themselves. Still others avoided pressuring their peers into repaying them. The borrowers who disliked the group loan design recognized that their preexisting social ties, that helped people survive during war, were threatened by the stress around surveillance and recouping debts. Friendships were threatened, sometimes even sacrificed, in the face of such interwoven responsibilities. These interpersonal battles were created by the microcredit group model design.

About a tenth of the interviewed borrowers complained about the costliness of the interest rates levied by the institutions. Many felt they were, in general, too high; one angrily noticed the increase from one loan to the next that was exacted upon her group. Indeed, the MFI interest rates rose over the study period; both of the major MFIs in Juba did this strategically to recoup the funds they had lost to poor repayments and other unanticipated costs of doing business in a new town. In any case, borrowers noticed that the loan capital was expensive against the counterfactuals: alternative sources of capital and no microcredit at all.

A couple of former borrowers voiced disappointment that their microfinance provider had either closed, or shifted services away from the offering they had been first using. These borrowers speak to a demand that would remain unmet. As will be detailed in greater length in the coming chapters, the Juba microcredit industry moved away from servicing their initially intended demographic within a few short years of its inception.

THE CHALLENGES WERE MANY BUT WHAT BROKE THE CAMEL'S BACK?[5]

Many people stopped borrowing for reasons similar to their complaints. However, while such struggles are instructive for future program design, the vast majority left for reasons completely different than what they listed as their biggest challenge. In other words, not all struggles were so great that they pushed borrowers out. For example, one former borrower despised that "some group members move away and this will force the members around to pay on their behalf," but inferred that this struggle was surmountable when she cited that her reason for quitting was "because commodities prices are going higher and it will become difficult for me to pay back the loan." For this person, adapting to the market was harder than adapting to the group obligations. Another explained that the worst part of borrowing was "the weekly payment is not easy since price of goods are high in market," yet the reason she departed was not because of the dueling sales and payment schedules but because, "I have enough of my own capital." For this person, dealing with the market challenge on its own was easier than thinking the constraints and risks involved with taking out another loan.

Of the microcredit procedural issues that caused the borrowers to stop, only the group dynamic issue was cause enough for quitting in the end. While onerous, the interest rate and the weekly payment schedule were not named as the reasons per se, the latter only referred to vaguely as a function of the general troubles within the economy. In other words, the borrowers saw the impossibility of the two systems functioning simultaneously but they did not blame the MFI practice directly.

Each borrower had decision-making thresholds throughout the loan and business processes. Sometimes they had the chance to innovate and choose which items they could sell, or like a quarter of former members, found alternative sources of capital. Others had no option to try something new. Some were too ill to work in a way that paying off the debt was possible. Furthermore, some people had the autonomy to choose whether to stop or continue borrowing while others had their peers or the lending agency rules making the choices for them. Not all the problems faced by borrowers were insurmountable, but those that were deserve further analysis.

LEAVING VERSUS BEING DROPPED

Some borrowers chose to leave while others were kicked out. The MFI could remove borrowers due to delinquency, for example. Surveyed borrowers left by their own volitions as often as they were disqualified. Disqualified borrowers included those who left because their peers had failed to pay and no one covered for them. For example, one man said his least favorite part about microcredit was that "sometimes some of our members are unable to pay back in time." The reason he no longer borrowed was grounded to the reality that he and his colleagues were barred from the system: "It is because one of our members has not cleared payment, so we are unable to get more." So while he was frustrated by the group co-guarantee demands, what ended the group ultimately was the fact that they were not allowed to continue because members did not follow through on their commitment to cover when a member did not make their payment.

On the other side were borrowers who credited their departures with being ill, or because their business failed. If they did not pay off the debt before quitting, that is, the business failed so greatly or the illness impinged business and in turn loan payments, I included them in the disqualified tally also. In short, I erred sorting on the side of "delinquency theories," where the borrowers failed on a procedural basis, because that was the thesis laid down by the industry.

QUIT WHILE THEY ARE AHEAD

Half of the former borrowers left by choice, and those were divisible equally by "success stories" and ones that evade the analyses written on the Juba microcredit situation to date. The former did well with the loans. Such participants chose to leave because they had their own capital or because they found a source better than the MFIs. Others, frustrated by aspect of the market or the banking procedures, clearly indicated that they quit after clearing payments to the MFI. These people chose to quit while they were "ahead."

First, the less-told stories, or people who quit while they were ahead. A quarter credited their departures with no longer needing microcredit. They quit because they were doing well enough to move forward without credit. Their businesses either had improved or the loans served them well enough to have a reserve of cash or they were satisfied without loan capital. "My business grew up," said a three-time former borrower, who fared well selling beer, soda, and sugar in Minuki market. The loans "have improved my clothing and shoe business," said another, former four-time Muru borrower who sold goods delivered from Khartoum. Not feeling any difficulties with microcredit, she declared that she was "not leaving it for good at the moment," and might return if possible someday. Another complaint free four-timer was an Acholi woman who sold sugar, soap and beans. She left because, "my business was grown."

What set the people who succeeded but quit apart from the others who failed? I asked all the participants a series of open-ended questions and did many rounds of sorting and analysis in efforts to find a common thread. The characteristics and activities of these former successful borrowers were greatly varied. They had little in common by way of what they sold, the size of their businesses, the length of time they participated, or how they devised their groups. They did not hail from the same demographics, when classified in terms of ethnicity. Nevertheless, the successful quitters had all been in Juba for quite some time; all were in Juba at or before the 2005 peace agreement.[6] This subgroup of borrowers also all received loans in the early wave. This meant that not only did they earn their profits before the competition surged, but they also knew the Juba business landscape much more intimately, and better heeded the warning signs about the peacetime economy. They got out while the going was good, while they were "ahead." There is an old fable about a frog not noticing that the water it was in was getting hotter. These people felt the heat and leaped out.

Take for example a young Muru woman from Yei who moved to Juba right when the CPA was announced. She used her loan for cassava flour, millet, maize, and cooking oil, a completely ordinary spread. She was one of the few who would sometimes track supplies from Uganda to Yei (rather than wait for shipped supplies), and she struggled when some group members moved away. She said the burden was overridden by how much profit she got from the loans, so much so that she was able to build a house after borrowing three loans. But despite her great financial success, she said she ultimately quit after completing her third loan cycle "because commodity prices are going higher and it will become difficult for me to pay back the loan when I borrow." Her choice to quit was an assessment that the risks of commodity prices were too great to bear.

Another interesting feature about this cluster is that most (all but two) went onto different, larger businesses after borrowing. They were innovators, and had the ability to scale. One such borrower was Amer, a Juba native. She had a business selling beer, cake, and bread. She got enough profits from doing that for two loan cycles that she was able to use the earned capital, and transition to a new business selling clothes.

This is noteworthy: not all borrowers were inept at doing postwar business and not all borrowers were failures. These examples can be seen as good news that microfinance works in terms of stabilizing or growing small businesses. The success stories were the kind of news that the practitioners would be quick (arguably, too quick) to celebrate. Practitioners might simultaneously bemoan that these savvy borrowers did not continue. Such borrowers were privy to something: borrowing eventually failed to reveal its utility. And such participants are worth understanding better so as to learn what features could have kept them.

QUIT WHILE THEY ARE BEHIND

Next are the stories told less often. The other half of those who left by choice (a quarter of all former borrowers) left because *something was not right.* These people did not leave because they had raised their standards of living. They were getting behind and became concerned that moving forward with microcredit would be detrimental.

Sarah, a middle-aged woman I met in Juba in mid-2013, lamented on how much the price of microcredit debt had risen. Sarah was a borrower who quit because the "high interest rate on the loan discouraged me so much since profit is lower." When Sarah was borrowing, she was selling maize only, and remarked that she was at least able to send her children and an orphan she was responsible for to school during that time. They were getting by. When things became difficult, however, she had to in turn make difficult choices. She undertook a cost-benefit calculation to bet on whether her profits could possibly match or exceed the cost of loans (including not just the price of interest, but time and social energy, too). This Madi, born in Juba, did not have exposure to MFIs elsewhere. Her judgment was based on watching competition and interest rates rise there in Juba. As the interest rate became too high, she deemed the costs of borrowing were greater than the benefits. After quitting microfinance, she opted to diversify her offerings, and added onions, tomatoes, lemon, and other vegetables to her shop, in hopes of luring more customers. She, like those who quit while they were ahead, had a sense that the continued credit was least favorable risk to make in the equation. The MFIs lost many likeminded customers as a result.

Rachel, another woman I met with, told me, "I am no longer doing microfinance because of this: there is no customer like there were in 2009," when she moved to Juba from Yei in search of business opportunity. Importantly, as she clarified, this was not because there were fewer customers in Juba—after all, the population had grown. Instead, it was because her business no longer drew in any customers. Unfortunately, the population did not demand the commonly sold goods she had to offer (cooking oil, tomatoes, eggs, beans, posho flour, and onions) in a substantially profitable way. What did she do to deal with the dilemma? In 2011, she quit the loans, but not the business, and then kept selling the same goods.

Those who got out while the going was good were onto something. They could detect the potential failures, and even dangers, of microcredit before they were widely apparent.

Borrowers like these women were winners (from being earlier in the market like Amer), and losers from the transitioning market (like Rachel, without leeway to innovate). Being a "winner" in this realm largely depended on purchasing power and sufficient awareness of the market trends, including growing costs of borrowing alongside diminishing profits. Both winners and losers, however, soon regarded the credit not as a solution, but rather as an impediment to overcoming economic challenges.

THE LIMITS OF MICROCREDIT UNDER DURESS

Underlying microfinance's noble intentions was a dangerous pattern being repeated in Juba, and beyond: the pricing out of those who could not afford the debt, in favor of more stable business clientele. This problem, coupled with the worsening prospects of the postwar South Sudanese market, made the threats to MFI portfolios even clearer. The Juba microcredit backers and strategists soon relied on their growing cost-covering policies to cast off the riskiest, poorest clients—and they did. While the MFIs were right roughly half of the time, they were wrong the other half. The borrower experiences demonstrate how and why this winnowing was actually a problem.

Borrowers who were removed from the programs were, in large part, causing a hit on the overall MFI portfolios, which the institutions needed to fix in order to stay in business. The MFIs in Juba were not unwise to contemplate the risks posed by the economy and a transitioning populace, but ironically, they underestimated the risk assessed by the borrowers themselves. The pendulum swung from the struggling, unsatisfied customers to the failing institutions, and then right back to the remaining customers, who became unsatisfied as debt costs were raised. The MFIs lost "bad" or fledgling borrowers who left by choice, who were at the cusp of advancing but recognized that the credit was no longer useful under the going conditions. The MFIs lost even "good" customers, or borrowers who left because their businesses were succeeding as well as others. Shifting resources away from these clients who needed them most was not, in other words, the wisest tactic.

The problems that clients faced—the import dependence, the saturated competition, the group troubles, and higher interest prices—test the boundaries of microcredit best practice. The postwar transitioning economy—with unpredictable import emphasis and border issues—rendered pricing unreliable. Meanwhile, the competition between borrowers was quickly saturated.

Some commercially minded analysts might suggest that the lesson based on these findings from Juba case is that there should be more preconditions[7] to post-conflict lending. Such preconditions would suggest that the MFIs should not become involved until met. And that is essentially what happened:

the MFIs eventually declared that the key problem undermining their models was the tough economy in Juba.

The lending models offered (and then rescinded) were understandable in the larger realm of microfinance moving toward sustainability, but they were ill suited in this new place. Any tailoring requires the institutional will and support to pull it off. Instead, borrowers were merely offered a "take it or leave it" product. Some took it as long as it was offered, but a great many left it too.

This exploration of the borrowers' dilemmas points to additional areas of blame including the particular credit formula that was laid out by MFIs. Former borrowers were willing to critique the program models. Numerous borrowers began seeing microfinance not as a source of prosperity, but as a danger and risk. Both successful and struggling micro-entrepreneurs determined that microfinance could not help them much at its given price point and under such economic circumstances. They felt that debt worsened their odds at succeeding in the unstable marketplace, and also increased the unwanted interpersonal drama in such a dynamic environment. Microfinance did not help in an already complicated market and an already complex social world.

There will always be people who default. However in this case, there were also large shares of clients who had enough of a positive track record, but faced circumstances beyond their control, and could not ultimately succeed with credit. They were savvy enough to know borrowing anymore was unwise, given the conditions of the loans. That rationality is, perhaps ironically, what banks should want in customers. These groups taught us that there was more potential ahead if they had not been given up on. The analysis herein demonstrated that borrowers past and present might have continued if the MFIs had been able to implement a handful of small program modifications. This view would charge that there should be more flexible program conditions made to accommodate them.

Like any responsive firm, microfinance institutions can reconsider the models they implement. The flashpoints of concern described in this chapter also highlight areas in which the MFIs might have been able to reform its policies and practices, and engage borrowers to stay before it was too late. Those who had complained about the market forces could have received better education to redress them. Resources to deal with group tensions could have made a huge difference. Tailoring the payment schedules could have, too. Besides, the MFIs had already invested costs into client recruitment, their original debt capital, and some training. We can surmise that retaining and helping clients through the crises would create loyalty and a foundation for future growth. All that was ultimately lost. While borrowing and running businesses were rarely easy, all the participants I met had the will to continue chasing their dreams by whatever means they could.

NOTES

1. Some might worry there exists some response bias here. As with any social behavior, people tend to say things that are socially agreeable. Participants could color their responses if they thought the enumerators or translators might take their responses back to the MFI and get them into trouble, for example. But recall from Chapter 4 that each and every participant knew, from the process of acquiring informed consent, their answers would not be associated with them individually.

2. These figures summarize BRAC's entire time providing microcredit. The earlier years had more import dependence: more trade and less agriculture. Once people grew more settled and property rights re/assigned, more began farming, particularly in the rural areas. Significantly lower rates of agricultural practice in Juba.

3. Based on surveys I did in a Ugandan study in 2007.

4. Based on the maize and dura figures shared by respondents in this study.

5. As with the reasons borrowers liked and disliked microfinance, these responses were axial coded into categories. For instance: some dubbed the complex postwar economy culprit for why they quit, others their own business' failure to thrive, or factors endemic to the microcredit replication that is practiced in Juba.

6. It was not the case that every borrower who was in Juba prior to the CPA succeeded, however, so this common thread did not predict success. And it was not the case that everyone who was there before the CPA quit. Some kept borrowing. Others who were there early did not borrow until later, and so on.

7. Karen Doyle, *Microfinance in the Wake of Conflict: Challenges and Opportunities* (Washington, DC: USAID, 1998).

Chapter 8

"They Think Food Grows On Trucks"

An industry diagnosis

All the Juba MFIs were dealing with people in transition, in a community in transition, all within a new nation in transition. People were coming from everywhere. There was no unified economic paradigm to which the MFIs could refer while escorting these communities into "modern capitalism." They were reaching out to a demographic that was transitioning to a new formulation of market economics, as well as marketing a new development tool.

Microcredit practice is not only a movement of capital, but of ideas. With money came ideas about disciplining repayment, empowering clients, creating profits, and enhancing participant well-being. The field level personnel worked as intermediaries in between the donor policies and client experiences. They were trained to think about clients based on generalized notions of human behavior, and also more specifically about the behavior of poor people, postwar people, first-time borrowers, and so on. They were also trained to create and develop explanations about what was and was not working, for the sending agencies and funders abroad. "Modern man has used cause-and-effect as ancient man used the gods to give order to the Universe," said Henri Poincaré. "This is not because it was the truest system, but because it was the most convenient."[1]

From the beginning, the Juba MFIs struggled to achieve their aims. Some problems were due to factors beyond the MFIs control, such as market demolitions, exchange rates, import dependence, salary delays loans, and the inefficacy of group loan accountability. Other problems were internal to MFIs (recruitment, operations, monitoring requirements) but those were mostly inflexible procedures. But the most common field level explanations for why the Juba microcredit endeavor floundered came back to the borrowers themselves.

MFI personnel told two narratives that summated the challenges faced by borrowers who had been exposed to war. The first MFI theory for failure was that borrowers lacked social capital, which was discussed in Chapters 5 and 6. In this chapter, I analyze the second common MFI narrative, based on a series of remarks I heard from staff in Juba that were too common to ignore.[2] According to their narratives, the target population suffered from "dependency syndrome," referring to the idea that being acclimatized to aid discouraged beneficiaries from becoming independent entrepreneurs. These theories were woefully inadequate, but also detrimental to the developmental and financial enterprise in Juba. If left unchecked, they have the potential to undermine the entire MFI system.

DISCOVERING DEPENDENCY SYNDROME

In 2008, I spoke with a microfinance practitioner who had been involved in the microcredit sector from around the time of when the first branch had opened there. He was therefore also present for the first wave of in-migration to South Sudan. He relayed to me the way the UN repatriation programs did something right.

> With most of them, by the time U.N. brings them in, they come to their home areas where they have been before. The good thing with the U.N. is that they take them through steps. By the time you step off the truck, you know you get assistance for the next three months only, after that you are on your own. Maybe get some utensils and a hoe and an ax to start you off. So you have three months to prepare yourself. Either you are going to get into farming, or you are going to start the business you brought along with you.

In his explanation, the United Nations gave extensive warning that independence—the goal for the aid—was forthcoming. This MFI staff member placed his work with their businesses at the end of this sequence, as if the UN programs were preparing returnees for the economically independent journey. His comments thusly made clear his belief that microcredit was not relief but a debt to be repaid, and was conceptually set apart from other aid programs.

There was just one major hitch that curtailed the UN transition he outlined. On his telling, it was that returnees were resistant to the prospects of farming or conducting business. His explanation for why was:

> But of course, if you look at the economy, really here in Southern Sudan it's an agriculture economy. We're not industrial per se. I really looked at that. If

you look at twenty years of civil war, when this was started I was in secondary school, actually, yes I was in senior one, if you look at somebody who was five years old when the civil war started, right now he should be about 30 years. This person grew up relying entirely on relief, knowing nothing. He just knows food comes off a truck. So right now he wakes up and says hey mister, wake up, food doesn't come off a truck food comes from the soil. And he says 'no.' So changing that mindset is something we need to do before people will appreciate that. They can do it. And that for me is the biggest challenge: the dependence syndrome being removed from their minds. The [assistance community] love[s] to think in terms of development.

However, recently displaced people do not think food grows off a truck. This manager's point, made through hyperbole, was that his clientele's prior reliance on relief programs created dependency among them. To make his point, this manager focused on one instance of a client resisting the route to enlightenment. The hypothetical person he singled out took the tone of a disobedient child; this tone implied the community was stubborn, did not want to change its ways, and needed an overall attitude change in favor of better work ethic. Though the letter of his diagnosis was that returnees struggled from "knowing nothing"—a knowledge issue—the spirit of his storyline thus highlighted the belief that it was necessary to replace the relief attitude with one of which he called "development."

In this case, the microfinancier was discussing the process of development in the context of farming. He illustrated how needed it was, as if it were the archetypal South Sudanese job to adopt. Up to this point in the interview he spoke as an outsider—an overseer of the poor—and made apparent his adoption of the development industry discourse. Then, he suddenly shifted to a tone of solidarity: his pride in the country, symbols of national prosperity, and what he regarded as its virtuous traits. He continued:

It's not just waking up one day and saying lets go agricultural. It needs government intervention and everybody to come in to try to address it. I mean it's so shameful to really see tomatoes being imported from the neighboring country when you have the best type of climate and soil for agriculture. So I don't know how we're going to do it but we really have to do it.

I have had many years to contemplate this story I have heard, and in this time, have gathered many more stories with similar conclusions regarding dependency. I am not the only one to be struck by them. This interpretation of "dependency syndrome" is so prevalent among aid workers that it received substantial ink in the edited volume, *Deconstructing Development Discourse: Buzzwords and Fuzzwords*.[3] Furthermore, when Amy Kaler and John Parkins set out to do field research on food security in South Sudan in 2012, they heard such comments so frequently that they published an article entitled, "Food, Donors, and Dependency Syndrome(s) in South Sudan" analyzing these narratives from across many INGOs there.[4] Appealing to Kibreab, they place judgments about the "lack of initiative and motivation to work" as central to this prevalent diagnosis in the global South in general and in South Sudan in particular.[5] They distinguish this idea as cultural dependency, or "a dimension of human characters and habits of the heart and mind after decades of war and instability."[6]

While clearly the discourse of dependency syndromes is not unique to South Sudan, its deployment in its microcredit sector matters. The symptoms of the supposed South Sudanese dependency related in this chapter were not just used to describe the syndrome, but the failure of the microcredit project. Considering that multiple staff respondents used the "dependency syndrome" concept to describe the borrowers, I consider the meaning of the word "syndrome" here. Webster defines a syndrome as: a group of symptoms that consistently occur together or a condition characterized by a set of associated symptoms. In health sciences, a syndrome is diagnosed by observing a sufficient threshold of co-occurring symptoms, or signals. What follows are more analyses by staff, and an attempt at tracing what comprised the borrowers' symptoms.

BECAUSE THEY ARE POOR, NOT BECAUSE THEY ARE HARDWORKING

One day I interviewed a chairperson for the Microfinance Association of South Sudan (MASS). We spoke a lot about the issues faced by member MFIs and their borrowers. The conversation eventually turned to the chairperson's personal journey back home to South Sudan, and why he continued to stay despite the challenges of working there.

Suddenly, he shifted the conversation to the possibility of cash transfer programs that are coming into fashion as a poverty alleviation tool. Even Nancy Birdsall, an expert on development, has called Brazil's success with these programs the closest thing development practitioners have to a "silver bullet."[7] This assistance paradigm was troubling to someone entrenched in the purpose and value of microcredit. He went on to characterize the origins of dependency syndrome as follows:

> With cash transfers, there are rumors that government has plans. That money will end up in the bars and will never have the impact that they expect. Of course, NGOs are NGOs; they think they know the best thing people will want. They can make you poorer than you were before. One thing I believe, it creates

> the culture that, more income came because we are poor, not because we are really hardworking. So instead of making the best of the little we have, you can sit back and relax thinking to wait for the batch is coming. So you can spend it on things you really want to help you.

Unlike the NGO cash transfer project, he suggested that his microcredit project had the right sense of what people really need. What they needed was income tied to hard work. He continued:

> You'll see in the areas with lots of NGOs now, the common man doesn't want to do any farming or whatever simply because they say the "NGOs are there and they'll bring the food with it and life goes on." But they have arable land and they're capable, and they have the potential and everything. But because the NGOs are there, the dependency syndrome is so high among them. I think Central Equatoria, all Equatoria, where you find people try to make the best of what they have, but the other areas they have that mentality. That's my assumption about the cash handout; it'll have that impact rather than creating what the government thinks it will do.

His analysis was not new: academic theory has long debated such determinations about the merits of dependency mindset claims. Take for instance, Islah Jad who writes extensively on the consequences of institutionalizing NGOs. She points out how, compared with other means of societal organizing, the "NGOisation itself has cultural dimensions, spreading values that favour dependency, lack of self-reliance, and new modes of consumption."[8] Similar critiques have been levied at the global humanitarian system, for undermining the state's obligation to protect its citizens.[9] At the crux of these criticisms is the idea that such projects take resources and attention away the right kinds of independence or interdependence. As this respondent suggested, there is a spectrum of the dependency syndrome, and South Sudanese are extremely prone to it. Microfinance, from his vantage, endows the worthier pathway out of it.

CUSTOM, COWS, AND CAPACITY

I later spoke with a donor intermediary who weighed in on the challenges that existed from the launch of the microcredit industry in Juba. Unlike the others I spoke with, he saw these challenges as entry points and signposts for microcredit demand, rather than impediments to it. The first reason he listed for this was that there were no policies on the ground to guide the private sector, which thwarted many plans. But that lack of policy also created opportunity for the MFIs founders to try new things.

"The second was capacity for development," he said. "These were people who have been at war or in the refugee camps for so long, there was no possibility of them of having picked up something of the entrepreneurship."

Capacity is a buzzword all on its own when discussing development, and it is understandable that an expert—donor interlocutor would use it. Capacity refers to an ability or power to do something. The term was popularized in the 1980s with Amartya Sen's poverty assessments that focused on the poor's capabilities through a prism of functional freedoms and rights.[10] Deborah Eade pointed out how "capacity building originally drew on a generally left-leaning range of intellectual and political traditions, but is today commonly used to further a neo-liberal 'pull-yourself-up-by-your-bootstraps' kind of economic and political agenda."[11]

By deploying the language of capacity in light of the challenges of development, this respondent also centered the syndrome on the lack of exposure. This lack of capacity to engage entrepreneurial activities after war, on his telling, provided an opportunity for microcredit institutions to provide locals with greater opportunity in general, and through enterprising in particular. Since development was regarded as impossible without something new to shift the paradigm, the absent skills needed for entrepreneurship must be introduced.

> However, teaching did not come so easily, he said.
>
> It's not easy. First of all, to change the mindset is difficult. We have been trying to preach to the pastoral community for example, to commercialize their animals. There are just too many. If we were to commercialize these animals, I think everybody would have a trade here, but we cannot. Because the mindset is trained not to allow this to become commercialized otherwise their social fabrics will break down. These are the feelings. In order to invest in that and try to change them, it becomes risky for a bank—a bank that also needs to survive. So that's why we are struggling.

Just "too many" cattle, he said, of a people who consider the more the merrier, and have for centuries. Cattle, I have been told by countless South Sudanese, are part of the family. Children are often named after favorite cows and grief is felt upon their passing. The long traditions around cattle keeping are even documented in E. E. Evans-Pritchard's ethnography of the Nuer who during the 1950s said, "It is more than a possession, more even than part of his social personality—it is a point of meeting between soul and spirit that therefore becomes a sacramental character."[12] The respondent's use of the word "preach" evoked the depth of the beliefs that shaped the "mindset."

The enlightenment that he then "preaches" from his institutional pulpit involved a new way of working with the economy, wherein commercializing was the gospel exemplar. Capitalism was postured as a new, superior faith system. His analysis of the mindset regard commercialization, for instance, as mutually exclusive with the current social fabrics. The existing social-economic customs, which did not yield monetarily as much as possible, thusly were at odds with what MFI systems were trying to achieve.

It is risky, he said, for the MFI to undertake evangelism among new borrowers. Borrowers without a commercial mindset are costly. The training required to convert people to prioritize profits over social customs is costly. And the respondent was trained to recognize these costs, given that he was an advocate of the commercial model of microfinance (compared to the poverty model), which sought to reduce overhead wherever possible.

I spoke with another Juba funding director that had a long experience working in between microcredit agencies and their supporters abroad. Like the last respondent, the one of his employers' primary interests was seeing commercial microcredit succeed in terms of financial sustainability. He spent most of his days in the Juba office interfacing with MFI management. He began his reflection with industry-centric language about the financial literacy:

> The issue has to do with financial literatures. A lot of people there need loans, but they only know about banks. They don't know MFI can give them a lot. They go to the bank and the bank asks them, "what question do you have?" They say, "I don't have a question." They don't know you don't go to bank for a loan. They don't know about MFI that doesn't require a physical collateral. These are issues with time. This is why we have the association: to improve financial literacy. But it requires funding to be rolled out. People will be financially enlightened. They will know alternative sources of credit, not just a bank.

The scenario used, that a prospective client had intentionally entered a bank but did not have questions when meeting face-to-face with a banker, was another narrative hyperbole. While surely any South Sudanese who had gone to the effort of entering a bank would be capable of asking for something while there, the tale suggested that they did not even know where to begin. Nevertheless, his point illustrated the long distance such locals had to go before reaching "enlightenment."

The key point of this storyline was the idea that the path to enlightenment, another phrase evoking spiritual awareness, was financial literacy. Compared to other practitioner narratives that characterized dependency as a lack of work skills or morale, this turns our attention lack of knowledge of how finance works. Funding could solve the shortcoming, which, as stated of the prior respondent, was also a key concern for this commercial microcredit proponent. Enlightenment also relied on familiarity bred over time, by seeing bank loans in practice and observing their effects, which he said, "can give them a lot."

INDEPENDENCE IS A NEW BALLGAME

In another 2009 interview, the CEO of a Juba MFI described what he had observed through the prism of his institution's mandate. He explained that the Juba experience was different than those in neighboring countries, where he had worked prior.

> But it is the challenge of paradigm, which is common to post conflict. They are used to handouts, used to NGOs. The loan concept is foreign. The culture of [South] Sudan is very rough; they are used to war. After many years in camps, they are now teaching them independence. It's a new ballgame altogether.

Independence, according to the CEO, could be taught. His story indicates that the syndrome was marked not by unwillingness but instead by lacking proper exposure. He again identified the borrower naivety symptom when he elaborated on the role of financial customs in the new ballgame.

"They always talk about interest rate," he gave another example. "Interest doesn't make sense to them because even if they are not Muslim, they grew up under Islam." The target population was inculcated to believe that charging and paying interest is sinful. Since microcredit always includes interest rates, this was at odds with systems they were brought up with. This was an attention-grabbing realization because the public narrative on the Southern Sudanese independence at the time of interview was pointedly about breaking from Northern Sudan's Islamic legal tradition. A new South Sudan would subsequently not comply with Islamic banking laws, and MFIs were one of many departures from the northern traditions. But the transition to believing that interest was not only not nefarious but also virtuous would require exposure.

Though he saw dependency as a trend among post-conflict populations, he also recognized a feature that differentiated the South Sudanese from other beneficiaries: he brought home how honesty was a virtue. This made his comments about borrower ignorance more interesting as he contrasted the South Sudanese virtues with their ostensible failure, in the eyes of the institution, to pay on time.

> But they are strict. Honest. They will tell you if they don't have the money but will pay next week. You better believe it they will.

In his example, not making timely payments was regarded as less a worrisome character flaw because he could count on their integrity, eventually. Though late payments were major issues at the time of the interview, he spoke as if tardiness was forgivable because their honesty counterweighted it. While for others dependency was associated with a corrupt work ethic, his narrative associated the hope for learned independence signaled by honesty and strictness.

He restated that dependency was not an issue of will or capacity, but instead a matter of cultural dissonance. He also explained that the beneficiaries' default was not to sit back, and resist change; in fact, they are eager for the new prospects.

"Those outside of country camps benefited because they were exposed to skills. People here want to understand badly."

SCARS AS CREDIT SCORES

"The biggest problem is cultural," said an MFI leader in a 2012 interview, during a period in which his MFI organization was scaling back drastically on loan services. "They completely lack a culture of credit." Despite having suffered from massive arrears because of the market demolition and other technical issues, it was clear that he considered culture to be the primary culprit of his bank's demise. His evidence? Toward the end of the first interview, the boss showed me a picture on his computer screen and turned to me, saying, "Head cutting like this—can you believe it? Look at them, look at what they're doing still this day to their bodies. They will do this but still not work. They're not anywhere close to ready for credit."

On his screen were photos of people with traditional facial scarification patterns, called *Gaar* in Nuer. The scars are part a long-lasting ritual performed at adolescence, and are extremely common Dinka, Shilluk, and Nuer as well as many other cultures in Ethiopia, D.R.C., Suriname, and even the United States.

To this MFI leader, these body modifications were indictments on their capability to understand microfinance. The markings symbolized backwardness and primitivism.

Scars made on the surface of their skin during adolescence had surely healed by the time he observed them coming in to do business. Yet somehow his analysis surmised that, their physical appearance still evidently had major bearing on their capacity for entrepreneurialism in the present world.

THE MALPRACTICE OF MISDIAGNOSIS

Anthropologist Barbara Harrell-Bond dubbed "dependency syndrome" as a blanket term used for all the undesirable social behavior found. However, she observed in 1986 about a region not far from Juba, "Like all blanket terms, it can hide more than it reveals, and in the case of the Sudan, this way of categorizing refugee behavior leads to the wrong diagnoses of its cause and thus inevitably, wrongly aimed aid projects."[13] Even back then, the tendency to generalize this population pervaded humanitarian practitioner communication. This blanket diagnosis has continued, and using the token phrase is problematic for a variety of reasons, but here it was used as a way to characterize the population as a lost or exceedingly difficult cause.

Within the folds of their blanket language, MFI personnel gave nuanced portrayals of the "dependency syndrome." In describing this illness, their descriptions included:

- Lacking knowledge (financial literacy, how to cultivate or do business)
- Lacking capacity (skills, abilities)
- An ineffective attitude (response to perverse incentives, resisting "hard work" and capitalism)
- An incompatible culture (too social or traditional rather than commercial)

As expressed by Paul Harvey and Jeremy Lind, the dependency discourse allows people to shift the blame away from the "poverty, destitution or conflict that creates chronic crises."[14] In Juba, it inhibited microcredit practitioners from seeing how the Sudanese war specifically perpetuated chronic economic insecurity among its citizens. In fractured, post-conflict environments, people are forced to think and act in the short-term. For instance, writes Samuel Rutherford, "When [the poor] do not save it is because of lack of opportunity rather than lack of capacity."[15] Awa M. Abdi's research on refugees in Somalia concluded similarly that the refugees were dependent on aid "due to lack of alternative livelihoods rather than 'dependency syndrome.'"[16]

I introduced this dependency idea as one of a syndrome, per the usage of the term in the field. While it is true to that syndromes often involve multiple symptoms that then yield diagnoses, it also is true that for some syndromes, not every symptom shows itself in every case. Some symptoms, additionally, can be signals for many different issues. A cough, for instance, can be a symptom of a cold, a virus, or a bacterial infection. Each requires a different remedy; a virus cannot be treated with antibiotics. A syndrome must therefore be accurately diagnosed before treatment can be prescribed. But the dependency discourse instead justified the microcredit industry's failure, and inhibited microcredit practitioners from properly identifying ways to improve their practices.

In order to prescribe more effective microcredit, the terms in question require being broken down and situated in the broader context. While it remains difficult to test the veracity of the industry staff stories, the magnitude of hyperbole combined with the relative distance each kept from regular interface with the borrowers makes me suspicious. Nevertheless, if these theorized symptoms are true, each would entail a different policy response. If borrowers lack knowledge, the prescription might be more training. If they lack awareness, sensitization might be key. If they lack the will to adapt, the prescription might be to better incentivize in order to encourage them to. If it is culture, the prescription might the need to ready for the long haul. A thorough examination of the troubles was in order, and yet all of these presumed that the troubles rested within the clients themselves. Prescribing effective microcredit in contemporary Juba required a wider lens.

The MFI operators placed the onus on certain dimensions of dependency—namely, the locals' cultural dependency—but failed to reckon with others at work in South Sudan. As Kaler and Parkins (2015) point out, this focus on cultural dependency ignores the aid industry's reverse dependency, the nascent country's import dependency, and the multiple layers of its structural dependency that were all very apparent during this period in South Sudan. No person who has spent an hour in Juba would dare say that the import-dependent market was simple. Time and time again, otherwise satisfied borrowers told me that the biggest threat to their business was not a dependency issue, but rather the market conditions and the incompatibility of the market flows with the institutions' unvarying loan payment schedule. Dissatisfied borrowers tended to dislike the interest rate and the intragroup social tensions inherent to the loans themselves. Neglecting analysis of the other dependencies at work had a substantial impact on why these borrowers were in the frustrating situation they were.

INDEPENDENCE, REALLY?

To receive "freebies" has long been viewed as a social failure. Anthropologists and sociologists alike have inquired about the social nature of gifts, and one of the most-cited early scholars on this is Marcel Mauss, who argued that gift giving elicits reciprocity. Pierre Bourdieu's concept of symbolic domination has also been applied to humanitarian grants and loans, in that the transfer of funds creates a dangerous power dynamic between giver and receiver.[17] Indeed, Mauss' early writings elaborated on how the gift "not yet repaid debases the man who accepted it, particularly if he did so without thought of return."[18] Aid organizations that give handouts are targeted as responsible for failing to incentivize productive citizenry. Indeed, this is the central thesis of Dambisa Moyo's best-selling *Dead Aid*. Moyo is an ardent microcredit proponent.

Microcredit uses the dependency narrative concerning "handouts" to justify its existence. As Paul Harvey and Jeremy Lind point out, "Dependency discourses in these contexts represent a way of justifying a strategic shift from the provision of relief to more 'developmental' approaches."[19] It is this belief that fuels microfinance institutions as they claim the capacity to tap into the entrepreneurial spirit of beneficiary populations and bring borrowers to long-term self-sufficiency. As such, microcredit practitioners in the field need to guard against fomenting dependency and also preach concepts such as autonomy and sustainability.

The truth is, MFIs have dependencies of their own. While different from donation-based assistance, practitioners still need a certain type of dependency from their borrowers. In fact, unlike aid, microcredit depends on dependency: loan capital is return-seeking capital. The microcredit sector depends on capital coming back. It needs borrowers that not only repay, but also remain within the system and graduate to larger, more cost effective, and profitable loans. This places the token ideal of independence in awkward relation to their real raison d'etre. That MFIs preach autonomy is not only ironic, but stands to undermine the loan procedure's very working fabric.

In the microcredit industry's rush to advocate for the personal responsibility of poor people, forgotten from the dependency syndrome conversation has been a question about its functions for society. Most people read Harrell-Bond's seminal work as one of the foremost contributors to this concept of dependency. But her inquiry really centered on the counter-social tendencies among Ugandans who were displaced in southern Sudan in the early 1980s. "What [she] had failed to anticipate was . . . the extent to which the demands of individual survival undermined social values. . . . The real and apparent lack of support for each other, the refusal to cooperate under circumstances where co-operation appears to be advantageous, and the prevalence of destructive and anti-social behavior puzzles and frustrates aid workers and researchers alike."[20] Through this critical analysis, Harrell-Bond suggested that a level of desperation led people to behave antisocially, as if survival was a competition. I now posit that preaching independence should be carefully considered in this light.

The goal of independence can be harmful. Economist Guy Standing makes a simple but crucial point that carries into this analysis: "Dependency may be juxtaposed with 'independence' . . . who could possibly favour the former, a supine condition? Well, this simplistic imagery could be challenged by the claim that most of us are dependent on others in many ways. Biologically, the human species has survived through mutual dependency and collaboration. Recognition of our dependencies is a healthy response to our humanity."[21] Echoing Harvey and Lind, "The concept of interdependency is helpful in reframing the debate around dependency." They suggest instead we try to understand assistance within the "complex web of interdependencies that make up livelihoods under stress in crises."[22]

It is possible that the independence ideal may have cost the Juba MFIs. It was never clear the extent to which these mores were impressed upon borrowers. However, one event that impeded returns, for example, was the market demolition that occurred in 2008. Markets were demolished to build new roads, so borrowers were displaced. This provided people an opportunity to take the money they were loaned and run. So, some borrowers ditched the loans, and their capital did not return to the MFIs.

The delinquents who vanished after the demolition felt little obligation to MFIs (the return-seeking dependence) or co-borrowers. They calculated of the worth of maintaining loyalty with the MFIs (getting future, and likely larger loans) against the cost of never receiving another chance, but also not having to repay their loans. There was also a social calculation: the trade-off between reciprocity and friendship among co-borrowers coming to an end versus continuing to develop. A landslide vanishing act for one cost others taken to task for their share. Group loan shirkers were not so dependent on the loans that they came back. They burnt bridges between themselves, the MFIs, and/or each other because this appeared to be the optimal choice. This may not be a holistic picture of economic self-reliance, but it does imply they did not see a long game reason to comply with some of various social contracts. Neither the social contracts between borrowers or the literal contracts between borrowers and MFIs can afford to have the borrowers behave entirely independent.

Microcredit practitioners will never avoid the webs of social relations required for their efforts, and especially during times of transition like in the post-CPA resettlement period in Juba. That said, the social interdependence might also have cost microcredit efforts in Juba. Social customs tested microcredit. While I never met a borrower who felt that cattle keeping was more important than entrepreneurialism, many borrowers I met felt that friends should not be subject to reprisal for non-payments. In these cases, the MFI independence norm sounded like a Faustian bargain; it threatened the social conventions in place. While these priorities frustrated the MFIs, they were a far cry from the rote dependency narratives depicting ill-prepared, lazy beneficiaries with little hope of conforming to the demands of modern entrepreneurialism. Indeed, such social customs may actually be keys to understanding the thresholds of what borrowers value.

Repayments in Juba were lower than the magical 95 percent celebrated by MFIs the world over not because borrowers preferred to take handouts, and not because they were unwilling to put in the time necessary to repay. However, instead of reckoning with the all these complexities, field level employees indexing the dependency trope served to trigger a generalized policy response from those with whom the staff was conversing.

The real power of these dependency discourses was in their power to persuade the industry lifelines, the donors and programmers, upon which the local MFIs were dependent. The local MFIs were dependent upon their donors for debt capital outlays, the debt ratings of their creditors, upon their willingness to furnish auxiliary monetary support, upon the programmatic requirements from headquarters, and metrics for success laid down to them. Despite the Juba MFIs having varied public stances on the commercial and poverty models, all struggled to retain support. Each had to justify its projects to donors that did not want to spend "extra" on training but instead wanted to see the banks run solvent on their own. The fieldworkers knew the rules inside these semiotic communities: their supporters would wince at the idea of servicing beneficiaries that could not be productive enough, that had a long road ahead of them, or that had bad attitudes, as these would thereby threaten efficient returns.

Hasty diagnosis without thorough examination is dangerous. Discourses have material consequences, and these that promote sustainability and fear dependency proved to divert support from life-saving projects in Sudan and Malawi.[23] This book charts how the discursive power of sustainability pushed the Juba industry to shift its the goalposts from reaching the poorest people to simply yielding returns. The effect was to have the organizations scale back from the riskiest borrowers.

More than just a rhetorical overstep, the dependency syndrome generalization overlooked very real phenomena. These views left crucial blindspots to the lived nature of events happening among the very folks they claimed to speak for and had material consequences. It neglected to recognize how an import-dependent market suited their replicated lending model. It ignored the sacred values—dependency, vulnerability, and community—relevant for their own program's operations. The dependency buzzword was the perfect culprit to avoid these complex matters. The wrong medicine was prescribed. Like many have said before me, if the concern is that people become dependent rather than what is required to advance them along, we are deeply misguided. Instead of prescribing this pill again, MFIs might benefit from attending to a few more tests.

NOTES

1. As cited in Anna Leahy, *Constituents of Matter* (Kent State University Press, 2007), 3.
2. I anonymized names and MFI identifiers in portions of the excerpts presented in this chapter. There was a bit of an analytical trade-off in doing so. Staff at multiple levels of all three local MFIs and the coordinating agencies characterized them with

remarkable similarity, but there were some nuances that could have amplified the MFI-centric storyline of the text. Nevertheless, I felt it more important to do so given the subject matter.

3. Andrea Cornwall and Deborah Eade, *Deconstructing Development Discourse: Buzzwords and Fuzzwords* (Rugby, Warwickshire: Practical Action, 2010).

4. Amy Kaler and John R. Parkins, "Food, Donors, and Dependency Syndrome(s) in South Sudan." *Sociology of Development*, 1, no. 3 (2015).

5. Gaim Kibreab, "The Myth of Dependency among Camp Refugees in Somalia 1979–1989." *Journal of Refugee Studies* (1993), 330.

6. Amy Kaler and John R. Parkins, "Food, Donors, and Dependency Syndrome(s) in South Sudan." *Sociology of Development*, 1, no. 3 (2015).

7. Jonathan Tepperman, "Brazil's Antipoverty Breakthrough: The Surprising Success of Bolsa Famílía." *Foreign Affairs* (2016).

8. Islah Jad, "NGOs: between Buzzwords and Social Movements, in Cornwall and Eade." In *Deconstructing Development Discourse: Buzzwords and Fuzzwords*, edited by Andrea Cornwall and Deborah Eade (Rugby, Warwickshire: Practical Action, 2010), 195.

9. Alex De Waal, "Is Famine Relief Irrelevant to Rural People?" *IDS Bulletin*, 20, no. 2 (1989).

10. Amartya Sen, *Development as Freedom* (New York: Knopf, 1999).

11. Deborah Eade, "Capacity Building: Who Builds whose Capacity?" In *Deconstructing Development Discourse: Buzzwords and Fuzzwords*, edited by Cornwall, Andre and Eade, Deborah (Oxford: Oxfam/Practical Action, 2010), 206.

12. E. E. Evans-Pritchard, "The Sacrificial Role of Cattle Among The Nuer." *Africa: Journal of the International African Institute*, 23 no. 3 (1953), 184.

13. Barbara E. Harrell-Bond, *Imposing Aid: Emergency Assistance to Refugees* (London: Oxford University Press, 1986), 283.

14. Paul Harvey and Jeremy Lind, Dependency and Humanitarian Relief: A Critical Analysis. Report, Humanitarian Policy Group (London: Overseas Development Institute, 2005), 18.

15. Samuel Rutherford, "The Poor and Their Money: An Essay about Financial Services for Poor People." Essay, (Institute for Development Policy and Management University of Manchester, 1999), V.

16. Awa M. Abdi, "In Limbo: Dependency, Insecurity, and Identity amongst Somali Refugees in Dadaab Camps" *Canadas Journal on Refugees*, 22 no. 2 (2005), 6.

17. Doreen Indra, "The Spirit of the Gift and the Politics of Resettlement: The Canadian Private Sponsorship of South East Asians." In *The International Refugee Crisis: British and Canadian Responses*, edited by Vaughan Robinson (1993); Tomohisa Hattori, "Reconceptualizing Foreign Aid," *Review of International Political Economy*, 8, no. 4 (2001).

18. Marcel Mauss, *The Gift: Forms and Functions of Exchange in Archaic Societies* (London: Lowe and Brydone Printers, 1967).

19. Paul Harvey and Jeremy Lind, Dependency and Humanitarian Relief: A Critical Analysis. Report, Humanitarian Policy Group (London: Overseas Development Institute, 2005), 16; see also Mark Duffield, et al., *Sudan: The Unintended*

Consequences of Humanitarian Action, Field Education Study (Report to the European Community Humanitarian Office, 2000).

20. Barbara E. Harrell-Bond, *Imposing Aid: Emergency Assistance to Refugees* (London: Oxford University Press, 1986), 283.

21. Guy Standing, "Social Protection." In *Deconstructing Development Discourse: Buzzwords and Fuzzwords*, edited by Cornwall, Andre and Eade, Deborah (Oxford: Oxfam/Practical Action, 2010).

22. Paul Harvey and Jeremy Lind, *Dependency and Humanitarian Relief: A Critical Analysis*. Report, Humanitarian Policy Group (London: Overseas Development Institute, 2005), 6.

23. Mark Duffield, et al., *Sudan: The Unintended Consequences of Humanitarian Action, Field Education Study* (Report to the European Community Humanitarian Office, 2000); Ann Swidler and Susan Cotts Watkins, "'Teach a Man to Fish': The Doctrine of Sustainability and Its Effects on Three Strata of Malawian Society." *World Development*, 37 no. 7 (2009).

Chapter 9

Autopsy

The fall of South Sudan's microcredit sector

When I say that microfinance failed in Juba, I am referring to the closure of the two main microcredit operations in town. At their height, these operations represented more than 90 percent of the microcredit market. The reasons for their closures meant that credit services to the *very poor* have all but vanished. What replaced them was not *micro*credit, and this has gravely important implications for what Roy called the "battle for the soul"[1] of the sector. The closures impacted some 40,000 South Sudanese poor in the short term, and countless more over the long term.

Below are theories for the failure, as formulated by various stakeholders I met in the field, as well as the reports of internal and external analysts. Each analyst has their own view of what constituted success or failure. Throughout this chapter, I highlight how the different actors involved determined their theories in light of what data and decisions were available to them. Through assessing these different interpretations, I craft my own analysis of why and how microcredit failed in South Sudan.

Nobody ever said it would be easy. Most research on post-conflict credit had not been done because the experiments were still unfolding. What little science had been done on post-conflict microcredit elsewhere offered warning after warning. But was Juba different, or were the warnings just not heeded?

As momentum behind microcredit grew and projects were unrolled, scholars and policy makers combined lessons from the test cases. One of the most broadcasted reports was by the International Labor Organization (ILO). In August 1999, just a few years before microcredit first arrived in South Sudan, there was a joint ILO/UNHCR technical workshop in Geneva attended by dozens of senior staff of hosting organizations devoted to discussing what is involved in post-conflict microcredit. There, participants discussed several themes, including challenges that were faced in previous cases, such as in

Cambodia and Mozambique. From an analysis of these, they devised a new set of guiding principles. The summary report indicated that microcredit in post-conflict regions is viable, as long as there is also 1) reasonable security, 2) adequate economic activity, and 3) population stability.[2] Of course, each of these preconditions is relative. Juba generally satisfied the primary criteria during the observation period, between the 2005 CPA and mid-2013.[3]

Earlier, in 1998, Karen Doyle penned a report sponsored by USAID that proposed "Preferred Conditions" for operating in post-conflict environments. The conditions for success listed in the Doyle report were more stringent. Her criteria included at minimum: commercial banks, an absence of hyperinflation, dense population, legislative structures, a skilled educated workforce, social capital, and trust in local currency and financial institutions.[4] These preferred conditions, also relative, were less present in Juba.

In 2002, the ILO and UNHCR collaborators created a training course, "Introduction To Microfinance In Conflict-Affected Communities," which extolled the viability. "Experience has shown that microfinance works in more environments than people thought possible. It seems that there are remarkably few environments where microfinance will not work," they celebrated.[5] The curriculum praised microfinance successes in conflict-affected communities, citing examples based on significantly varied credit program offerings around the globe: Cambodia, Bosnia, and Herzegovina, Kosovo, Palestine, Rwanda, Mozambique, Sri Lanka, Georgia, Tajikistan, and El Salvador.[6]

The well-circulated ILO and UNHCR reports rested their optimism on the faith that microfinance industry would work to develop rather than replicate past models. The report acknowledged that there exist challenges particular to operating MFIs in post-conflict regions, and consistently reminded its students of the need to adapt. It implied malleability should be expected on both partner agencies and the MFI doctrines.

In Juba, however, the malleability admonition received little more than lip service. When things soured, blame was directed toward things outside the scope of microcredit policy. The practitioners blamed the poor's lack of social capital and lack of business acumen or motivation. Almost everyone blamed the whacky economy. But no one dared to suppose the fault was actually within the donors' cost-effective mandates, prefabricated lending models, and resistance to invest in work to understand the borrower trends and needs on the ground.

SUMI'S FALL FROM GRACE

Recall that the initial support for SUMI was set to last five years. The USAID-Chemonics contract never promised to last beyond 2007, at which time the project, based on Washington "best practices," was expected to be a fully solvent, independent MFI. After the first phase of SUMI, the small banking institution entered a slow spiral of confusion, which found it begging for support. SUMI was "at a crossroads" according to the Chemonics 2008 final report.

The Chemonics farewell report is illuminating because it demonstrates the reckoning between the policy-makers' planned model and those who implemented it day-to-day. This partial autopsy, delivered to the donors who held the much-needed lifeline in their hands, described what happened during the first five-year phase of SUMI.

Overall, the summary of the Chemonics self-evaluation declared its work successful, "based on both client demand and repayment experience." In those first five years, SUMI was established, opened five branches serving more than 6,000 clients, had an outstanding portfolio of more than USD$2.7 million, had cumulative disbursements totaling more than $7.1 million, and a qualitative repayment rate over 90 percent. The report listed numerous positive statistics.

Key results included:

- Hired and trained SUMI staff
- Developed policies and procedures for SUMI
- Developed targeted loan products, including group, salary, and individual loans
- Appointed an initial board of directors and guided the MFI to board elections
- Provided ongoing training to board members on their roles and responsibilities
- Supported SUMI in conducting outreach and marketing activities

Yet despite Chemonics' optimistic analysis of its own performance, SUMI was struggling. The report did not examine how these bullet points met or fell short from the targets. It did not situate results within goalposts. The project fell short (300k) of the previously published $3 million loan portfolio goal. The report included no clear review of targeted populations like displaced people, the very poor, and women. The report described the challenge of having "fewer women than men operate in the market," but did not list the practical effects of this. Vague declarations of success like, "the number of women participating in the market increased significantly," provided insufficient information to determine whether SUMI was ready to be weaned.

The Chemonics report did include subtext that indicated SUMI was not on solid ground, but it understated the gravity of it. The report outlined how "it was vital that the MFI be managed as a business to be viable and sustainable."[7] These were signals of SUMI struggling to meet the demands from above, in particular with regard to not being satisfactorily commercial. What prevented SUMI from becoming self-sustaining according to the business model?

One of the biggest problems that SUMI had was making a case for continued, poverty-focused funding, because it had sparse records to prove that its operations were successful and deserved more support. By 2007, SUMI received an independent audit by Price Waterhouse Coopers, which deemed SUMI's account balances below par. Chemonics defended SUMI from the Price Waterhouse Coopers (PwC) auditor's analysis for failing to understand post-conflict complexities. It was in this defense of its performance, which played to the broadness of SUMI's original and ambitious aims, that Chemonics analysts appealed to the poverty lending side of the debate. Chemonics reasoned that "PwC looked strictly at accounting and did not consider the microfinance perspective." The auditors gave "no consideration to either the SUMI business plan, or the reality of where an MFI should be at this stage of its development. PwC assumed that SUMI should have been operating all along with a sophisticated computerized loan tracking system. Such an expectation is valid for a commercial bank, but it goes against best practices in microfinance."[8]

USAID in-house discord over microfinance policy made implementing and evaluating its program difficult. A few years later, in part due to the new legislation requiring better records, USAID disciplined the field-level organization for failing to comply with the new benchmarks. At this point, the audit showed that Chemonics and SUMI indeed did not make the numbers. Far too few loans had been repaid. USAID paid Chemonics to launch SUMI without requiring or furnishing a way to create a paper trail, and the Chemonics infrastructure had little reason to prove itself until this point. The Chemonics response to PwC evoked certain frustration, for being unable to implement the work required while being, in its perspective, under-supported. SUMI and Chemonics staff bankers, though still employed at this time, were in a bind.

The data collected by different actors spoke over one another, pointing to different metrics of analyzing success. The field staff had manual payment receipts; borrower experiences that were collected by the agencies amounted to single paragraph success stories at best.[9] The donors mainly sought to know portfolio returns in the paper trails. Headcounts. Proof—of a narrow variety—was a pawn of the actors with the power.

On the whole, the Chemonics sunset report concluded with advocacy that SUMI go on: "SUMI, as a young institution in a complex post-conflict environment, needs additional support," it declared. Despite being "well on its way to becoming an independent Sudanese-run private sector business,"[10] SUMI was not quite ready for independence. Having exhausted the loan fund provided by USAID, SUMI needed to grow its capital base because, "although

SUMI is able to cover its operating costs, it does not generate enough revenue for much-needed expansion, capacity building of personnel, or product development."[11] Knowing it was dependent on further support, Chemonics analysts could only *ask* its donors for help for the fledgling institution.

Mercifully, SUMI received a little more funding. In 2008, SUMI received USD $56,000 worth of technical assistance (TA) from the South Sudan Microfinance Development Facility (SSMDF), earmarked for getting its paperwork in order.[12] The technical assistance went a long way toward increasing capacity and gathering data, but it did not solve the SUMI capital shortfall.

When I met with staff from SUMI in late 2009, they were thrilled to have finally received an information system—computer database software. Whenever I heard of their challenges, I next heard them speak as if the new technology would solve the tribulations. One staffer told me: "We are constantly growing, we have now opened our sixth branch in Wau. We were trying to consolidate into five branches. But we can now expand again because we have the automated MIS [Management Information System]. Before we were on the manual MIS, so now we've gotten a computerized one, then at least efficiency and productivity are improved." He spoke as if he thought the new technology could correct the MFI's income shortage, even in the specific branch expansion issue he described. However, SUMI's problems expanded far beyond unorganized paperwork, or its lack of technical capabilities. Underlying its funding problem, as noted, were issues of not only collecting client data to trace the impediments to repayments, but also its capacity to make verifiable claims to future funding.

SUMI could march on, but it became apparent that it was no longer the USAID favorite. In 2008, USAID proudly reported their launch of the Southern Sudan Microfinance Forum (to become MASS) and another new investment of note: "the establishment of a second MFI—Finance Sudan."[13]

FINANCE SUDAN'S TRANSFORMATION

"By that time," Finance Sudan's chairperson reminisced to me from a 2012 vantage, "it was challenging. This company was actually collapsing. The countries' challenges were beyond the business expectations." Finance Sudan was struggling. In its early years under the American Refugee Committee (ARC), FSL had low repayment ratings, and donors and the MIX Market were paying close attention. The 2009 repayment rates were just as terrible: their portfolio at risk for more than thirty days, (or overdue payments), was at 42 percent, a far cry from the 5 percent range championed by microcredit advertising the world over. At the time, Finance Sudan's return on investment was less than 67 percent, nowhere near full solvency. Something had to give beyond what ARC grants could offer.

At about that time, Finance Sudan was bought and became a company guaranteed by shares, changed its name to Finance Sudan Limited (FSL), and hired a new manager with extensive experience by field management standards (given that attrition rates were high). Oketi had ten years of experience in microfinance, having managed branches in Kenya and in Uganda during its conflict. He told me proudly that he was "posted mostly in branches that had challenges. I used to go turn them around."

Oketi received a phone call in the spring of 2010 from the board chairman for FSL, and another from one of the former directors and shareholders in Uganda Microfinance Limited that had just two years earlier been bought by Equity Bank, one of Kenya's giants. Oketi recapped:

> So they called and told me, "We know you have a lot of experience in microfinance and especially in dealing with the higher branches. Once we shut down this operation in South Sudan, can you come and make a miracle for us?" I said, "it's not a miracle, I will just go do three months and start up with consultancy, I will do a review of the business operations and see how we can sort the business and if it's worthwhile, I will say yes and if it's not, I will say just shut your investment and move on."

SPECTACLE, CONFUSION, AND MOMENTUM

FSL did not initially move on. Despite the 2010 audit and noted struggles, there was still a push to make microcredit work in South Sudan. "Historic stuff" began a Sudan Watch article about *Southern Sudan's First Microfinance Conference*.[14] The impending referendum, with an independent South Sudan within reach, created an era of boundless hope throughout Juba. The conference was a spectacle, appealing to the faith in finance and entrepreneurialism for the soon-to-be country. USAID and SSMDF funded the conference, clearly denoting their interest in growing and improving the sector.

The July 2010 USAID conference in Juba was a microcosm of the engine that ran the microcredit machine. Thousands of dollars were spent on the meeting, which took place in a nice hotel.[15] More than a hundred practitioners and technical experts from around the world attended, "to exchange views about the state of microfinance in southern Sudan and develop a strategy to build the sector, which is still in its infancy."[16] The South Sudanese practitioners relayed challenges like the low financial literacy among the target population and high transaction costs, and received guidance from visiting guests from around the world. The guest speakers, drawing on neoliberal fundamentals, charged that the industry could grow by "focusing on the basics," which the field practitioners would soon learn just meant optimizing a shoestring budget.

The key themes presented to practitioners included active listening and adaptation to the local demands. The MicroSave Africa[17] director, for instance, championed the need to perform market research so as to modify services, explaining how, "the smallest adjustment to a loan product can sometimes transform a product utilized by a few hundred borrowers to one that benefits thousands, and the only way we can change is to listen to our clients."[18] He boasted that MicroSave had been doing this for Finance Sudan during the restructuring year where the mantras advocating for client feedback satiated reporters and persuaded prospective donors. But it would take more time to witness whether the community would heed his call for active listening, responsive inquiry, and tailoring microcredit for South Sudan.

"Microfinance is dynamic and SUMI will adapt to change as it grows. I envision that SUMI, in the future, will be a bank,"[19] said Lokule Edward, then-managing director of SUMI to reporters. By the summer 2010 conference, SUMI was still tied with BRAC as the largest MFI in South Sudan, and held the respect of the community by virtue of having been there first. SUMI was show ponied throughout the conference, and media mentions of it focused almost entirely on great news. And yet, in lieu of its internal turmoil, even SUMI's initial supporters had already begun going public with their support of its competitors instead.

The conference signaled the donor community's confidence in the continuing, if not new, support for the microfinance sector; after all, it would not have been organized if they saw microcredit as hopeless. "The microfinance sector," declared the US Consul General in Juba Ambassador, "has the potential to transform millions of lives." There was indeed a spike in support of the South Sudanese microfinance sector following the conference as early donors shifted their attention back to the sector, and new entrants joined in to help.

Directors of the United Nations Capital Development Fund (UNCDF) were also smitten by the hopeful ethos coming from the pre-Independence conference. They committed over US $7 million to financial service providers in southern Sudan through a program called MicroLead.[20] The UNCDF directors named the program MicroLead with careful intention. Funding was concentrated on retail financial service providers with "proven business models" rather than new market entrants—market leaders that could "rapidly scale-up their own operations offering a variety of products and services while accelerating the pace of sector development" would access funding.[21] The MicroLead architects did not hide their favoring of "market leaders" for this funding; they even promoted it. They judged that the industry's "enabling" regulatory environment was moving in "the right direction," and, combined with promised funding by other major donors, beckoned to the agency that this bandwagon was worth jumping on. UNCDF's explicit goal was to more than double the number of borrowers in Southern Sudan through "an ambitious strategy of combining support to a range of local institutions and market leaders" by 2013, which meant moving away from serving the very poor.[22]

MicroLead was intended to support savings-led financial and technical service providers. Its many partners included: UNCDF, the Bill, and Melinda Gates Foundation, The MasterCard Foundation, Governments of South Sudan, Liberia, Bhutan, Timor-Leste, Sierra Leone, Democratic Republic of Congo, Rwanda, Ethiopia, Lao PDR, Vanuatu, Solomon Islands, and Samoa. Its specific mission was to "increase sustainable access to client-centric financial services, particularly savings services, for low-income populations."[23] This rests under the logic that savings are important, and gives banks money to mobilize. While the sustainability buzzword was pervasive across many development domains, the savings component was even more acutely synchronous with the norms circulating among financial inclusion advocates, and was endorsed by influential actors in the field, including the Innovations for Poverty Action, the Consultative Group to Assist the Poor, and the Women's World Banking. Indeed, out of the seven million committed in South Sudan, a noteworthy share went to Equity Bank; a bank that neither needed the money nor was trying to reach the MFI target audience.

The 2010 MicroLead grant had a soft but ostensible bend toward the Washington consensus on poverty and its neoliberal underpinning. This included training and certifying local auditors to ensure regimented payment tracking, as well as filtering support through the commercial advocates' favored channels: sending senior staff and management to Boulder Microfinance Center, getting the Bank of South Sudan "access CGAP Policy cadre or its equivalent," and technical assistance to be filtered through the SSMDF.

In the summer of the 2010 conference, SUMI underwent serious institutional changes at the governance and management levels. It formed a new board and appointed a new CEO, to redress challenges like high PAR, high staff turnover, diminishing liquidity, and operating inefficiency. But something was amiss.

The new CEO of SUMI, Vincent Olweny Oywak, expressed large concerns as he was in the dark about how his MFI was going to forge ahead and succeed. In October 2010 he went on record in the local newspaper over the "unexplained irregularities and lack of transparency in the management of donor funds intended for microfinance institutions." Speaking as a voice for his other affiliation with the Microfinance Association of Southern Sudan (MASS), Vincent voiced concern that "despite the millions of dollars committed to the sector, only a scant amount has been accessed by some of the member institutions." Specifically, he "alleged that some donor funds were being directly channeled to a foreign owned microfinance institution based in Southern Sudan rather than going to small businesses."[24] Vincent was concerned that the industry support was shifting away from the "right" MFIs, including his own SUMI.

In November 2010, SUMI appealed to SSMDF for additional funding to reschedule its loans. The SSMDF insisted that they could not move forward, "without an audit report, realistic business plan and a proper evaluation of the impact the rescheduled loan would have on the financial position of SUMI." SUMI had not been audited since Price Waterhouse Coopers in 2007. After three months of delay, in February 2011, SSMDF approved US$59,646 in Technical Assistance funding, but only "to meet the cost of a financial audit and a revision of the business plan."[25] More assistance was needed, and in more areas, yet this became another strike-out in requests for the much-needed debt capital.

The year 2010 marked a reorienting for SSMDF leadership and priorities. In September, the institution revised its plan in order to "make SSMDF more relevant and responsive to the challenges facing the microfinance industry." The most significant transformation was that the "new strategy" was to be committed to "Greenfield MFIs with potential to become viable financial institutions." The objective was not new: "ensure that MFIs are focused on building sustainable institutions that will stand the test of time."[26] As mentioned earlier, the mandate to service sustainable MFIs was at odds with the poverty finance model. In 2010, the SSMDF gave Finance Sudan—one of the foreign MFIs that worried SUMI CEO Vincent—a substantial sum of loan funds: US$300,000.

Despite its expected commitment to the World Bank's preferred strategy of commercial microcredit over the poverty model, signs were soon flashing that microfinance was moving away from this. By the date of independence for South Sudan, the Bank brought in new agendas to the landscape. The revised Bank plan marked the day when microfinance receded from the World Bank priority agenda. In a 2013 interview, one World Bank staffer illustrated the personal side of change—after repeatedly mentioning SME or "small-to-medium enterprise" he self-edited his vocabulary, replacing it with "micro enterprises." SMEs were the exemplars of loans for the "slightly less poor," and poverty lending advocates contend that they fail to reach those who need credit the most. However, to commercial microfinanciers, SMEs are perfectly sensible and desirable.

The World Bank plan for promoting micro-entrepreneurship (US$ 4.4 million, or double what was allocated to traditional MFIs) officially established a business plan competition (BPC). More than half of all private sector monies were allocated to 200 small entrepreneurs to the tune of US$20,000 each.[27] Twenty grand, it is worth noting, is not *micro* credit.

The World Bank money was disbursed as a guarantee so that the key stakeholders[28] who had formally invested were Kenya Commercial Bank-South Sudan and Equity Bank who provided the BPC loans.[29] Both are private banks. I learned how poorly those grants had performed in a 2012 interview with a person who worked for the World Bank microcredit initiative in Juba.

> It is not actually part of microfinance, but it is a complement to it. We decided in terms of support to microenterprises, in order to make sure the economy grows, you have to support the microenterprises with some bigger entrepreneurs. The analysis came from, say for example, the tea sellers in the streets who are supported by this microfinance scheme. But now, they have to get sugar, they have to get tea and coffee outside the country. So why don't we do it by picking some who have become our formidable entrepreneurs to grow the sugar within.
>
> Then we decided also to come up with another scheme. This was a supplement, so that we could groom a few members of the community who could take up this bigger. I wouldn't call it SME, it's not SME as such because we couldn't fit it into the international definition of SME. But at least something related to that. We wanted to go into production so that we can be able to service this industry, which is growing very big, because our main bag was the microenterprises. But out of that we wanted to have some sort of support scheme within the country. So we picked through what we called a Business Plan Competition, which was actually a business idea competition.

He added that they picked sixty entrepreneurs for training on business management and other issues related to enterprise development. After that, they chose to fund the best forty-five because the budget could only support that many. He told me that since most of these people were "unbankable," without collateral to support any individual loan scheme, they set up a collateral scheme to guarantee for them, facilitated through the banking system, where they deposited the BPC prize money. Winners opened accounts and started sourcing loans from there. "Now currently, out of the 45, 17 are doing extremely well," he said. Fewer than half. "What happened to the rest?" I asked.

> The others, they're people who are used to the donor syndrome, they just saw it as a donation and they just disappeared into thin air. We're not worried about that. We said that even if we could only build up three of them, that would be a something because we could use them as a lantern to attract others to do a similar thing for the future. So that's what allowed us to be approved for the second phase. Because of this success they extended another 12 months, and even for a bigger amount. So it is approved for another year.

The Bank might have been happy, but I was shocked by the poor repayment rates of these large loans. He concluded our interview by describing the future of World Bank support of traditional microfinance—small loans for the poor.

> But after three months microfinance will not receive anymore World Bank funding. They will have already done their bit through the MDTF, because what they wanted to do was to create a foundation, a system, a forum. A system is there, the forum is there, the institutions like SSMDF are already created so the only thing for them is the government supporting. But unfortunately the government doesn't have that so [he laughed] we're hoping they do, or even that the donors do come in and continue supporting.

Oketi, the gentleman hired to come turn Finance Sudan around, took the job in the spring of 2010. He is a self-proclaimed hero in its ascent story. Many believed in his abilities as well, as evident by surges in funding flows, and the institution portfolio.

"Luckily enough when I came, I did a review of the internal operations," he told me in 2012. "And I looked at the markets, the kind of plans they sort. I looked at what they offer differently, I looked at the human resources and then also their policy and procedures." Oketi's 2010 overhaul of FSSL was, more than anything, a product differentiation because, he told me, "we were basically the only group lending." He explained his prescriptions to me as follows:

> We saw that sector of the microfinance, especially the salary people like the NGO and some of the state government needed services from us, so I had to create a salary loan product that take care of employees who are South Sudanese. I think that also increased the product lending, because now we are also attracting quite a of number these salary people. They had no any other option except us. The banks were not offering credit to them and so we needed these clients.

Oketi's proposed modifications satisfied the new Kenyan owners of FSL, but they knew they could not achieve the ambitious market rate aims if they continued in partnership with the refugee NGO. Servicing loans to people who were lucky enough to have salaries was not part of the mission to serve refugees who desperately needed credit. So in 2011, ARC sold its stake to allow FSL to transform into Finance South Sudan Limited (FSSL), a company limited by shares.[30] This transformation freed up Finance Sudan from any prior obligation to serve the much poorer customers.

Finance Sudan's transformation was very much facilitated by USAID's fresh boost of support at that time—so much support that USAID counted "the turnaround of Finance Sudan from an MFI on the verge of failing to one that now stands at the forefront of the industry" among its "major successes."[31] By 2011 and officially a private firm, Finance Sudan started getting funding from almost all the donors in the sector. Once the smallest actor on the scene, Finance Sudan was now leveraging most of the support that had previously been allocated to the other MFIs.

But this growth in funding, and the addition of a new branch, did not amount to greater client outreach. In fact, the overhauled Finance Sudan was reaching far *fewer* borrowers than it did as an NGO; according to MIX Market figures, FSL had 5,400 borrowers in 2011, 4,020 borrowers in 2012, and 2,416 in 2013. In just two years, the company halved the amount of borrowers it distributed loans to.

Finance Sudan became less inclusive than it was initially designed to be, because it had to make extra efforts to create a sustainable institution. FSSL at this point closed northern branches in the cities of Wau and Malakal, which were losing the most returns due to the economic downturn brought by the oil conflict between South Sudan and Sudan, and the closure of the borders. The institution saw the costs of closely monitoring the branches and having unpaid loans as too high to stay in these areas, and saw it as a risk that threatened the sustainability of the entire institution.[32]

An FSSL worker explained the situation in a 2013 interview.

> So, that current situation was not a very good experience for us in 2012. 2012 passed of course with some challenges and strategically as an institution we decided to take a very big step and learn from our mistakes and say how do we overcome these challenges? The key thing is we had to go through a process of business realignments, and to really put them into place. The situation in South Sudan, with or without oil we must do business. As I said, we transformed into a company limited with shares and the shareholders did not want us to shut down and leave the operation. Even as a stakeholder, we build such a big stake in the community, I think it will be a waste for the industry. Actually for the industry, if Finance South Sudan decides and shut down and then the industry is shutting down because currently we have the biggest microfinance institution and the others have refugees which are very small.

Finance Sudan stayed ahead of what its leadership regarded as its biggest struggles by choosing sustainability over funding the poorest. This approach satisfied the supporters of the Washington consensus on poverty.

AN UNEXPECTED FAREWELL

I had no idea things could have devolved to the extent they did. My first day on a fieldwork trip in the summer of 2012, I went to visit MFI administrators, staff, and borrowers. I had developed theories based on the prior fieldwork and wanted to see what these people thought. This is an important test of ethnography: that it ring true with those whom it is about.

My first stop on that trip was with Vincent, the SUMI director. He was based at the head office in Juba. It was a good thing I arrived when I did; they were in the process of packing the office and closing up shop. There was only one other person left in the whole two-story office facility.

The research I had done up to that point in no way suggested the microcredit sector in South Sudan was thriving, but I simply had never heard of an MFI that was completely incapacitated like SUMI—and certainly not one with such a wide reach. The MFI in Adjumani, Uganda with whom I had done research had suffered losses with the CPA out-migration from Uganda, but it continued offering services to those who had remained. Even despite the sparse paper trail, I reasoned that MFI was bought by massive Equity Bank, so there must have been *some* asset or capital base left worth an investor's attention. I was not expecting to hear what had actually happened.

Vincent listed off the challenges SUMI had been facing, and they were the same that everybody else had said. Borrowers were not able to make ends meet, and his staff did not have the resources to adequately support them. SUMI started closing poorly performing branches in 2009, but by 2012, it was down to just two branches in town. They were continuing service with them while they deal with the lost assets before closing down completely. Despite the moving boxes, he held hope that with the right changes to the system, SUMI could turn things around.

He explained how, for a while, there was a sliver of hope for USAID to come through with a round of funding after the first term of the contract. He reminded me that, since its birth, SUMI was dependent on a USAID grant. In 2011, continued support seemed likely. USAID had promised SUMI US$1.5m, conditioned on one thing: if they could find an "international strategic partner" agency. But none was approved by the SUMI Board and USAID. So, USAID funding was cut off. Once more, SUMI sought support from the South Sudan Microfinance Development Facility (SSMDF).

But, SSMDF weighed in to express their concerns, "As a company limited by guarantee, SUMI does not have clear ownership. The lack of clear ownership unwittingly compromises Management and Board accountability." Neither owned by USAID nor its implementing partner agency Chemonics, SUMI had no owner to speak of. There was no agency or firm whose stakeholders had a vested interest in the institution's fate. SSMDF refused to provide further support on these grounds. Their report's last mention explained: "This has impacted negatively on the performance of the institution whose future currently lies in balance."[33]

In many ways, and in spite of how it unfolded, Vincent agreed with the orders that SUMI should find clearer ownership. In our follow-up meeting, Vincent waxed poetically about the ownership of "the means of production." He knew ownership was where the power of change lived in any corporation, and he knew well that laborers could not do much without the strength of its ownership sharing the same vision. This applied to him as much as it did the borrowers: he was powerless in the management-but-not ownership of his MFI.

"People call their work capacity building," he said, "but they work with the same people over and over again; it doesn't penetrate the rungs of society." He saw the solution to this as cooperative savings and regulated credit unions. He had even gone to the Bank of South Sudan to propose locally owned credit unions but, he said, they did not fully entertain microfinance concepts, as "their primary focus was banking in addition to the lack of a microfinance policy and/or regulatory framework." That, he said, was one of the big problems; that people knew the loan money "was from donors far away, no MFIs were emphasizing that need for the local ownership opportunity, and the government is more comfortable with business people running things for everyone else."

Vincent told me that SUMI was not the only MFI that was dying out in the field. BRAC too had begun rescinding its credit services in several branches, he had heard at a microfinance association meeting. I was due to pay BRAC another visit anyway. In 2012, I asked the BRAC staff for a little more explanation, and if possible, data, about what went wrong with their microfinance endeavor. True to their research and reflection form, they scheduled a meeting in which we could review a Powerpoint slideshow presentation they had prepared.

In the meeting, the BRAC staff explained that their model was transitioning away from providing microfinance. Their lead researcher told me: "We try to find out how microfinance was working in the beginning and how it went through with demands, and how it grew up, and the challenges that we faced with the operations. We had information; the group meetings after the group formations, then the members' business here, you can see some of the members being visited and at their business places and doing these things."

Challenges and barriers they discussed, cited here from their PowerPoint presentation, were:

- Low economical viability
- Migrations as a result of demolition, land demarcation and resettlement
- Loss of business
- Money transaction
- Tribal conflict
- Insecurity
- Poor internal road communication
- Staff-related issues
- Money stuck in Nile Commercial Bank
- Less possibilities of extension due to low population density (Scattered)
- Inadequate communication networks

The researcher and an upper-level staffer went on to tell me how frustrating it was to scale back lending. Between the millions of dollars lost in the Nile Commercial Bank and the fact that borrowers just did not continue paying back into the system, they felt they had run out of options. They relayed this dismay to headquarters.

"It was a heartbreaking situation," said a former high-level decision-maker from BRAC International in an interview. BRAC's holistic model was funded not by one "impact first" impact investor, but by several different funders. Each contract was earmarked separately for development activities (grants) and loans. It was up to the direction of BRAC International, which coordinated all the franchises outside Bangladesh, whether the Juba directors could try anything new within the funding constraints. Despite having some grant funding from which they could draw and subsidize new program experiments, the commercial debts BRAC carried from its borrowers had to be repaid. If not, those who lent to BRAC, could drop BRAC International's credit score. The grant funds simply could not fill the growing gap in what was needed to achieve BRAC's holistic poverty outreach model.[34]

On the ground, BRAC first tried to right the ship and repay its debts by downsizing. In 2010, management in Juba noticed some outreach programs were a bit too costly, so they merged 16 branches to reduce the cost of operation and closed three branches altogether, bringing the total number remaining in South Sudan from 45 down to 26. It was not nearly enough, but they kept marching through 2011. That year, they introduced staff performance incentives and fired underperforming staff. They had a branch review analyzing their operating system and documentation. Yet, they were still being spread too thin. No amount of scaling back was enough to reach the debt obligations.

BRAC was not coming close to the needed portfolio balance. That year it also tried something relatively controversial among poverty finance advocates, to fill the gap: it increased the interest rate to match the market rate, and introduced twenty installment loans. It still was not enough money, and definitely not fast enough for the institution. The staff in Juba argued that the challenges were just too great, and mostly outside of BRAC's control.

The challenging postwar economy received most of the blame from microcredit observers in and outside the new country. As with BRAC outposts in Sierra Leone and Liberia, efforts to provide credit in South Sudan faced major challenges specifically due to its postwar status.[35] A 2015 UNCDF *Microfinance Greenfields In Challenging Environments* report reasoned that, "the BRAC methodology . . . works in places with basic security, a stable and relatively dense population and significant levels of existing economic activity." Instead, operating challenges, a sparse and mobile population and low levels of economic activity "prevented the model from working."[36] The

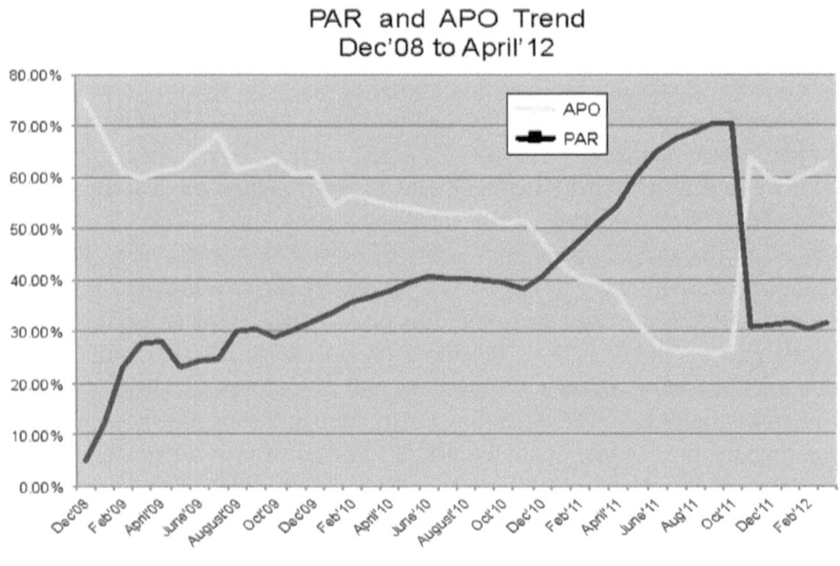

Figure 9.1 BRAC Portfolio at Risk 2008–2012. *Source:* Courtesy of BRAC.

postwar particularities would be charged as the difference between the failures in South Sudan and BRAC's otherwise successful models.

A World Bank manager based in Juba, one who advocated that even the poorest South Sudanese were credit-worthy, took issue with such post-conflict blaming analyses. He analyzed BRAC's microcredit failure differently. He explained in a 2013 interview that BRAC, "started an ambitious program going to seven states with a lot of branches." He continued:

> The problem, according to me, is not the market. It is the model. The model BRAC brought was Bangladesh model. We see that Bangladesh and South Sudan have a lot of disparities between the populations. I have not been to Bangladesh but from my reading, you can get a lot of people in a few kilometers. In South Sudan, the distance between villages is quite long. So then, we cannot have several offices spread all over. Then the system stability will be questionable. The ideal model in microfinance: one branch has to be sustainable.
>
> BRAC may not tell you that, but from our assessment that could be reality. The market is not difficult. In microfinance, say a loan, there is no bad plan, there's only the policies which are really bad. It's how you design the policies that will lead to how your client will respond to your policies. With the right policies, they will follow.

Bangladesh (or Uganda or Kenya, or Tanzania) is not South Sudan. Though BRAC received much praise for the ground-up work it completed over forty years in Bangladesh, part of its success was in its homegrown nature, keeping a finger on the pulse of its own community issues, and problem solving approaches. BRAC had an array of programs, but each was fabricated from the Bangladeshi context. Even Duval, whose prism for success was defined by "outreach and sustainability" (i.e., closer to Washington than Bangladesh) pointed out how, "there was virtually no adaptation of BRAC's microfinance model"[37] in South Sudan. Ironically, the BRAC microcredit model was praised for being adaptive, but failed to do more than apply its one-size-fits-all template, assuming it could reach economic prosperity in any context.

BRAC's holistic social service model was admirable. Its monitoring and evaluation diligence, too, especially compared to its peers who did little, and revealed less. Still, BRAC's microcredit endeavor met its match in the organization's limited, prefabricated options for applying said learning. Governed almost entirely by donors far away, BRAC's options for making adaptive decisions were limited because of the grants it received. The debts were inflexible and the donations were too few to let BRAC field operations behave in the ways they are praised for doing elsewhere. While donors and investors to BRAC must have admired its model, not enough donors came through to realize it.

Finally, in 2012, BRAC had to give up on microcredit in South Sudan. It closed sixteen more lending branches that year, and its strategists resolved to shift from microfinance to targeting adolescent girls and the ultra poor (TUP) models they had from Bangladesh. BRAC's Ultra Poor program has now been gaining traction in recent years around the world. Generally it is seen as a social safety net program, which assists its participants to improve their livelihoods so as to eventually access mainstream development services. In South Sudan, it was a necessary replacement for microcredit in the immediate term. A staff person explained the model as follows:

> In Bangladesh and outside Bangladesh, we have an initiative for those who are ultra poor, who have no capacity or ability to utilize microloan. Through this program, we provide some technical, training and monitoring support to these beneficiaries. Besides this support, we have a safety net project. If they have health incident, education requirement or need food, for that case, we'll give them some support during this project period. That way they won't utilize their capital for their consumption. This way, we will be latching them for two years. Within these two years, we hope they will pick up capital, there we'll test them for setting this objective, then we switch over to microfinance. This is suitable and effective buoy for microfinance in South Sudan.

While the local staff characterized the shift as an issue regarding local capacity deficits, the decision to prescribe the TUP instead of credit demonstrated the organization's unwillingness—and inability—to provide microloans without adequate auxiliary support. According to the BRAC paradigm, lending to borrowers who faced so many shocks that they would not be able to use debt well would be dangerous. In the Juba case, the subsidies required for "real" microcredit were not an option. The bigger picture, as understood by those at the funding helm, painted the constraints of South Sudan combined with the constraints of the total grants available to BRAC. In short, BRAC decision makers found it was easier based on their funding earmarks to offer the Ultra Poor program than expensive credit, but probably not necessarily better.

The BRAC field staff went on to discuss his view of the financial service providers who chose to stay in the South Sudan microcredit industry.

> So far I know that all MFIs are facing loss of programming. And some of these MFIs are not lending microloans; they are providing other loans. Basically, it is not microfinance. As an institution, we cannot do this. We are not a business institution. We like to provide this support in a proper manner, with all loans. Which is why we are thinking to develop a good microfinance model for South Sudan, which will be a sustainable and effective model. You know that BRAC is working with a holistic approach, that's why.

His comments, aligned with the BRAC vision, were razor sharp. Giving loans without proper support, he emphasized, was not microcredit. Business models were not good for the poorest. What became of the remaining Juba microfinance industry was not, by definition, microcredit at all.

TRANSITION TO PROFITS

When the South Sudan microfinance industry donor-investors began evaluating how to surmount the challenges they were facing, they looked to the MFIs that were able to be sustainable without support. The shift in focus overshadowed any remaining poverty-driven approach.

Given its still-unfolding relationship with federal microcredit policy, USAID's chasm between relief and development was growing clearer by its 2009 *Guide to Economic Growth in Post-Conflict Countries* report. It crafted scaffolding for the bifurcation of free aid and loans, by emphasizing the tenets of lending to clients—that loans must be repaid. It also suggested facilitated activities to make clear the distinction between aid and loans.

> When supporting microfinance, donors must ensure that relief services and microfinance services are kept separate. In the immediate aftermath of a conflict, the NGOs supporting MFIs often are the same NGOs that provide humanitarian assistance. This can be a practical arrangement, as these organizations typically are familiar with local clients, enabling them to quickly identify those with the greatest needs. Donors must make it clear, however, that grant assistance should

> never be offered as forgivable loans; this practice can have negative long-term effects on future loan repayment. NGOs providing both microfinance and grants must clearly separate the two activities to avoid confusing clients about their loan repayment obligations.[38]

Though the debates around commercial microcredit increased accountability, the Washington Consensus on Poverty eventually won out. John Owens' 2013 USAID's *Microfinance Experiences over the Past 25 Years* report looked back on its history and surmised the transition to a commercial model has been beneficial overall, even deeming it an evolution:

> After struggling for decades with targeted and directed credit programs for the rural poor and small enterprises, USAID evolved its programs in the late 1980s to focus on specialized microenterprise credit institutions, emphasizing sustainability, better accountability, measurement of progress, and later, cost-effective outreach.[39]

In practice, this meant USAID administrators and allocators shifted attention and finance upstream. No longer interested in subsidizing finance activities, USAID let SUMI go under. USAID refused to support SUMI in the way required in this environment and no other donor came to fill the whole operating gap. This was largely because SUMI's portfolios were tarnished by a host of challenges. Attempts to rectify pitiable performance were focused on the wrong things as most of the blame was directed away from those doing the reflecting. Instead of dealing with the internal problems, the MFIs hedged their bets on *sustainability*.

The rise and fall of SUMI was a consequence of debates and subsequent policies happening in the United States as the neoliberal argument was winning. Any openness to a "gray" area or poverty-focused microcredit narrowed as donors chose sustainability over poverty outreach. There is little reason to believe that there was anything the borrowers or field staff could have done—apart from perfect performance—to convince the agency to choose the latter, and continue the endeavor with the initial inclusive and charitable vision.

By 2012 all signs pointed to USAID becoming more invested in mainstream banking than microcredit. This was seen in how USAID chose to pursue FSSL instead of SUMI, and also in its disbursal of private financing from its Development Credit Authority (DCA) in South Sudan the same year. This was the first time the DCA would be directed to South Sudan since the fund began in 1999.[40] Through the DCA leverage, US$7 million total private capital was mobilized to all the big banks—Equity Bank, Kenya Commercial Bank and Finance South Sudan Limited—serving those better off than the very-poor.

Finance Sudan ascended because of its ultimate commitment to turning profits. It did what it had to do to maintain them. Not only did USAID turn in its direction, but so did other investors who agreed with this commercial microcredit orientation. Mattijs Renden, a Cordaid program officer (FSSL) wrote a piece with his colleagues who were contracted to support Finance Sudan entitled, *The (im)possibility of financial inclusion in South Sudan.* In it, the group echoed a familiar Washington consensus refrain about how "microfinance in post conflict countries is no different from elsewhere in that microfinance institutions should always make their products appropriate to their clients' needs, be vigilant regarding defaults, and work as efficiently as possible to keep costs low." They only saw one real way to do this, anywhere: exclusion. Unsurprisingly, they were sympathetic with how "the challenges in South Sudan forced FSSL to be somewhat less inclusive than it had wished to be and to make extra efforts to make the institution sustainable" agreeing that exclusion of the very poor should take a back seat to sustainability. They then affirmed that FSSL's closure of fledgling branches in northern cities were remedies for when the "costs of loan losses and close monitoring of the branches became too high."[41] Cordaid's logic in support of FSSL, choosing to work with the financial institutions that "ensure that productive financial products are made available to the economically active in a sustainable way"[42] was thus understandable. NGO contractors of a company with shareholders would naturally make such an argument in support of their work.

FSSL grew in prominence such that by the end of the study period, it had leveraged most of the funds that had been previously awarded to institutions such as BRAC and SUMI.[43] How did Finance South Sudan Limited start off on weak foundations and then go on to garner such a massive support base, while the others fell apart? Why did donors give funds to Finance Sudan, and not to the others? I asked the Finance Sudan CEO in 2013. His response was simply: "We have proven to be efficient."

THE OTHER EAGER FINANCIER LURKING IN TOWN

Equity Bank Limited is an important actor to understand in this story because it came to the scene at a later moment and in many ways exemplifies the industry supporters' increasing romance with the profitable finance paradigm. Though Equity established operations in South Sudan in 2009, I had never once understood it to be a microfinance institution, according to the World Bank sector map I had been following for interviews. Instead, it was understood by locals around town to be a full-fledged bank where upper-class entrepreneurs and employed workers deposited wired funds back home to Kenya.

Equity is a Kenyan bank with more than twenty years of experience in mainstream banking and microfinance services. Having faith in the profitable "success" of its model, and in light of its vast portfolio that could hedge risk, it sought to expand its services to neighboring countries by way of a Greenfield investment subsidiary. Having learned from experience when it bought Uganda Microfinance Limited (UML) in 2008, Equity Bank Limited (EBL) recognized that, as one manager interviewed said, "the Equity Bank model doesn't favor acquisition [of other banks]—it's impossible to convert staff and management of an existing institution to our culture."[44] EBL opted therefore to forge greenfield subsidiaries in which it could write its own rules.

According to Duval's report, the Equity endeavor in South Sudan was one of bank's riskier implementations, but also stood to gain the most, given that it had the largest potential demand. Equity established operations according to its model in South Sudan in 2009.[45] Much like the others in the business in South Sudan, Equity faced several major struggles due to the region's independence in 2011, the economic crisis in 2012, and violence in 2013. "In light of this particularly challenging environment, EBL South Sudan has achieved impressive results," judged Duval's analysis.[46] By the end of 2013, EBL South Sudan was profitable and serving close to 86,000 active depositors.[47] It is almost miraculous, especially compared to the relatively peaceful period in which SUMI and BRAC were working. Duval wrote that Equity managed to succeed in this environment where others had failed "by capitalizing on the technological investments and shared services provided by EBL headquarters in Kenya." This was true in part, but such capital also came from many other sources outside of Kenyan business people.

In a 2013 interview with a field manager of the World Bank project, I asked if Equity was dealing in loans. He replied:

> Yes. Equity had a very good chapter to open to South Sudan because of what actually it aims to do. It aims to open the unbankable communities so as to become bankable. We were trying but it has become too costly for us. Because we're not just looking at the current wholesale, retail kind of businesses, we know that those cannot be sustainable. We know that for Equity to be able to grow, we need to have a productive unit on the ground and the only way to do that is to take bigger risk, go to the production areas and spark up production.

Equity had a lot of support in shouldering the high operations costs. Its resulting size was what was needed to facilitate the Bank's agenda for promoting larger businesses on the production chain. The World Bank Group's International Finance Corporation (IFC) announced in March 2012 that it extended a US $100 million loan to Equity Bank Group "to support lending to small and medium businesses, agricultural projects and women entrepreneurs" in various East African countries and including South Sudan.[48]

Investors chose Equity because it made money. UNCDF was also drawn to Equity. MicroLead "took substantial financial risks" in SUMI and Finance Sudan, which Duval characterized as "young unproven" financial service providers (FSPs) in the complex post-conflict country. But there was tremendous appeal in a much less risky choice. "Investments in large, proven commercial entities like Equity Bank, by contrast, offer less financial risk (deep capital pockets, experience, strong governance, established procedures, etc.)."[49] Equity had built a "nice base" by focusing on transactional income (mainly foreign exchange), small-to-medium enterprises (SMEs) doing cross-border trade, banking government employees, entire NGOs, and other "big players."[50] By targeting larger flows, its endeavor proved to be sustainable.

The truth is, Equity is not—and never was—a microcredit agency in Juba. Its South Sudan strategy entailed many other kinds of loan products as it serviced 40 percent more SME loans than microloans, and eighty-three times more consumer loans to salaried employees. Duval noticed the archetypal shift upmarket. She wrote, "if deposit and loan sizes are taken as a proxy for the income level of clients, it would seem that generally loans are provided to a more affluent clientele than are deposit services. This pattern fits with global experience that low-income clients, when presented with appropriate products, prefer to save rather than borrow."[51] That is one way of framing it; saying that low-income clients would prefer not to borrow loans seems to justify an industry shift away from microcredit access for the very poor. While Duval wrote that, "EBL has made an effort to reach the low-income microenterprise sector,"[52] the loans it disbursed ended up being much larger than those provided to typical poor borrowers. Equity furnished a total of ninety-four loans in 2012, whose average size at distribution was a whopping US$1,283.

"Well I wouldn't say microfinance loans. They could be small loans, but they are not microfinance loans," an SSMDF staffer said when I asked about Equity's work in 2012. He had no problem saying as much. This donor intermediary for the Bank can be understood as the local comfort with the shift admonished the industry actors above.

Equity grew. It had its own funding, but also managed to gobble a good share of funding from donors who had previously been financing other MFIs that actually targeted the *very poor*. And despite its extremely large "micro"loans to the less poor, it garnered huge amounts of attention. The bank is ranked highly on CGAP's MIX Market website, which is a guide to potential donors who are trying to find "good" microcredit providers to invest in. According to the site, Equity is meant to promote financial inclusion for the poor and anyone else who is investing. What would be unclear to this audience, however, is whether the investment in Equity will likely turn a return (yes) or whether it is offering holistic microcredit options to the poor in Juba (no).

AND THE FALL . . .

This book began with two dominating MFIs that comprised over ninety percent of the microcredit market. They were the largest, and initially held missions to serve the poorest populations, many from post-conflict regions. Neither of them are lending today. SUMI operators closed their doors because their capital fund was starved by their donors; BRAC withdrew its credit services in favor of TUP ultra-poor social support services for the same reason, even if the process was slightly different. What began as the smallest MFI in Juba became the last MFI of the first three standing to continue lending, and it is also the largest in the industry today.[53]

The microcredit industry moved upstream—or up market. In response to pressure from the neoliberal mindset in the West, MFIs became mainstream banks. They shifted to targeting the more well-off borrowers rather than the very poor who urgently needed the services the most. What loan capital SUMI had once accessed soon shifted to Finance South Sudan and Equity, profiteers with loans too large and too expensive for very poor entrepreneurs. Less poor borrowers received larger loans.[54] Those funding the Juba MFIs cast their votes for this shift. The poorest left behind were intended to be caught by a subsidized safety net, but only if they were lucky enough to receive access. This was hardly guaranteed. Social services were again reduced to being the only appropriate option for the poor.

USAID devised a haphazard MFI with SUMI and did not provide enough support for it to succeed in offering microcredit to the poorest as first intended. It could have better provided support for MIS, external evaluation, and product modifications (i.e., modified loan schedules), among other needed improvements. It was unsurprising that SUMI could not rationalize scarce taxpayer funds to meet both its outreach goals (number of borrowers) and solvent rates of return payments. When SUMI chose the latter, its program died, and USAID swiftly redirected its support to an MFI with a less

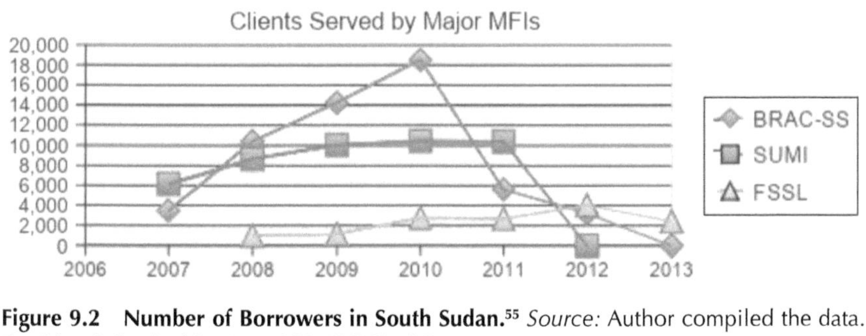

Figure 9.2 Number of Borrowers in South Sudan.[55] *Source:* Author compiled the data. Frankfurt School of Business/ SSMDF Final Report 2013.

costly business model directed to borrowers that were financially better off. Though SUMI professed interest in poverty lending in its messaging and marketing, USAID politics got in the way, and the supporters of the MFI were not willing to take the risk with their investments to accomplish its original ambitious agenda.

If any one MFI should have made the poverty lending approach work in Juba, it would have been BRAC. BRAC was an organization that was, in principle, committed to unveiling a holistic microcredit model that could adapt to circumstance and had the strongest research unit from which it could do this. BRAC also had the broadest set of program strategies to try out, and a staff generally ready to apply the broader organizational ethos in practice. However, BRAC's holistic program models were still not supported well enough to be flexible in a new setting.

BRAC International's charitable grants had their limits, too, and they soon ran out. Its investors became increasingly interested in commercial returns that would come from market-based policies, and had strict expectations. None were willing to subsidize the work necessary to achieve true microcredit that serves the very poor. The same ideological preference toward commercialization, or against the gray zone, showed itself for BRAC, just later in the sequence than for the other MFIs. BRAC's commitment, too, was undercut by the black and white binary.

Constraints from above kept the Juba microfinance industry from living up to its promises to help the poor on the ground. MFIs could not experiment and modify to the extent that the context demanded them to in order to succeed. I will show in the next chapter how these MFI ideological shifts in South Sudan specifically paralleled the broader global picture in the "battle for the soul of microfinance." Contrary to the perception by many spectators, the particular post-conflict challenges in Juba appear less to blame than the guiding supporters' power to wield their desires away from aid and toward commercial

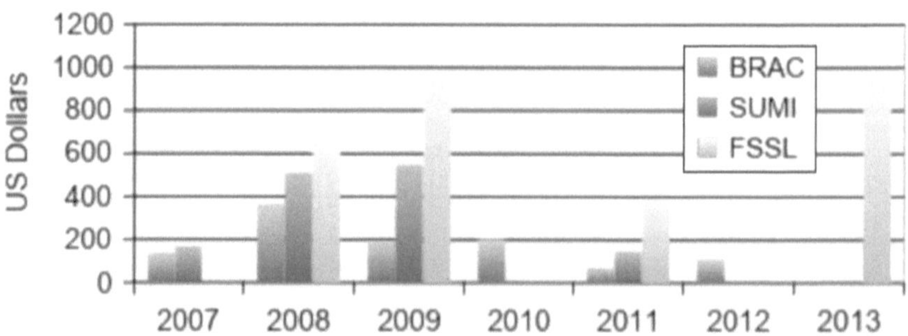

Figure 9.3 Average Loan Size of Three Principle MFIs.[56] *Source:* Author compiled the data. Frankfurt School of Business/ SSMDF Final Report 2013.

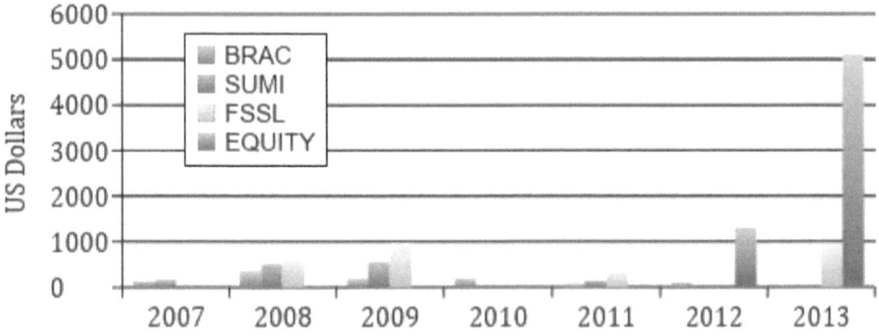

Figure 9.4 Average Loan Size, Three Principle MFIs Plus Equity.[57] *Source:* Author compiled the data. Frankfurt School of Business/ SSMDF Final Report 2013.

banking. Juba's post-conflict features—its strange market, nascent state and local governance, so-called dependent community, and fragmented social networks—were merely scapegoats; MFIs should have invested and adapted to address these complexities, not just run away from them.

NOTES

1. Josh Leon, "Poverty Capitalism: Interview with Ananya Roy." *Foreign Policy in Focus* (2011).
2. See Karen Doyle, *Microfinance in the Wake of Conflict: Challenges and Opportunities* (Washington, DC: USAID, 1998).Geetha Nagarajan, *Microfinance in Post-Conflict Situations: Towards Guiding Principles for Action* (Geneva: ILO, 1999).
3. Conflict broke out in South Sudan in December 2013.
4. Karen Doyle, *Microfinance in the Wake of Conflict: Challenges and Opportunities* (Washington, DC: USAID, 1998).
5. Patience Alidri, et al., Introduction to Microfinance In Conflict-Affected Communities: A Training Manual (International Labour Organization and United Nations High Commissioner for Refugees, 2002), 18.
6. Tasmin Wilson, "Microfinance During and After Armed Conflict: Lessons From Angola, Cambodia, Mozambique And Rwanda" (Concern Worldwide & The Springfield Centre For Business In Development, 2002) found how lenders in Cambodia were willing to accept various forms of payment and quantities of interest. Mozambique had a variety of microcredit offerings supplied, particularly in urban areas.
7. Chemonics International, *Sudan Agricultural Enterprise Finance Program Final Report* (USAID, 2008), 5.
8. Chemonics International, *Sudan Agricultural Enterprise Finance Program Final Report* (USAID, 2008), 18.

9. I noticed the same "success story" of a woman named Esther appeared in almost every USAID report on its South Sudanese microfinance endeavors, even after SUMI had closed its doors.

10. Chemonics International, *Sudan Agricultural Enterprise Finance Program Final Report* (USAID, 2008), 37.

11. Chemonics International, *Sudan Agricultural Enterprise Finance Program Final Report* (USAID, 2008), 38.

12. The Frankfurt School of Management, *Southern Sudan Microfinance Development Facility (SSMDF)—Final Report* (Juba: South Sudan Microfinance Development Facility, 2011).

13. Chemonics International, *Sudan Agricultural Enterprise Finance Program Final Report* (USAID, 2008).

14. Sudan Watch, "MicroSave-Africa - USAID Sponsors Southern Sudan's First Microfinance Conference." *Sudan Watch* (2010).

15. SSMDF contributed $10,000 USD "discussed actions that needed to be taken to ensure increased outreach and sustainability of the microfinance sector in Southern Sudan." (Frankfurt School of Management, *Southern Sudan Microfinance Development Facility (SSMDF)—Final Report* (2011), 25). No other contribution amounts were shared.

16. USAID, Sudan Monthly Update, July 2010.

17. A CGAP, UNDP and DFID initiative.

18. USAID, Sudan Monthly Update, July 2010.

19. Sudan Watch, "MicroSave-Africa - USAID Sponsors Southern Sudan's First Microfinance Conference." *Sudan Watch* (blog) (2010).

20. Also: UNCDF and UNDP put in $4 million USD budget for 2010–2013.

21. UNDP, "Building an Inclusive Financial Sector in Southern Sudan" Project Document. 2010.

22. UNDP, "Building an Inclusive Financial Sector in Southern Sudan" Project Document. 2010.

23. UNCDF, "UNCDF in South Sudan." UNCDF, South Sudan, n.d.

24. Julius N. Uma, "South Sudan: 10,000 Micro-businesses at Risk of Collapse." *Sudan Tribune* (2010).

25. Frankfurt School of Management, *Southern Sudan Microfinance Development Facility—Final Report* (Juba: South Sudan Microfinance Development Facility, 2011), 21.

26. Frankfurt School of Management, *Southern Sudan Microfinance Development Facility—Final Report* (Juba: South Sudan Microfinance Development Facility, 2011).

27. According to the 2012 Emergency Project Paper on a Proposed Grant to the Republic of South Sudan, The World Bank Financial and Private Sector Development, "Business Plan Competition (BPC) for existing businesses and start-ups. A total of US$4 million will be earmarked to support 200 entrepreneurs with sub-grants in the amount of US$20,000 to be used as block collateral for loans provided by commercial banks. Another US$0.4 million will be allocated for the preparation, technical assistance and M&E for the BPC. Under this component, some of the loans

will be used to finance activities across different sectors such as light manufacturing, services, poultry farms, and agriculture."

28. According to the report, stakeholders included the Ministry of Commerce, the implementing agency Industry and Investment as MFIs and their clients, BPC winners, and the GOSS in general.

29. World Bank, "Project Information Document (PID) Appraisal Stage: *Private Sector Development Project Report* (2011).

30. Linked In, "Finance South Sudan Limited LinkedIn Profile." Linked In, Finance South Sudan, n.d.

31. ACDI/VOCA, "South Sudan." *ACDI/VOCA* pamphlet, (2013).

32. Mattijs Renden, et al., "The (im)possibility of Financial Inclusion in South Sudan." *The Broker* (2013).

33. Frankfurt School of Management, *Southern Sudan Microfinance Development Facility (SSMDF) – Final Report* (Juba: South Sudan Microfinance Development Facility, 2011).

34. Courtesy of BRAC.

35. Whereas BRAC closed the South Sudan microfinance program altogether, it "significantly retract[ed] operations in Sierra Leone and Liberia." Ann Duval, *Microfinance Greenfields In Challenging Environments: BRAC's Experience In Three Post-Conflict Countries In Africa* (UN Capital Development Fund, 2015).

36. Ann Duval, *Microfinance Greenfields In Challenging Environments: BRAC's Experience In Three Post- Conflict Countries In Africa* (UN Capital Development Fund, 2015), 7.

37. Ann Duval, *Microfinance Greenfields In Challenging Environments: BRAC's Experience In Three Post- Conflict Countries In Africa* (UN Capital Development Fund, 2015), 7.

38. USAID, *Guide to Economic Growth in Post-Conflict Countries,* 2009.

39. John Owens "Studying the Past, Looking to the Future: USAID's Microfinance Experiences over the Past 25 Years: An Impression from the Field." *USAID's Microfinance Consortium,* (2014).

40. USAID, "USAID and Banks Launch Partnership To Expand Farmers' Access To Credit In South Sudan." *Press Release* (2012).

41. Mattijs Renden, et al., "The (im)possibility of Financial Inclusion in South Sudan." *The Broker* (2013).

42. It also selected Rural Finance Initiative (RUFI). RUFI was such a small MFI during the study period that, while I did meet a couple of its borrowers, I did not get to trace its staff or history.

43. BRAC's funding was predominately from its own fountain. However, some of their funding was coming from UNCDF and Internet philanthropists, via Kiva. When I refer to available funding, I mean those latter two sources, which were, when BRAC chose to focus its efforts on the TUP program, allocated instead to FSSL.

44. Ann Duval, *Increasing Financial Inclusion in East Africa: Equity Bank's Agent-Driven Model* (Microlead, UN Capital Development Fund, 2014).

45. Ann Duval, *Increasing Financial Inclusion in East Africa: Equity Bank's Agent-Driven Model* (Microlead, UN Capital Development Fund, 2014).

46. Ann Duval, *Increasing Financial Inclusion in East Africa: Equity Bank's Agent-Driven Model* (Microlead, UN Capital Development Fund, 2014), 2–3.

47. Operational self-sufficiency, according to Duval 2014, was 128 percent.

48. Neha Sud, *Equity Bank Group and IFC Team up to Expand Access to Finance in East Africa* (Washington, DC: International Finance Corporation, 2012).

49. UNCDF, "UNCDF in South Sudan." (2013), 26.

50. Interview with EBL Senior Manager in headquarters cited in Duval 2014.

51. Ann Duval, *Increasing Financial Inclusion in East Africa: Equity Bank's Agent-Driven Model* (Microlead, UN Capital Development Fund, 2014), 8 acknowledged that,"there is no clear correlation between loan size and economic status of the borrowers."

52. Ann Duval, *Increasing Financial Inclusion in East Africa: Equity Bank's Agent-Driven Model* (Microlead, UN Capital Development Fund, 2014).

53. Data Sources: Dec 2012–2014 active borrowers (MIX); Dec 2012–2013 GLP MFI Data, BRAC-SS Annual Reports 2007–2013; 2009–2011 Frankfurt School of Business/ SSMDF Final Report 2013, UNCDF Microlink.

54. The commercialization processes can be observed by loan size amounts, whereby larger loan averages mean less poor people are reached. See, for example: Robert Cull et al., "Financial Performance and Outreach: A Global Analysis of Leading Microbanks." *The Economic Journal*, (2007). Some, like Beatriz Marulanda and María Otero, "The Profile of Microfinance in Latin America in Ten Years: Vision & Characteristics." (*Boston MA: ACCION International*, 2005), have dissented that evolved borrowers with good payments and then larger loans can conflate the math. While very possible elsewhere, those moderators seem highly unlikely in Juba. Only half of Juba borrowers continued for two or more group loans, with unchanging terms. Only four percent of borrowers took four loans, and completing five was the benchmark for graduating. No borrowers I interviewed had "graduated" to individual loans.

55. Data Sources: Dec 2012–2014 active borrowers (MIX); Dec 2012–2013 GLP MFI Data, BRAC-SS Annual Reports 2007–2013; 2009–2011 Frankfurt School of Business/SSMDF Final Report 2013, UNCDF Microlink.

56. Data Sources Dec 2012–2014 active borrowers (MIX); Dec 2012–2013 GLP MFI Data, BRAC-SS Annual Reports 2009–2013; 2009–2011 Frankfurt School of Business/SSMDF Final Report 2013, UNCDF Microlink.

57. Data Sources Dec 2012–2014 active borrowers (MIX); Dec 2012–2013 GLP MFI Data, BRAC-SS Annual Reports 2009–2013; 2009–2011 Frankfurt School of Business/SSMDF Final Report 2013, UNCDF Microlink.

Conclusion

Can We Learn From the Parable of South Sudan?

Practitioners, supporters, and observers wrote off Juba as a failure of the post-conflict scenario. The Juba post-conflict context entailed several features, namely: the demographic disruption associated with the return of refugees, internally displaced persons, capitalists, and aid workers hailing from fragmented social networks created largely outside the country during the conflict; the institutional changes associated with nascent state and local governance, nascent legal frameworks, and reliance on international actors for social services; the high costs associated with rebuilding deteriorated physical infrastructure, including buildings and accessible roads; and the unequal access to resources and opportunity amongst Juba citizens.

What these post-conflict features meant for the fate of microcredit ultimately depended on the theorist's perspective. Such perspectives were shaped by an array of interests, ideological favoritisms and knowledge networks. Ideas that resulted had very visible consequences for populations in Juba, and the microcredit industry at large.

The field-level institutional practitioners had three main theories about how the Juba post-conflict features affected microcredit being conducted there. The first was that the borrowers lacked the necessary social capital to make payments. The second was that the borrowers had too much of a dependency ethos. And the third was that the market was too troubled for borrowers altogether. The fact that the industry generally did not theorize about the role of institutions or inequality is consistent with the microcredit culture; the focus on the individual, financial unit of analysis largely precludes concern with addressing the structural causes of poverty.

According to the commercially minded practitioners, supporters, and observers of microcredit, offering loans to the very poor became impossible in South Sudan early on principally due to the high costs and demographic disruption. This included factors such as long distances between offices, the high costs of travel, and market instability. It was very expensive to operate an MFI in Juba. Likewise, these local market configurations stacked the odds against the borrowers. There were multiple regions involved, absence of local industry, import dependence, unpredictable trade circuits, the currency exchange market, and the tough client competition associated with the population influx. In this depiction, borrowers simply did not have the capacity to manage such macro level complexities.

From this industry vantage, certain social factors worsened the situation further, such as the varied meanings of money and work, the levels of exposure to finance and entrepreneurship, and the newly reformulating social networks. If social ties and social practices did not contribute to payments and the other desired capitalist outcomes, many argued that there was not enough social capital and not enough spirit of independence present among the borrowers, which threatened the MFIs' solvency. The industry personnel regarded social issues as impediments.

Together these economic and social challenges compromised the success of micro-entrepreneur businesses, and caused too few borrowers to make satisfactory payments. In the end, the creditors' balance sheets were negative. Cost covering and poverty outreach became mutually exclusive. The banks then switched their primary goal to cost covering, leaving poverty outreach behind.

The end of Juba microcredit was warranted in the commercial paradigm, but a more holistic-minded analysis shows that the industry departure was premature. Unlike the industry analyses outlined above, this text revealed that there might have been more possibility for microcredit success than this industry vantage allowed it to see.

Furthermore, this theory argues that the failure of South Sudanese microcredit primarily grew out of the ill-suited program boundaries, which were buttressed by ideological biases originating faraway. The top MFIs delivered products that they had designed elsewhere. The MFIs offered varieties of credit that did not match many borrowers' demands. The credit programs were brought in from abroad, and the MFIs expected that the social norms and economic opportunities that made them function elsewhere would be present in Juba. They were not. Juba is not Dhaka. South Sudan is not Bangladesh. It is not Afghanistan or Mozambique. The postwar dynamics differed greatly from other microcredit contexts.

This book showed several critical flashpoints wherein the delivered models did not anticipate Juba's postwar particularities. For instance, while industry observers assumed that social capital would be destroyed after the war, I showed in chapters 5 and 6 that social ties were very much present, but that they functioned differently than the industry training had allowed them to anticipate. Chapter 5 demonstrated that wartime diaspora networks ended up shaping which borrowers entered loan programs, and which borrowers were left out of them. Chapter 6 discussed the processes by which borrowers created trust and converted it locally. In particular, it found that trust evolved through experience and that borrowers often sought to protect social bonds even at the expense of economic success. Chapter 7 showed the extent to which the postwar market influenced prospects for microcredit businesses, but also highlighted the social and economic temporalities that had hampered the using the debt well. In short, there were ways in which microcredit may have worked out—and worked out well—if certain accommodations had been made.

The replicated models should have been responsive enough to accommodate to the complexities of social ties in the group formation process, the composition of borrower enterprises, and the specific ways co-borrowers received payments from one another. The field practitioners could have been able to accommodate the patchy social networks created during the war and work to expand outreach more evenly, if they had been given the chance to do so. As it was, for instance, the MFIs had no resources to support the borrowers who experienced social sanctions against getting co-borrowers to pay one another back. The MFIs also had no specific program for the unusually high fraction of total borrowers engaged in retail trade. Adapting was difficult.

The tailored, personalized work required for microcredit in Juba was costly by nature. But policy changes on the ground required approval from distant headquarters, and the ship was beholden to the strategies laid down many thousands of miles away. There was no room to develop the meaningful financial instruments to accommodate the particular demands because industry supporters were unable to look beyond the standard commercial model. The funding to support any new policy likewise was dependent upon actors very distant from the field.

Despite the volition of poverty-concerned theorists and practitioners, austerity was the mandate laid down by those sending the capital. It was problematic that the debt was inflexible. When given, the subsidies attempting to smoothen the gap between borrower capacity and loan terms were too little or too late. Technical assistance grants from the major backers were limited to improving in-house matters (like staff incentives), not toward client investments (like reduced interest rates). In this context, the price of debt owed by the MFIs and the costs of purchasing credit only escalated over time. This laid the burden at the feet of borrowers, and the borrowers could not or did not want to pay up.

The material consequence was that microcredit became a misnomer in Juba as fewer micro loans were issued to the poorest segment of the population. Loans grew larger, more expensive, and more difficult for the poorest to attain. The little loan product differentiation that was done by the MFIs was far from sufficient; it made the loans more expensive and less inclusive.

Despite beginning their programs with different ideal ways to procure credit, both SUMI and BRAC were ultimately hamstrung by debts that could not accept losses. The Juba industry supporters responded to the post-conflict circumstances by either moving upstream to better off customers, or abandoning credit provision altogether in exchange for other safety net approaches. Instead of directly addressing the challenges of financing poor entrepreneurs in Juba, the practitioners with power gave up. Practitioners gave up on upwards of some forty thousand business-owning poor people, and left behind the population they had philosophically set out to serve. And these borrowers did not have a chance to put the lessons they learned to use once the industry turned its attention away.

JUBA, WHERE THE BANGLADESH CONSENSUS AGREED WITH THE WASHINGTON CONSENSUS

While Juba's postwar particularities were unique in many ways, they were not an isolated departure from financing the poor. We must understand the Juba case as an example of a larger, global industry struggle.

The practicalities of market-based profit incentives were enmeshed in the ongoing debates about who the ideal microfinance clients are. In her 2001 book, *The Microfinance Revolution*, Marguerite Robinson drew a line in the sand that Ananya Roy called indelible. She elaborated upon Hulme and Mosley's 1996 delineation of eligible borrowers, describing them as people who had "the existence of a reliable income, freedom from pressing debt, sufficient health to avoid incapacitating illness, freedom from imminent contingencies and sufficient resources (such as savings, non-essential convertible assets and social entitlements) to cope with problems when they arise."[1] Robinson's "economically active poor" furthermore included "people who have achieved some but not necessarily all of these benchmarks, who have marketable skills or control over earning assets—and who are or could become creditworthy borrowers and savers in commercial financial institutions."[2] This book was published by the World Bank. As a leading voice for the commercial camp, Robinson argued that lending to the "extremely poor" would require subsidies, which she described to be as senseless as "trying to build a house by using a saw to hammer the nails and a screwdriver to cut the boards."[3] Instead, the poor below her threshold "should not be the responsibility of the financial sector. The food, employment, and other basic requirements needed to overcome desperate poverty are appropriately financed by government and donor subsidies and grants. These tools are properly the responsibility of ministries of health, labor, social welfare, and others, as well as of donor agencies and private charities."[4] Practitioners all over the world applied Robinson's framework, and it had little resemblance to the previously advocated notion that the poor could (or should) be entrepreneurial with a dose of capital. In fact, such a framework opposed the possibility, and entailed another leap of faith that safety nets for such people would indeed be cast without setting up practical policy that guarantees as much. This industry chasm only grew over time.

The side taking highlighted the quest for a clear if not reductionist framework. The "indelible line" became the "fork in the road," as Sam Daley-Harris said in an interview. "Resources for developing microfinance are limited," wrote Robinson, "and donors and governments must choose among options if microfinance services are to be made available to all who can use them."[5] Robinson's view held that the more commercial the services, the more efficient the business; she figured this would make the outreach greater. The Washington Consensus on poverty eventually interpreted subsidized finance as what Ananya Roy described as the "pollution of free money."[6] It encouraged the idea that only black or white strategies were palatable to donors. Market or charity. Loan capital or free donations. No gray. Thus began the dissent of the possibility of hybrid, holistic, subsidized, or impact-first microcredit.

Around the world, microfinance has moved away from its original promise to equip the poor towards a more formulaic and less accessible commercial enterprise. This book is the story of South Sudanese microcredit, but it parallels the broader story concerning the trends of the MFI industry in recent years. In 2011, Juba microlending to the poor deteriorated just as this was happening in several other regions around the globe. The Microcredit Summit Campaign, which advocated for ensuring the poorest individuals received finance by tracking their share of the microcredit pie, revealed a sign of defeat beginning in 2011. Though the amount of investment in microcredit has been growing at a stable rate,[7] the sum of poor borrowers declined for the first time in the existence of the 13-year campaign. There were fewer borrowers altogether, but the decline occurred among the poorest clients.[8]

This was a worldwide trend that only got worse. The 2015 Microcredit Summit Campaign Report showed how microfinance expenditure bounced back overall, but the attention to the poorest did not. It dropped from 138 million down to 114 million borrowers.[9] If 2004 was the year that had the closest ratio of poorest to total borrowers at 73 percent worldwide, the gap widened to its largest at 54 in 2013. Loans grew larger while far fewer poor people had received them.[10]

The Microcredit Summit Campaign did significant amounts of theorizing to explain the global decline in poverty lending. Its 2013 and 2015 reports

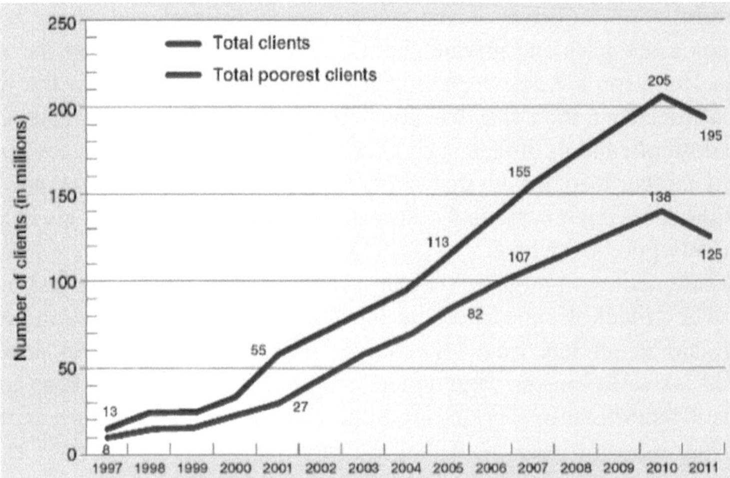

Figure 10.1 Global Number Borrowers and Poorest Borrowers, 1997–2011. *Source:* Larry R. Reed, Lisa Laegreid Gatti, and Anna Awimbo, Vulnerability: the state of the microcredit summit campaign report, Microcredit Summit Campaign, (2013).

held that backlash from the Andhra Pradesh crisis in India accounted for most of the reduction in poor clients worldwide. The headlines on over-lending and harsh collection practices precipitated a significant swath of funding pulled away from the banking industry as a whole. Another set of analysts wrote

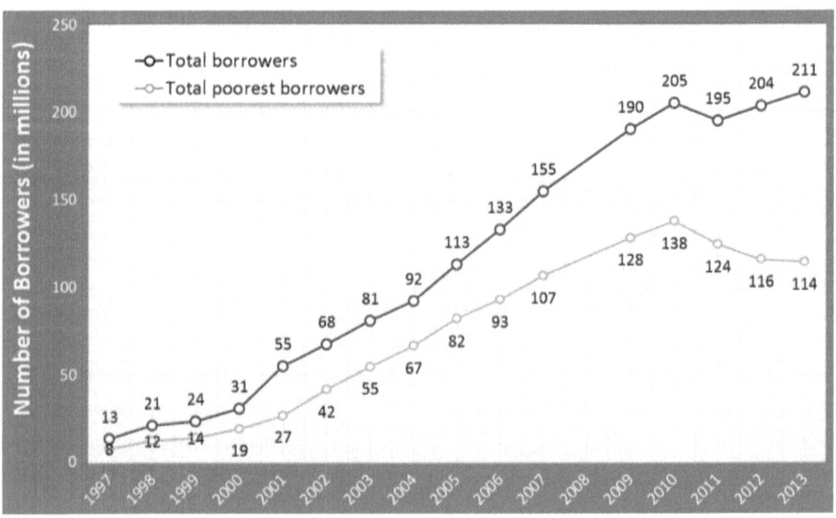

Figure 10.2 Global Number Borrowers and Poorest Borrowers, 1997–2013. *Source:* Larry R. Reed, State of the Campaign Report, State of the Campaign, (2015).

that the India crisis thereby "made borrowing expensive."[11] MFIs thus had to garner new capital and pass the costs elsewhere; many MFI portfolios lost returns, while others moved upmarket to clients that could better afford the debt burden. Most agreed that microfinance needed to ensure that lending practices do not become so dangerous looking ahead.

The data collected has been an indication of priorities held by the industry's power holders. The 2015 Report also highlighted how "patchy information" made it "hard to see which markets are overheating until it is too late." The question of which data can explain microfinance health has been an ongoing part of the debate and in turn, the practice. The authors argued that a myopic focus on measuring profit was impeding outreach to the poor: "For many years, the indicators used to measure microfinance performance have focused on numbers of clients and the sustainability or profitability of the institutions that reach them. These indicators tell us little about whether we are achieving the real aim of microfinance—helping people lift themselves out of poverty. Without tools to measure our ultimate ends, we satisfy ourselves by measuring our means instead."[12] It is easy to measure progress with financial, quantitative metrics, but much more difficult to measure it in qualitative terms that reflect the lives of borrowers. Likewise, conflating profitability with borrowers' well-being misses the mark entirely. In this way, the wrong metrics propagated ignorance about the details.

The BRAC Blog reported on the trend, too. The post argued that the body of microcredit data was actually getting richer and helped MFIs identify what was working. It even cited South Sudan as an example of where the NGO was "actually scaling down lending in some markets where we found it simply wasn't effective."[13] My prior knowledge of the case led me to read the post-mortem statement like a chicken-and-egg problem: Did the microfinance loans not reach the poorest people because the loans did not work, or did the loans not work because they were not being dispensed correctly?

Practical challenges haunted the reduction too. Not unlike the case of South Sudan, the Microcredit Summit Campaign speculated that investors had grown warier of risky markets serving the poorest. The next culprit was interrelated, donor fatigue: "less funding is coming in for groups that may need subsidies to build sustainable programs to reach poorer and more remote clients." Donors—a great many of whom are indeed return-seeking investors, but even those drawn to the ideological commitment of sustainability under the neoliberal paradigm—became tired of reaching the poor who offered smaller margins, and the market offered "few rewards" to the MFIs that did reach poorer, more remote clients. Such clients were costlier, in fact. The report suggested herd mentality also came into play, whereby MFIs opted to operate predominantly in locations where other MFIs already had done the "due diligence" and developed the market. In short, through a commercial perspective, the industry had understandable reasons to shy away from its most challenging clientele.

This commercial camp is gaining traction around the world. The commercial finance paradigm championed by actors such as the Washington, DC, agencies and the World Bank, presents itself as banking faithfully on the idea that the trickle-down effect will create opportunities for the poorest, eventually. To such actors, working directly with the poorest in this way is a lost cause. To such actors, commercializing as like what happened in Juba represents a healthy bloodletting that allows financiers to reach more and better prospects—even if they were not the very poor. However, not everyone shares the excitement.

Unsurprisingly, advocates of the poverty lending approach, like Sam Daley-Harris' RESULTs team and the Microcredit Summit Campaign, are critical of the commercial turn. Their worries are grounded in a fundamental faith that credit can help alleviate poverty, and should thus be inclusive of the poorest borrowers. Others have concerns regarding the effects of commercializing. For instance, some Marxist political economists might consider this an instance of the "financialization" of neoliberalism,[14] or the "increasing scope and prevalence" of interest bearing capital. This logic believes that its very nature enriches lenders as it "extract[s] its surplus (or interest) prior to the distribution of the remaining surplus across other capitals."[15] Thus, the expansion of commercial microcredit in Juba might be seen like any capitalist accumulative process; it widens the gap between classes, and can lead to crisis and recession.[16] Milford Bateman, drawing on the example of Bolivia's microcredit commercialization, warns that the process can create speculative bubbles and further saturate the "bazaar economy" instead of promoting long-term development via larger scale industrial support and locally adapted credit approaches.[17]

Juba is one of many cases that has revealed a deepening chasm in the microcredit industry whereby ideological intentions and material interests have pressured the industry to become more commercialized. Three chapters of this book in particular examined the degree to which certain ideologies gave way to concrete changes within Juba. Chapter 4, *Blueprints and Architects*, traced the intentions underlying the South Sudanese microcredit endeavor and its material scaffolding. It showed how the major MFIs, though originating in different locations, had begun with similar, lofty aspirations for responsibly providing credit to poor people. Several chapters discussed the ways in which practitioners were conditioned to blame the post-conflict ecosystem for the industry's failure. Meanwhile, chapter 8 focused on the particularly near-sighted theory that postwar borrowers themself were to blame for their circumstances. Chapter 9, *Autopsy*, instead traced the Juba microcredit industry's demise as happening when the largest industry supporters ultimately turned to more profitable investment vehicles. Ultimately, the Juba microfinance institutions were beholden to their own internal systemic dependencies, including their debt ratings, performance requirements from headquarters, and limited metrics for success. While supporters of microcredit were drawn to it from different ideological vantages, the most powerful voices ultimately overrode the demands coming from program participants themselves.

The Juba industry analysts blame the failure of microcredit in Juba on the region's complex post-conflict social-economy. However, I posit that these complexities were merely a scapegoat, and that the failure was instead due to the industry's profound resistance to invest in the work of listening to the demands on the ground and tailoring their approach accordingly. This negligence points to an ideological transformation in the industry in which business interests and the false notion of a finance-assistance binary won over the initial intention to provide inclusive support. While some detractors might say that Juba's postwar complexities were even more extreme than in other post-conflict societies and therefore too difficult to work with—perhaps the currency is more inflated, or the security more tenuous than in other cases—this begs the question, why set out on the mission in the first place?

RE-ENVISIONING MICROFINANCE FOR POST-CONFLICT ENVIRONMENTS

Wherever the poor are losing financial services, including in post-conflict contexts, microcredit must be "gray" in order to live up to its name. Compared with the commercial rates, this will be costlier for purveyors, and ideally cheaper for users. Relieved of the burdens of cost covering or profit earning, the benefits of microloans would still almost certainly be cheaper for the donors than direct aid alone. The central call to this action comes, perhaps ironically, from backers of Finance Sudan (the commercialized MFI that lured much of the industry support). The aim "to reach all people in need of appropriate and affordable financial products" according to Renden *et al.*, "cannot be achieved in just a few years. . . . For an investor, this requires both a long-term vision and the ability to accept losses."[18] In order for microcredit to work for borrowers in challenging places like Juba, therefore, the industry must be willing to spend more of both subsidies and time to support the right kinds of accommodations.

Genuine microcredit is attractive to supporters who believe that the poor are better served by an approach that is responsive to the input of the population served, and is strategically long-term in its outlook. It is for those who can stomach revision and let go of the idea of a one-size-fits-all template for doing business with poor people. Indeed, as the writers of the ILO/UNHCR curriculum made clear: "Relief organisations can learn about microfinance and adjust to its practice. Adjustments also have to be made in the practice of traditional microfinance to make it more suitable for the specific environments of conflict-affected communities."[19]

The "best practice paradigm is a fallacy," writes Morten Jerven.[20] A one-size-fits-all recommendation is inappropriate. Standardized programming, while efficient to roll out, cannot automatically supply the exact products that are needed in an enduring fashion. Generalizable impact assessment frameworks similarly cannot observe clients' complex individual, social, and economic demands. Both the financial tools delivered by practitioners, and the evaluations of them, must reflect the will of the people being served. Microcredit practitioners must improve upon both.

Post-conflict microcredit is not for the faint of heart, but it is for anyone who acknowledges that the poor want to make use of loans for their businesses in the recovery period. Indeed, there were a good number of poor borrowers who themselves felt the programs were useful overall; while they did not escape poverty, they nevertheless saw utility. And despite the many problems borrowers experienced in South Sudan, they also relayed many signs that these programs could succeed with the right changes and support. Many post-conflict entrepreneurs in Juba took pride in participating in it, and would have taken on more debt if the MFIs had altered the financial services to accommodate their demands. Former borrower determinations like these showed that they were market savvy enough to know that the offered program design offered less help to them than they would have going alone. These were "economically active" entrepreneurs that had the attitude that even the commercial microcredit approach philosophically seeks to enhance. These were successes upon which reflexive programs should have been built, not left behind.

It is a reasonable proposition that while the industry learns from its mistakes, so too do clients. Both should be afforded the opportunity to become more adept at retailing their goods in the local articulations of the post-conflict economy. There were many program features that could have been tailored and tested if the Juba industry had had the funds and wherewithal to realize them.

BETTER VISION BEGS BETTER DATA

If Juba is an indication of the global transfiguration toward commercial microcredit, the problem is that it falters on material interests justified by rhetoric that is theory driven, rather than on evidence that reflects what the poorest users said they needed. The global microfinance industry raised billions of dollars and heaps of praise by touting the industriousness of the poor, the autonomy the loans provided, and the responsibility they required. Indeed, these so-called empowering qualities were among the core rationale for introducing credit to stimulate the postwar economy in the first place. What is the vision for helping the poor now?

Ideas from practitioners about who the poor are and what they think they need should not matter. In other words, the driving ideologies from faraway should not override the demands from the ground. Instead, what the poor themselves say they need is more crucial than ever. Practitioners must attend to the poor's actual prospects for doing business and the specific challenges they want to overcome. This includes agency introspection as to why some want their products in the first place, why some want to continue but cannot, and why some leave frustrated. The practitioner community can stand to build services from the ground up in ways that are responsive to borrower demand. By suggesting that failed borrowers (including both those who failed to meet the loan terms and those who were failed by the vanishing lenders) should simply move back into the safety net needing populace, policymakers ignore the possibilities of everything in between.

Through subsidies, post-conflict microcredit will inevitably have more room to achieve goals that go beyond the financial metric. A microfinance industry committed to inclusion that promotes well-being for its clientele for all strata of a society, not just the better off, will have a fundamentally different set of criteria for moving forward. Freed from the cost-covering confines of commercial microcredit in such regions, the MFI mission could reorient to what possibilities remain for "fair and affordable" financial services.[21] There, agencies can promote both individual and social well-being. Such an effort is worth the investment.

A post-conflict microcredit that can be useful, and eventually sustainable, to its users must incorporate client voices. Part of the reformation will require leaving ideologies at the door in favor of evidence. This will entail shifting the question from what poor people *should* need to what they actually *ask for.* A robust research-based, demand-driven post-conflict microcredit requires an ear to the ground not just in terms of monitoring payments but also to the experiences of participants.

The common industry indicators will miss important facts on the ground. So long as the only microfinance institutional goal is repayment, evaluations will be limited to finance issues at the institutional unit of analysis. SUMI's learned obsession with getting an MIS was an example of the quest for accountability measures, and one that I agree was important. But surveillance on payments did little for the MFI without understanding the trials that clients struggled against. Moreover, the metrics of success must include not just economic gain, but also social well-being.

Researchers should try to attain as many records as are available. I recognize that even my retelling aspects of the borrower experience vis-à-vis the story arch of the industry transformation, was limited. This study was also limited by the scarce data collected by the participating MFIs. Even as I critique the limited prescriptive value of repayment rates, the math matters. Eventually, the necessarily gray poverty microfinance will need to reckon with the viable thresholds between zero (aid) and 100 percent return on investment (ROI). MFIs cannot afford to wait until later stages to collect data.

Focusing on a unique, situational approach to needs assessment is key. Post-conflict societies may share some general features, but are nonetheless different from one another and should be treated as such. Researchers and practitioners can benefit from understanding the worldview of each community on its own terms without injudiciously applying insights from or to other communities who have their own unique challenges and worldviews. Findings from one venue will seldom be entirely applicable to others. For example, the dynamic of groups' *de facto* organizing in exclusionary ways, recounted in chapter 5, may be particular to the social customs and networks of the Juba region. The anomaly illustrates the value of attention to all parts of the borrowing process, and can help future researchers identify the critical flashpoints that may be improved within the credit system. Findings like these exemplify why the in-depth listening, facilitated by open-ended questions described in chapters 2 and 3 is necessary. Although this means more work, resources, and time must be dedicated to research, these reforms will ultimately lead to a more successful system. It is the responsible way to move forward.

TAILORING PROGRAMS FROM THE GROUND UP: LESSONS FROM JUBA

No part of the multipronged borrowing process should be treated as given. Many program features can be custom-made. The case of South Sudan illuminated various flashpoints within procedures that should have been modified. The Juba microfinance borrowers saw challenges around group formation, group member business verification, and intra-group payment recovery. They also saw challenges from the market conditions, made clear with the distinct composition of import retail businesses there compared to other sites as well as the structural challenges of the currency and import regimes. I offer the following suggestions based on learning from open-ended questions to past and present program participants at that time in Juba. If this book says anything, it is that these suggestions are not a hard and fast proposal for other post-conflict sites but rather a possible guide.

First, the social contracts undergirding group composition warrant special attention in post-conflict settings. The socioeconomic world receiving micro-credit came from somewhere before. Social ties affect and are affected by the various components of the borrowing process, from group formation through contract completion. Microfinance must work within existing social systems, however fragile, and be attentive to the ways it entrenches or endangers them. While some of these factors cannot be entirely anticipated, they should be sought out in advance. Once recognized, they cannot be ignored.

Awareness of this should be applied early on in the process, even as soon as in determining client eligibility criteria. If certain subpopulations get left out of the system, tensions may arise. MFI practitioners should develop strategies to assess client eligibility afresh from the common industry-wide hands-off model. Juba group loan prospects bore the onus of determining prospective peer eligibility. Clients were tasked with verifying that others had been running their businesses for some period of time, and little more. This non-system did not work as planned. In chapter 5 we learned that it gave borrowers choice in theory, but was ultimately exclusive. Juba's micro-finance institutions favored certain groups of people through their hands-off practices. Still, many co-borrowers overrode the institutional criteria in favor of other proxy observations for confidence. For better and for worse, they managed the social and economic risks of group selection as they saw fit. Juba borrowers had their own inclusion litmus tests, ranging from observable things like knowing one another's homes to their displacement status, to how much they ate. While there were attempted shortcuts to intimacy, like home visits encouraged by the MFIs, they had little functionality. Researchers should work with locals to identify better predictors of success than the locally developed calculi. The result may, for instance, solicit that MFIs take on responsibility for the verification burden from the co-borrowers and evaluate them on individual bases.

And, as chapter 6 taught us, people love regardless of the capacity to earn money from love. Individuals also grouped themselves in distinctive ways from other contexts, and few Juba borrowers were willing to forego their friendships for economic ends. Many found it too difficult to insist their struggling friends pay them back, and even quit because of the group drama. Practitioners can learn from this: longstanding social ties, or "strong social capital," do not necessarily equate to success, and can sometimes even make imposing threats more difficult. These lessons teach us that new interventions require bridging with the prevailing social customs, especially those around transactions. Borrowers averse to quarrels may want resources for enforcing contracts and dispute resolution, for example.

Next, what borrowers do with their loans matters. In post-conflict markets that have felt infrastructural blows and rely heavily on imports, MFIs should tailor their loans to accommodate to the variety of enterprises undertaken by micro-entrepreneurs. The impacts of the post-conflict market made it so that Juba's client population was substantially more invested in import retail compared with other microfinance receiving venues. The microcredit model that had been implemented in rural, agricultural markets could not have been successfully replicated in a swiftly changing urban retail hub like Juba. Instead, MFIs must engage in an analysis of the composition of businesses undertaken by clients, as well as their chronicity, costs associated with borrower trades, and competitiveness is needed in order to inform policies.

In Juba, the dissonance between the MFI models and borrower business needs hinged upon the integration of markets. As described in chapter 7, Juba borrowers were working at the interstice between the import calendar, the debt payment schedule, and the timing of their own sales. Each contract had its own chronological requirement, and they were not in sync. Countless borrowers complained that the standardized weekly repayment schedule was "too fast" for them, and as the loan schedules did not match the import calendar, many wished the loan schedules could accommodate more time to allow for mobilizing business resources. Studies on programs in Bangladesh and India have found that adjusting the maturities in small ways—like creating a two-month delay in the first installment or extending the payment schedule from weekly to monthly—made a big difference in the amount borrowers earned from their businesses.[22] MFIs in contexts like Juba that have persistent repayment failures should be prepared to try similar adaptations as relevant to the local commerce constraints.

The demand for firmer foundations was obvious at many points of the process in Juba. Practitioners should train borrowers about microfinance (and follow through with training regimens) as well as the business climate—especially those who had not been familiar with formal finance in general or with the program in particular before the end of conflict. Coaching has been found to help raise borrower incomes, especially when modified to suit the limitations posed by local social networks.[23] Emerging markets like the ones in Juba might experiment with a strategy of mentorship from established business leaders or other more seasoned micro-entrepreneurs. Microcredit need not be sink or swim.

Much more can be done to support borrowers whose markets are saturated. The majority of Juba borrowers were selling portioned-out food to other poor people and there was tough competition. This problem was painstaking, and precluded them from finding ways of innovating their strategies. Practitioners and researchers should find out what borrowers need in order to break through the market holdups. They should develop and promote ways to forecast industry trends. Alternatively, the MFI inclusion criteria might need overhauling to include this consideration. MFIs might onboard the work of evaluating business competitiveness to ensure borrowers are poised for success. MFIs might even discard the individual loans within solidarity group format altogether, in order to co-create new models for co-operative group businesses.

Meanwhile, several potential clients also saw that the costs of borrowing were too high for what sparse profits were being made by the Juba micro-entrepreneurs. Given that some borrowers were "economically active" but weathered by lending terms and the structural problems of the economy, incoming borrowers and/or MFIs may need better loan products. Offering a more extensive variety of loan terms and sizes by sector might help. Reducing rather than raising interest rates is another approach that would likely yield positive results, especially for the poorest borrowers.

Lastly, in post-conflict markets where currency fluctuation is prevalent,[24] internationally funded NGOs and financial institutions themselves can bear the burden of foreign exchange rate risk[25] and are sometimes bound by institutional rules to provide funds in a particular state currency.[26] Where possible, MFIs might disburse debts in other currencies that are being circulated in the region, so as to help clients save time and conversion costs. Where impossible due to currency transfer and convertibility risks, MFIs might offer clients exchange rate education, bargaining techniques, or training on collective approaches to the challenge. This could help borrowers avoid the pitfalls associated with black market and rival currency rates.

THE GRAY

Many problems haunt the future of the microfinance industry. Some observers think the central problem is that commercial microcredit in difficult terrains is too costly to sustain, and thus begs redoubling on a formula which precludes the poor. But sustainability is not the solution to the problem microfinance is designed to fix. The problem is best described in the words of Adam Smith predating microfinance by two centuries: "Money, says the proverb, makes money. When you have got a little, it is often easy to get more. The great difficulty is to get that little."[27] Microcredit was meant to leverage finance for the poor. In Juba and so many other places, microfinance has failed to deliver.

Failure to follow through on finance to the poor yields many consequences. In Juba and around South Sudan, tens of thousands of people bought into an idea that could bring them out of poverty. They either left dissatisfied, or were left behind by the institutions whose supporters decided that their local economy and peculiar social worlds were too much work. Failures such as these might go unnoticed in public donor circles, but they do not by those on the ground. Each project that fails also diminishes trust in the product and in loyalty ahead. Another "tragedy," to borrow from Bill Easterly's lingo, is lost opportunity cost. All the time, money and energy spent on the wrong things are also not spent on the incremental doable things.

"Ironically for the founder of the idea that the poor can be a good credit risk," reads Easterly's telling of Muhammad Yunus' story, "the farmers didn't fully repay Yunus, and he lost money. But he persisted . . . visiting as many rural villages as possible to try to understand how to help. Yunus realized that very small loans to very poor people could make a big difference in their lives."[28] It was not ironic at all; it was instructive. The failure of microcredit in general, and in this post-conflict region in particular, was a systematic refusal to make a long-term investment in financing the poorest.

Post-conflict microcredit will remain impossible unless stakeholders insist the "micro" nomenclature is real. People who work in this domain do care about real solutions to problems. Just as the evolution of the Juba microcredit story had many fingerprints, any future will require a great deal of will from many actors who must push for the right information with the right incentives. Many contributors and observers must guarantee that loans are not commercialized unduly, and insist on research that ensures borrowers are not being coerced. Integrity to the name and to the thriving of clients is the responsibility of many, and should be the responsibility of the industry as a whole.

Donors must insist that microfinance be "gray" to succeed in more than the commercial sense, but in the original, broader vision of financial inclusion. The charity vs. investment binary must be broken. The funding gaps in places like Juba must be filled. Donors should be given better choices in more challenging places that need a combination of assistance and credit to succeed. Unforgivable, rated debts need to be paired with subsidies. Grants can support things like keeping interest affordable, technical assistance, hiring more staff and external researchers to better make the products offered function for participants. Even whereas donors might be unwilling to subsidize costly modifications such as those described here, there may be opportunity for the private sector credit bureaus to fill the screening gap.[29] Alternatively, "impact first" investing, in which financiers are willing to accept losses, deserves a conversation because even a 50 percent return is better than zero in such cases. In order for donors to allocate their funding to accomplish these aims, they must first be informed on the different prospects offered by microcredit in practice.

Reforming the donor circuits is the work of analysts and jargon interpreters, too. Not all microcredit is truly microcredit and not all microfinance is created equal. Advocates at all levels need to be able to know and find the difference. Empirical findings must be accessible to practitioners, experts, policymakers and laypeople. Investors need to know which varieties of microcredit they are funneling toward on the ground. As reflected by how Kiva.org's individual "peer-to-peer" lenders became such a large share of the industry, contributors of all kinds must be better informed.

This is also the work of scholars and of M and E professionals. The measurement and evaluation research can afford an overhaul. The status quo, which overwhelmingly counts repayments and numbers served advocated by the Microcredit Summit Campaign, helps but can go further. What gets counted matters, yet only very little is counted. A qualitative approach appears best suited to answer the deeper social questions that continue to puzzle quantitative data.

Finally, borrowers have always been clients. They need to be treated as such rather than as passive product recipients. This means allowing for a genuine malleability to the desires they put forth. This requires listening to what they need, so that MFIs can make supply meet their demand. Case by case evaluation research is thus needed.

Lest the cachet of "micro" be a front for ordinary finance, a renovation is in order. It is time to revisit a mission-first lending paradigm in challenging, even post-conflict, contexts. There is no one-size-fits-all solution. This has been a key lesson learned in many fields of development and needs to be applied to microcredit approaches as well, if it wants to be relevant on a larger scale. The goal needs to be reset back to the founding ideals of getting the poor capital so that it can support their development. The methods to getting there will have to be gradual, piecemeal, and responsive to the ideas of not just those with the purse strings. The programs must be inclusive. The participants must be centered. The viability of microcredit depends upon the attention of those who care more about people than bank solvency—the very principle that inspired its beginnings in the first place.

NOTES

1. David Hulme and Paul Mosley, *Finance Against Poverty* (London and New York: Routledge, 1996), 132.
2. Marguerite S. Robinson, *The Microfinance Revolution: Sustainable Finance for the Poor* (Washington, DC: The World Bank, 2001), 18.
3. Marguerite S. Robinson, *The Microfinance Revolution: Sustainable Finance for the Poor* (Washington, DC: The World Bank, 2001), 20.

4. Marguerite S. Robinson, *The Microfinance Revolution: Sustainable Finance for the Poor* (Washington, DC: The World Bank, 2001), 20.

5. Marguerite S. Robinson, *The Microfinance Revolution: Sustainable Finance for the Poor* (Washington, DC: The World Bank, 2001), 23.

6. Ananya Roy, *Poverty Capital: Microfinance and the Making of Development* (New York and London: Routledge, 2010).

7. Matthew Soursourian and Edlira Dashi, *Current Trends in International Funding for Financial Inclusion.* CGAP Donor Brief, World Bank Group (Washington, DC: CGAP Publishing, 2015).

8. Larry R. Reed, et al., *Vulnerability: The State of the Microcredit Summit Campaign Report,* Microcredit Summit Campaign (2013).

9. Larry R. Reed, *State of the Campaign Report*, State of the Campaign, 2015.

10. Larry R. Reed, *State of the Campaign Report*, State of the Campaign, 2015.

11. Kaur Prabhjot and Soma Dey, "Andhra Pradesh Microfinance Crisis and its Repercussions on Microfinancing Activities." *India Global Journal of Management and Business Studies*, 3, no. 7 (2013).

12. Larry R. Reed, Lisa Laegreid Gatti, and Anna Awimbo, *Vulnerability: The State of the Microcredit Summit Campaign Report,* Microcredit Summit Campaign (2013).

13. Oscar Abello, "Don't Fear The Data Reaper." *BRAC Blog* (2013).

14. Ben Fine, "Financialization from a Marxist Perspective." *International Journal of Political Economy*, 42, no. 4 (2013), 54.

15. Ben Fine, "Financialization from a Marxist Perspective" *International Journal of Political Economy,* 42, no. 4 (2013), 55.

16. See Costas Lapavitsas, "Financialised Capitalism: Crisis and Financial Expropriation." *Historical Materialism,* 17, no. 2 (2009) and Costas Lapavitsas, *Profiting Without Producing: How Finance Exploits Us All*, (London: Verso, 2013) for an alternative Marxist analysis, which focus far more on the possibilities for exploitation.

17. Milford Bateman, *Why Doesn't Microfinance Work?: The Destructive Rise of Local Neoliberalism*, (London & New York: Zed Books, 2010), 120. Bateman's analysis describes several proven and compelling alternatives to commercial microcredit in chapter 7 of the same text. His analysis does not juxtapose the "poverty lending" approach as the primary alternative; however, he does praise Venezuelan and Vietnamese microcredit banks that issued affordable, subsidized microcredit to businesses thoughtfully.

18. Mattijs Renden, *et al.*,"The (im)possibility of Financial Inclusion in South Sudan." *The Broker*, (2013).

19. Patience Alidri, Judith van Doorn, Mayada El-Zoghbi, Myriam Houtart, Dave Larson, Geetha Nagarajan and Caroline Tsilikounas, Introduction To Microfinance In Conflict-Affected Communities: A Training Manual, (International Labour Organization and United Nations High Commissioner for Refugees, 2002), 15.

20. Morten Jerven, *Africa*: *Why Economists Get it Wrong* (London: Zed Books, 2015), 127.

21. See Introduction Isabelle Guérin, Marc Labie and Jean Michel Servet The Crises of Microcredit, (London: Zed Books, 2015).

22. Manohar Sharma and Manfred Zeller, "Repayment performance in group-based credit programs in Bangladesh: An empirical analysis." *World Development*, 25, no. 10 (1979) Erica Field, Rohini Pande, John Papp, and Jeanette Park, "Repayment flexibility can reduce financial stress: a randomized control trial with microfinance clients in India." (PloS one, 2012) Erica Field, Rohini Pande, John Papp, and Natalia Rigol, "Does the classic microfinance model discourage entrepreneurship among the poor? Experimental evidence from India." *American Economic Review*, 103, no. 6 (2013).

23. Lars Berge, Ivar Oppedal, Kjetil Bjorvatn and Bertil Tungodden, "Human and financial capital for microenterprise development: Evidence from a field and lab experiment." *Management Science,* 61, no. 4 (2014) Alejandro Drexler, Greg Fischer, and Antoinette Schoar, "Keeping it simple: Financial literacy and rules of thumb." *American Economic Journal: Applied Economics,* 6, no. 20 (2014) Martin Valdivia, "Business Training Plus for Female Entrepreneurship? Short and Medium-Term Experimental Evidence from Peru." (PIERI Working Papers, 2014).

24. Currency fluctuation is common to not only many post-conflict states, but also many transitioning states. See Ken Vander Weele and Patricia Markovich, "Managing High and Hyper-Inflation in Microfinance: Opportunity International's Experience in Bulgaria and Russia." *Microenterprise Best Practices,* (2001) for an analysis of microfinance in high- and hyperinflation periods in Bulgaria and Russia.

25. Peter R. Crabb, "Foreign Exchange Risk Management Practicesof Microfinance Institutions." *ESR Review,* 6, no. 2 (2004).

26. Scott Featherston, Elizabeth Littlefield and Patricia Mwangi, "Foreign Exchange Rate Risk In Microfinance: What Is It And How Can It Be Managed?" CGAP Focus Note No. 31, (2006).

27. Adam Smith, *The Wealth of Nations*, Book 1. (London: Methuen & Co, 1776)

28. William Easterly, *The White Man's Burden: Why the West's Efforts to Aid the Rest Have Done So Much Ill and So Little Good* (New York, NY: Penguin Press, 2006) 120.

29. Field *et al.* "Microfinance: Points of Promise" Harvard Kennedy School Faculty Research Working Paper Series, 2016.

Glossary of Abbreviations

ARC	American Refugee Committee
BOSS	Bank of South Sudan
BRAC	Bangladesh Rural Advancement Committee
CGAP	Consultative Group to Assist the Poor
CPA	Comprehensive Peace Agreement
FSL	Finance Sudan Limited
FSSL	Finance South Sudan Limited
GDP	Gross Domestic Product
GOSS	Government of South Sudan
ICRC	International Committee of the Red Cross
IDP	Internally Displaced People
IMF	International Monetary Fund
IOM	International Organization for Migration
IPA	Innovations for Poverty Action
JAM	Joint Assessment Mission
MASS	Microfinance Association of South Sudan
MDG	Millennium Development Goals
MDTF	Multi-Donor Trust Fund
MFI	Microfinance institution
MIS	Management Information System
MIX	Microfinance Information Exchange
NGO	Non-governmental organization
NIF	National Islamic Front
ODA	Official Development Assistance
OECD	Organization for Economic Co-operation and Development
PPP	Purchasing power parity
RCT	Randomized control trial

SME	Small-to-medium enterprise
SPLA	Sudanese People's Liberation Army
SSLM	Southern Sudan Liberation Movement
SSMDF	South Sudan Microfinance Development Facility
SSP	South Sudanese Pound
SUMI	Sudan Microfinance Institution
UNCDF	United Nations Capital Development Fund
UNDP	United Nations Development Programme
UNHCR	United Nations High Commissioner for Refugees
USAID	United States Agency for International Development

Bibliography

Abbink, Klaus, Irlenbusch, Bernd, and Renner, Elke. "Group Size And Social Ties In Microfinance Institutions." *Economic Inquiry* 44, no. 4 (2006): 61–28.

Abbink, Klaus, Irlenbusch, Bernd, and Renner, Elke. "Group Size and Social Ties in Microfinance Institutions." *Paper presented at the annual meeting for the Royal Economic Society*, Coventry, England. (April 7–9, 2003).

Abdi, Awa M. "In Limbo: Dependency, Insecurity, and Identity amongst Somali Refugees in Dadaab Camps." *Canadas Journal on Refugees* 22, no. 2 (2005): 6–14.

Abello, Oscar. "Don't Fear The Data Reaper." *BRAC Blog* (blog). (February 21, 2013). http://blog.brac.net/2013/02/dont-fear-the-data-reaper/.

ACDI/VOCA. "South Sudan." *ACDI/VOCA* pamphlet (July, 2013).

Achwan, Rochman. "Microfinance Institution, Social Capital and Peacebuilding: Evidence from West Kalimantan, Indonesia." *University of Indonesia, Center for Research on Inter-group Relations and Conflict Resolution* (2007).

Adams, Dale W., Graham, Douglas H., and Von Pischke, J. D. (Eds.). *Undermining Rural Development with Cheap Credit.* Boulder: Westview Press, 1984.

AED. *FIELD-Support LWA: Quarterly Report.* Washington, DC: United States Agency for International Development, 2011.

AED. *FIELD-Support LWA Award: Quarterly Report.* Washington, DC: United States Agency for International Development, 2010.

Agier, Isabelle and Szafarz, Ariane. "Subjectivity in Credit Allocation to Micro-entrepreneurs: Evidence from Brazil." *Small Business Economics* 41, no. 1 (2013): 263–75.

Alexander-Tedeschi, Gwendolyn and Dean Karlan. "Cross Sectional Impact Analysis: Bias from Dropouts." *Perspectives on Global Development and Technology* 9, nos. 3–4: (2010): 270–91.

Alidri, Patience, van Doorn, Judith, El-Zoghbi, Mayada, Houtart, Myriam, Larson, Dave, Nagarajan, Geetha and Tsilikounas, Caroline. Introduction To Microfinance

In Conflict-Affected Communities: A Training Manual. (International Labour Organization and United Nations High Commissioner for Refugees 2002)

Alldén, Susanne. "Microfinance and Post-conflict Development in Cambodia and Timor-Leste." *Sojourn: Journal of Social Issues in Southeast Asia* 24, no. 2 (2009): 269–84.

American Refugee Committee. "About Us." Arcrelief, About Us. http://arcrelief.org/about.

Anderson, Elizabeth S. "What Is the Point of Equality?" *Ethics* 109, no. 2 (January 1999): 287–337.

Anderson, Mary B and Woodrow, Peter J. *Rising from the Ashes: Development Strategies in Times of Disaster.* Boulder: Westview Press, 1989.

Armendariz de Aghion, Beatriz and Morduch, Jonathan. *The Economics of Microfinance.* Cambridge: Massachusetts Institute of Technology Press, 2005.

Atil, Melody. *Expanding the Provision and Impact of Microfinance in Southern Sudan.* Juba: World Bank Southern Sudan Office, 2009.

Banerjee, Abhijit Vinayak, Amsden, Alice H., Bates, Robert H., Bhagwati, Jagdish N., Deaton, Angus, and Stern, Nicholas. *Making Aid Work.* Cambridge, MA: Boston Review Book, MIT Press, 2007, 23–24.

Barley, Stephen R., "Semiotics and the Study of Occupational and Organizational Culture." *Administrative Science Quarterly* 20 (1983): 393–413.

Basher, Md. Abul. "Empowerment of Microcredit Participants And Its Spillover Effects: Evidence From The Grameen Bank Of Bangladesh." *The Journal of Developing Areas* 40, no. 2 (2007): 173–183.

Basu, Priya and Srivastava, Pradeep. "Exploring Possibilities: Microfinance and Rural Credit Access for the Poor in India." *Economic and Political Weekly* 40, no. 17 (2005): 1747–56.

Bateman, Milford. *Why Doesn't Microfinance Work?: The Destructive Rise of Local Neoliberalism.* London and New York: Zed Books, 2010.

BBC, "South Sudan becomes an Independent Nation." https://www.bbc.com/news/world-africa-14089843 (July 9, 2011).

Beijuka, John. "Microfinance in Post-conflict Countries: The Case Study of Uganda." *International Labor Organization* (1999).

Bello, Walden. "Is the Structural Adjustment Approach Really and Truly Dead?" *Business World* (1999). Available at https://www.tni.org/en/article/is-the-structural-adjustment-approach-really-and-trully-dead.

Bennett, Jon, Pantuliano, Sara, Fenton, Wendy, Vaux, Anthony, Barnett, Chris, and Brusset, Emery. "Aiding the Peace: A Multi-donor Evaluation of Support to Conflict Prevention and Peacebuilding Activities in Southern Sudan 2005–2010." *Ministry of Foreign Affairs of Denmark*, U.K. (December, 2010).

Berenbach, Shari and Guzman, Diego. "The Solidarity Group Experience. Growth and Equity through Microenterprise Investments and Institutions Project." *Action International* (1992).

Berge, Lars, Oppedal, Ivar, Bjorvatn, Kjetil, and Tungodden, Bertil. "Human and Financial Capital for Microenterprise Development: Evidence from a Field and Lab Experiment." *Management Science* 61, no. 4 (2014): 707–722.

Berold, Robert, ed. *Introduction to Microfinance in Conflict-Affected Communities.* Geneva: ILO, 2002.

Besley, Timothy and Coate, Stephen. "Group Lending, Repayment Incentives and Social Collateral." *Journal of Development Economics* 46 no. 1 (1995): 1–18.

Bhalla, Ajit and Lapeyre, Frederic. "Social Exclusion: Towards an Analytical and Operational Framework." *Development and Change* 28, no. 3 (1997): 413–33.

Birdsall, Nancy and Fukuyama, Francis. "The Post-Washington Consensus: Development after the Crisis." *Foreign Affairs* 90, no. 2 (2011): 45–53.

Birdsall, Nancy and Kinder, Molly. "The U.S. Aid 'Surge' to Pakistan: Repeating a Failed Experiment? Lessons for U.S. Policymakers from the World Bank's Social-Sector Lending in the 1990s." *Center for Global Development*, Working Paper No. 205 (March 17, 2010).

Birdsall, Nancy, Malik, Adeel and Milan Vaishnav. "Poverty and the Social Sectors: The World Bank in Pakistan 1990–2003" Washington, DC: World Bank Operations Evaluation Department, 2005.

Blanchard, Lauren Ploch. "Sudan and South Sudan: Current Issues for congress and US Policy." Congressional Research Service, Library of Congress (October, 2012). https://www.fas.org/sgp/crs/row/R42774.pdf.

Blayney, Robert G. and Otero, Maria. *Small and Micro-enterprises: Contributions to Development and Future Directions for Aid's Support.* Report for the Employment and Enterprise Development Division. Washington, DC: USAID, 1985.

Block, Fred L. and Somers, Margaret R. *The Power of Market Fundamentalism: Karl Polanyi's Critique.* Cambridge, MA: Harvard University Press, 2014.

Bohannan, Paul. "The Impact of Money on an African Subsistence Economy." *The Journal of Economic History* 19, no. 04 (December, 1959): 491–503.

Bornstein, David. *How to Change the World: Social Entrepreneurs and the Power of New Ideas.* Oxford: Oxford University Press, 2004.

Bourdieu, Pierre. *The Logic of Practice.* Stanford, CA: Stanford University Press, 1990.

Boyce, James K. and O'Donnell, Madalene. *Peace and the Public Purse: Economic Policies for Postwar Statebuilding.* Boulder, CO: Lynne Rienner, 2007.

BRAC. "Creating Opportunity for the Poor." BRAC, Home. http://www.brac.net/.

Brahimi, Lakhdar. *Report on the Panel on United Nations Peace Operations.* United Nations General Security Council: 55th session, August 21, 2000.

Bruett, Tillman. *Supporting Microfinance in Conflict-Affected Areas.* CGAP Donor Brief 21. Washington, DC: CGAP Publishing, 2004.

Buchanan-Smith, Margaret and Maxwell, Simon. "Linking Relief and Development: An Introduction and Overview." *IDS Bulletin* 25, no. 4 (October 1994): 2–16.

Burki, Hussan-Ban. *Unraveling The Delinquency Problem (2008/2009) In Punjab – Pakistan* (October 2009) MicroNote No: 10 Pakistan Microfinance Network.

Caplan, Bryan. *The Myth of the Rational Voter: Why Democracies Choose Bad Policies.* Princeton, NJ: Princeton University Press, 2007.

Carroll, Peter and Kellow, Aynsley. *The OECD: A study of Organisational Adaptation.* Edward Elgar Publishing, 2011.

Cassar, Alessandra, Crowley, Luke, and Wydick, Bruce. "The Effect of Social Capital on Group Loan Repayment: Evidence from Field Experiments." *The Economic Journal* 117, no. 517 (2007): F85–F106.

Castillo, Graciana Del and Del Soto, Alvaro Del Soto. "Obstacles to Peacebuilding." *Foreign Policy*, no. 94 (Spring 1994): 69–83.

Charity Navigator. "Giving Statistics." Charity Navigator, Index. http://www.charitynavigator.org/index.cfm?bay=content.viewandcpid=42#.U7w7RfmICSo.

Chemonics International. *Sudan Agricultural Enterprise Finance Program Ninth Quarterly Report*, 2005.

Chemonics International. *Sudan Agricultural Enterprise Finance Program Tenth Quarterly Report*, 2005.

Chemonics International. "A Component of the: Southern Sudan Agricultural Revitalization Program (SSARP) Second Annual Workplan." *Agricultural Enterprise Finance Program* (October 1, 2003–September 30, 2004). http://pdf.usaid.gov/pdf_docs/Pdabz514.pdf.

Chemonics International. *Sudan Agricultural Enterprise Finance Program Final Report.* USAID, April 30, 2008.

Cheston, Susy and Kuhn, Lisa. "Empowering Women through Microfinance." In *Pathways Out of Poverty: Innovations in Microfinance for the Poorest Families*, edited by S. Daley- Harris (pp. 167–228). Bloomfield: Kumarian Press, 2002.

Chouliaraki, Lilie. "Distant Suffering in the Media." In Inaugural Public Lecture by Professor Lilie Chouliaraki, LSE (February 27, 2008). 1–19. http://www.lse.ac.uk/media@lse/study/pdf/ChouliarakiLSEPublicLectureDistantSuffering.pdf

Churchill, Winston S. *The River War: An Historical Account of the Reconquest of the Soudan.* London: Longmans, Green and Co, 1900.

Cirri, Simon. "Serial Entrepreneur Finds Success in Microlending." *Business Daily*, March 16, 2015. http://www.businessdailyafrica.com/Corporate-News/Serial-entrepreneur-finds-success-in-microlending/-/539550/2655642/-/item/0/-/sie8itz/-/index.html.

Clemens, Michael and Sandefur, Justin. "Mapping the Worm Wars: What the Public Should Take Away from the Scientific Debate about Mass Deworming." *Center for Global Development* (July 30, 2015).

Cohen, Louis, Manion, Lawrence, and Morrison, Keith. *Research Methods in Education* 5th edition. London: Routledge, 2013.

Collier, Paul, Elliott, V. L., Hegre, Havre, Hoeffler, Anke, Reynal-Querol, Marta, and Sambanis, Nicholas. *Breaking the Conflict Trap: Civil War and Development Policy.* Washington, DC: World Bank, 2003.

Collins, Robert O. *A History of Modern Sudan.* Cambridge: Cambridge University Press, 2008.

Comaroff, Jean and Comaroff, John. "Christianity and Colonialism in South Africa." *American Ethnologist* 13, no. 1 (1986): 1–22.

Corbett, Edward P. J. and Connors, Robert J. *Classical Rhetoric for the Modern Student.* New York: Oxford University Press, 1965.

Cornwall, Andrea and Eade, Deborah. *Deconstructing Development Discourse: Buzzwords and Fuzzwords.* Rugby, Warwickshire: Practical Action, 2010.

Crabb, Peter R. "Foreign Exchange Risk Management Practices of Microfinance Institutions." *ESR Review* 6, no. 2 (2004): 51–63.

Cramer, Christopher. *Civil War is Not a Stupid Thing: Accounting for Violence in Developing Countries*. London: Hurst and Co, 2006.

Cramer, Christopher. *Violence in Developing Countries*. Bloomington, IN: Indiana University Press, 2006.

Crépon, Bruno, Devoto, Florencia, Duflo, Esther, and Pariente, William. "Estimating the Impact of Microcredit on Those Who Take It Up: Evidence from a Randomized Experiment in Morocco." *Economics* (May, 2014).

Cull, Robert, Demirgüç-Kunt, Asli, and Morduch, Jonathan. "Financial Performance and Outreach: A Global Analysis of Leading Microbanks." *The Economic Journal* 117, no. 517 (2007): 107–133.

Daley-Harris, Sam. *Reclaiming Our Democracy: Healing the Break between People and Government*. Philadelphia, PA: Camino Books, 1994.

Daley-Harris, Sam. "State of the Microcredit Summit Campaign Report 2005." *The Microcredit Summit Campaign* (2005).

Dasgupta, Partha. *An Inquiry into Well-Being and Destitution*. Oxford: Oxford University Press on Demand, 1995.

Dees, Gregory J. "A Tale of Two Cultures: Charity, Problem Solving, and the Future of Social Entrepreneurship." *Journal of Business Ethics* 111, no. 3 (August 17, 2012): 321–34.

Derrida, Jacques. *The Ear of the Other: Otobiography, Transference, Translation*. University of Nebraska Press, 1985.

De Sousa-Shields, Mike, Navarrete, Juan, Panday, Nabina, and Hanson, Lene. *Microlead Midterm Evaluation*. UNCDF Report, February 11, 2013.

De Waal, Alex. "Is Famine Relief Irrelevant to Rural People?" *IDS Bulletin* 20, no. 2 (1989): 63–7.

Dewey, John and Gilbert Ross, Ralph. *The Middle Works*, vol. 13. Edwardsville, IL: Southern Illinois University Press, 1983.

Dichter, Thomas. "Introduction," In *What's Wrong with Microfinance?* edited by T. Dichter and M. Harper (pp. 1–6). Warwickshire: Practical Action Publishing, 2007.

Doyle, Karen. *Microfinance in the Wake of Conflict: Challenges and Opportunities*. Washington, DC: USAID, 1998.

Drexler, Alejandro, Fischer, Greg, and Schoar, Antoinette. "Keeping it Simple: Financial Literacy and Rules of Thumb." *American Economic Journal: Applied Economics* 6, no. 20 (2014): 1–31.

Duffield, Mark, Jok Madut Jok, David Keen, Geoff Loane, Fiona O'Reilly, John Ryle, and Philip Winter. *Sudan: The Unintended Consequences of Humanitarian Action, Field Education Study*. Report to the European Community Humanitarian Office, The University of Dublin, Trinity College, 2000.

Duflo, Esther; Banerjee, Abhijit; Glennerster, Rachel; and Kinnan, Cynthia G. "The miracle of microfinance? Evidence from a randomized evaluation." *National Bureau of Economic Research* no. w18950 (2013).

Duflo, Esther, Banerjee, Abhijit, Glennerster, Rachel, and Kinnan, Cynthia G. *The Miracle of Microfinance? Evidence from a Randomized Evaluation*. No. w18950. National Bureau of Economic Research, 2013.

Duval, Ann. *Increasing Financial Inclusion in East Africa: Equity Bank's Agent-Driven Model.* Microlead, UN Capital Development Fund, 2014.

Duval, Ann. *Microfinance Greenfields in Challenging Environments: BRAC's Experience In Three Post- Conflict Countries In Africa.* UN Capital Development Fund, 2015.

Easterly, William. "Why Does Foreign Aid Fail?" *Big Think* (September 6, 2007). http://bigthink.com/videos/why-does-foreign-aid-fail.

Easterly, William. *The White Man's Burden: Why the West's Efforts to Aid the Rest Have Done So Much Ill and So Little Good.* New York, NY: Penguin Press, 2006.

The Economist. "The Path through the Fields; Bangladesh and Development." *The Economist* (November 3, 2012).

Edward, Peter. "The Ethical Poverty Line: A Moral Quantification of Absolute Poverty." *Third World Quarterly* 27, no. 2 (2006): 377–93.

Elyachar, Julia. "Empowerment Money: The World Bank, Non-Governmental Organizations, and the Value of Culture in Egypt." *Public Culture* 14, no. 3 (2002): 493–513.

Enclude. Principles: "The Principles that Inform our Work and Worldview" Accessed on http://encludesolutions.com/about/principles.

Enterprise Development. "We're on a Mission to Help the Poor End Poverty." Accessed on www.endpoverty.org.

Entman, Robert. M. "Framing: Toward Clarification of a Fractured Paradigm." *Journal of Communication* 43, no. 4 (1993): 51–8.

Evans-Pritchard, Edward Evan. *Nuer Religion.* Oxford: Oxford University Press, 1956.

Evans-Pritchard, Edward Evan. *The Nuer: A Description of the Modes of Livelihood and Political Institutions of a Nilotic People.* Oxford and New York: Oxford University Press, 1902–1973.

Evans-Pritchard, Edward Evan. "The Sacrificial Role of Cattle Among The Nuer." *Africa: Journal of the International African Institute* 23, no. 3 (1953): 181–98.

Fafo Institute for Applied International Studies. *Independent Evaluation of the Multi-Donor Trust Fund-South Sudan (MDTF-SS).* World Bank, July 25, 2013.

Featherston, Scott, Littlefield, Elizabeth, and Mwangi, Patricia. "Foreign Exchange Rate Risk In Microfinance: What Is It And How Can It Be Managed?" CGAP Focus Note No. 31 (2006).

Feldman, Martha S. *Strategies for Interpreting Qualitative Data.* Qualitative Research Methods Series, Vol. 33. Newbury Park: Sage, 1995.

Ferguson, James. "Formalities of Poverty: Thinking about Social Assistance in Neoliberal South Africa." *African Studies Review* 50, no. 2 (2007): 71–86.

Fiala, Nathan. "Stimulating Microenterprise Growth: Results from a Loans, Grants and Training Experiment in Uganda." *SSRN Electronic Journal* (2013). DOI: 10.2139/ssrn.2358086.

Field, Erica, Holland, Abraham, and Pande, Rohini. "Microfinance: Points of Promise" in *Evolving Approaches to the Economics of Public Policy: Views of Award-Winning Economists*, Jean Kimmel, ed. Kalamazoo, MI: W.E. Upjohn Institute (2016): pp. 11–32.

Field, Erica, Pande, Rohini, Papp, John, and Park, Jeanette. "Repayment Flexibility can Reduce Financial Stress: A Randomized Control Trial with Microfinance Clients in India." *PloS one* 7, no. 9 (2012): e45679.

Field, Erica, Pande, Rohini, Papp, John, and Rigol, Natalia. "Does the Classic Microfinance Model Discourage Entrepreneurship Among the Poor? Experimental Evidence from India." *American Economic Review* 103, no. 6 (October, 2013): 2196–226.

Finca. "Mission and Vision." Accessed December, 2008. www.villagebanking.org/site/c.erKPI2PCIoE/b.2603941/k.BBB2/Mission_and_Vision.htm.

Fine, Ben. "The Developmental State Is Dead-Long Live Social Capital?" *Development and Change Development and Change* 30, no. 1 (1999): 1–19.

Fine, Ben. "Financialization from a Marxist Perspective." *International Journal of Political Economy* 42, no. 4 (2013): 47–66.

Frankfurt School of Management. *Southern Sudan Microfinance Development Facility (SSMDF) – Final Report*. Juba: South Sudan Microfinance Development Facility, 2011.

Fraser, Nancy and Gordon, Linda. "A Genealogy of Dependency: Tracing a Keyword of the US Welfare State." *Signs: Journal of Women in Culture and Society* 19, no. 2 (1994): 309–36.

Fukuyama, Francis. *Trust: Social Virtues and the Creation of Prosperity*. New York: Free Press, 1995.

Galak, Jeff, Small, Deborah, and Stephen, Andrew T. "Microfinance Decision Making: A Field Study of Prosocial Lending." *Journal of Marketing Research* 48, no. SPL (2011): S130–S137.

Gallardo, Joselito, Ouattara, Korotouomou, Randhawa, Bikki, and Steel, William F. "Microfinance Regulation: Lessons from Benin, Ghana, and Tanzania." *Savings and Development* 29, no. 1 (2005): 85–96.

Garang, Kuir ë. *South Sudan Ideologically: Tribal Socio-Democracy, SPLM Ideologues, Juba Corruptocrats, Khartoum Theocrats and their Time-Frozen Leadership*. Calgary: The Nile Press, 2013.

Geertz, Clifford. *Peddlers and Princes: Social Development and Economic Change in Two Indonesian Towns*. Chicago: University of Chicago Press, 1963.

Geertz, Clifford. "Religion as a Cultural System." In *The Interpretation of Cultures: Selected Essays*. Fontana Press, 1993.

Gehlich-Shillabeer, Mareen. "Poverty Alleviation or Poverty Traps? Microcredits and Vulnerability in Bangladesh." *Disaster Prevention and Management* 17, no. 3 (2008): 396–409.

Ghatak, Maitreesh. "Group Lending, Local Information and Peer Selection." *Journal of Development Economics* 60, no. 1 (1999): 27–50.

Gibson-Graham, J. K. *The End of Capitalism (As We Knew It): A Feminist Critique of Political Economy*. Cambridge, MA: Blackwell Publishers, 1996.

Gibson-Graham, J. K. (2003). *A Diverse Economy: Rethinking Economy and Economic Representation.* Retrieved 2010, 3–3 from http://www.communityeconomies.org/papers.php.

Gilens, Martin. *Why Americans Hate Welfare: Race, Media, and the Politics of Antipoverty Policy*. Chicago: University of Chicago Press, 2000.

Gilpin, Robert and Gilpin, Jean M. *Global Political Economy: Understanding the International Economic Order*. Princeton, NJ: Princeton University Press, 2001.

Giné, Xavier, Jakiela, Pamela, Karlan, Dean, and Morduch, Jonathan. "Microfinance Games." *American Economic Journal: Applied Economics* 2, no. 3 (2010): 60–95.

Glaeser, Edward L., Laibson, David I., Scheinkman, Jose A., and Soutter, Christine L. "Measuring Trust." *Quarterly Journal of Economics* 115 (2000): 811–46.

Glaser, Barney G. and Strauss, Anselm L. *The Discovery of Grounded Theory: Strategies for Qualitative Research.* New Brunswick: Adline Transaction, 1968.

Global Humanitarian Assistance. "South Sudan Key Figures 2012." *Development Initiatives*. Accessed http://www.globalhumanitarianassistance.org/countryprofile/south-sudan

Global Partnerships. "About us." Global Partnerships, About Us. Accessed December, 2008. www.globalpartnerships.org/sections/aboutus/aboutus_mission.htm.

Godquin, Marie. "Microfinance Repayment Performance in Bangladesh: How to Improve the Allocation of Loans by MFIs." *World Development* 32, no. 11 (2004): 1909–26.

Gonzalez, Henry, and El-Zoghbi, Mayada. *Where Do Impact Investing and Microfinance Meet?* Washington, DC: Consultative Group to Assist the Poor, 2013.

Goronja, Natasa. "A Microfinance in Post-Conflict Countries: Bosnia and Herzegovina." Paper prepared for September ILO conference, available from the Haje Schutte, 1999.

Government of the Republic of Sudan and the Sudan People's Liberation Movement. *Chapeau of the Comprehensive Peace Agreement.* New York: United Nations Peacemaker, 2004. Accessed in 2009.

Graham, Carol. *Safety Nets, Politics, and the Poor: Transitions to Market Economies.* Washington, DC: Brookings Institution, 1994.

Grossman, Herschel I. "Foreign Aid and Insurrection." *Defense Economics* 3, no. 4 (1992): 275–88.

Gutiérrez-Nieto, Begoña, Carlos, Serrano-Cinca, and Molinero, C Mar. "Social Efficiency In Microfinance Institutions." *Journal of the Operational Research Society* 60, no. 1 (2007): 104–19.

Guyer, Jane I. *Marginal Gains: Monetary Transactions in Atlantic Africa*. Chicago: University of Chicago Press, 2004.

Haase, Dwight. "Banking on the Poor." *Contexts: American Sociological Association.* (2012).

Harper, Malcolm. "What's Wrong with Groups?" In *What's Wrong with Microfinance?* vol. 35 no. 48 edited by Thomas Dichter and Malcolm Harper (pp. 35–48). Practical Action Publishing in association with GSE Research, 2007.

Harrell-Bond, Barbara E. *Imposing Aid: Emergency Assistance to Refugees.* London: Oxford University Press, 1986.

Harrison, Graham. "Financing Peace?" In *Peacebuilding, Power, and Politics in Africa,* edited by Devon Curtis and Gwinyayi A. Dzinesa (pp. 158–71). Athens: Ohio University Press, 2012.

Harriss, John and De Renzio, Paulo. "'Missing Link' or Analytically Missing?: The Concept of Social Capital, An Introductory Bibliographic Essay." *Journal of International Development* 9, no. 7 (1997): 919–37.

Harvey, Paul and Jeremy Lind. *Dependency and Humanitarian Relief: A Critical Analysis*. Report, Humanitarian Policy Group, London: Overseas Development Institute, 2005.

Hashemi, Syed M., Schuler, Sidney Ruth, and Riley, Anne P. "Rural Credit Programs and Women's Empowerment in Bangladesh." *World Development* 24, no. 4 (1996): 635–53.

Hattori, Tomohisa. "Reconceptualizing Foreign Aid." *Review of International Political Economy* 8, no. 4 (Winter, 2001): 633–660.

Haughton, Jonathan. "The Reconstruction of War-torn Economies." *Harvard Institute for International Development* (June, 2018).

Hermes, Niels and Lensink, Robert. "The Empirics of Microfinance: What do we Know?" *The Economic Journal* 117, no. 517 (2007): F1–F10.

Higgins, Bill. "Natalie Portman Gets Behind Microfinance for Third World." *Pret-a-Reporter* (2011).

Hoos, Karin. "Urban People: Too Poor to Save Money? The Case of Micro Deposit in the Philippines." *Philippine Quarterly of Culture and Society* 38, no. 1 (2010): 75–83.

Hopkins, Jim. "Ebay Founder Takes Lead in Social Entrepreneurship." *USA Today* (2005).

Hudon, Marek and Sandberg, Joakim. "The Ethical Crisis in Microfinance: Issues, Findings, and Implications." *Business Ethics Quarterly* 23, no. 4 (2013): 561–89.

Hulme, David and Mosley, Paul. *Finance Against Poverty* vol. 2. London and New York: Routledge, 1996.

Hunt, Juliet and Kasynathan, Nalini. "Pathways to Empowerment Reflections on Microfinance and Transformation in Gender Relations in South Asia." *Gender and Development* 9, no. 1 (2001): 42–52.

Hutchinson, S. E. *Nuer Dilemmas: Coping with Money, War and the State*. Berkeley and Los Angeles: University of California Press, 1996.

Hutchinson, S. E. "A Curse from God? Religious and Political Dimensions of the Post-1991 Rise of Ethnic Violence in South Sudan." *The Journal of Modern African Studies* 39, no. 2 (2001): 307–31.

Indra, Doreen. "The Spirit of the Gift and the Politics of Resettlement: The Canadian Private Sponsorship of South East Asians." In *The International Refugee Crisis: British and Canadian Responses*, edited by Vaughan Robinson. Palgrave, 1993.

Innovations for Poverty Action. "School-Based Deworming: Scaling Effective Solutions." Accessed http://www.poverty-action.org/deworming.

International Finance Corporation. *Implementation Completion and Results Report on a Multi Donor Trust Fund Grant in the amount of USD 10.02 Million to the Government of South Sudan and Government of South Sudan Financing of USD 0.6 Million for the Southern Sudan Private Sector Development Project.* Washington, DC: The World Bank, 2015.

International Finance Corporation. *Interim Strategy Note (FY 2013-2014) For the Republic of South Sudan.* Washington, DC: The World Bank, 2014.

IOM International Organization For Migration and South Sudan Relief And Rehabilitation Commission. "Sudan Spontaneous Return Tracking Report." May, 2009.

IRIN. *South Sudan: Briefing – Life Without Oil.* Juba: IRIN News, 2012. http://www.irinnews.org/report/94858/south-sudan-briefing-life-without-oil.

Isabelle Guérin, Marc Labie and Jean-Michel Servet. *The Crises of Microcredit.* London: Zed Books, 2015.

ITAD Bennett, Jon, Kluyskens, Jups, Morton, James, and Poate, Derek. *Mid-Term Evaluation of the Joint Donor Team in Juba, Sudan.* Oslo, Norway: Norwegian Agency for Development Cooperation, 2009.

Jad, Islah. "NGOs: Between Buzzwords and Social Movements, in Cornwall and Eade." In *Deconstructing Development Discourse: Buzzwords and Fuzzwords,* edited by Andrea Cornwall and Deborah Eade. Rugby, Warwickshire: Practical Action, 2010.

JAM Sudan. *The Report of the Sudan Joint Assessment Mission (JAM): Framework for Sustained Peace, Development and Poverty Eradication.* Vol. 1. Prepared by the UN and World Bank JAM team in collaboration with the GoS and the SPLM, 2005.

Jansen, Anicca. *USAID's contribution to Microfinance: From Microfinance to Financial Inclusion.* Washington, DC: USAID, 2014.

Jerven, Morten. *Africa: Why Economists Get it Wrong.* London: Zed Books, 2015.

Johnson, Douglas H. *The Root Causes of Sudan's Civil Wars: Peace or Truce.* Kampala: Fountain Publishers/James Currey, 2011.

Joseph, Nithya. "Mortgaging Used Saree-skirts, Spear-heading Resistance: Narratives from the Microfinance Repayment Standoff in Ramanagaram, India, 2008–2010." In *Microfinance, Debt and Over-indebtedness: Juggling with Money*, edited by I. Guérin, S. Morvant-Roux and M. Villarreal. London: Routledge, 2013.

Judy L. Baker. *Evaluating the Impact of Development Projects on Poverty: A Handbook for Practitioners.* Washington, DC: The World Bank. 2000.

Kabeer, Naila. "Beyond the Poverty Line: Measuring Poverty and Impoverishing Measures." In *Reversed Realities: Gender Hierarchies in Development Thought,* edited by Naila Kabeer (pp. 136–162). London: Verso, 1995.

Kabeer, Naila. "Conflicts Over Credit: Re-Evaluating the Empowerment Potential of Loans to Women in Rural Bangladesh." *World Development* (2001): 63–84.

Kabeer, Naila. "Resources, Agency, Achievements: Reflections on the Measurement of Women's Empowerment. Development and Change." (1999): 435–464.

Kahneman, Daniel and Tversky, Amos. "Prospect Theory: An Analysis of Decision Under Risk." *Econometrica* 47 (1979): 263–91.

Kaladhar, K. "Microfinance in India: Design, Structure and Governance." *Economic and Political Weekly* 32, no. 42 (1997): 2687–2706.

Kaler, Amy and Parkins, John R. "Food, Donors, and Dependency Syndrome(s) in South Sudan." *Sociology of Development* 1, no. 3 (2015): 400–16.

Kalpana, K. "Shifting Trajectories in Microfinance Discourse." *Economic and Political Weekly* 40, no. 51 (2005): 5400–09.

Karim, Lamia. *Microfinance and its Discontents: Women in Debt in Bangladesh*. Minneapolis: University of Minnesota Press, 2011.

Karim, Lamia. "Demystifying Microcredit: The Grameen Bank, NGOs, and Neoliberalism in Bangladesh." *Cultural Dynamics* 20, no. 1 (2008): 5–29.

Karlan, Dean, Sendhil Mullainathan, and Omar Robles. "Measuring Personality Traits and Predicting Loan Default with Experiments and Surveys." In *Banking the World: Empirical Foundations of Financial Inclusion*, edited by Robert Cull, Aslı Demirg-Kunt, and Jonathan Morduch (pp. 393–410). Cambridge: MIT Press, 2013.

Karlan, Dean S. *Microfinance Impact Assessments: The Perils of Using New Members as a Control Group*. Minneapolis: University of Minnesota Press, 2011.

Karlan, Dean S. "Social Connections and Group Banking." *The Economic Journal* 117, no. 517 (2007): F52–F84.

Karlan, Dean S. and Gine, Javier. "Group versus Individual Liability: A Field Experiment in the Philippines." *Center for Global Development Working Paper* no. 111 (2009).

Karlan, Dean S. and Valdivia, Martine. "Teaching Entrepreneurship: Impact of Business Training on Microfinance Clients and Institutions." *Review of Economics and Statistics* 93, no. 2 (2001): 510–27.

Karlan, Dean S. and Zinman, Jonathan. "Expanding Microenterprise Credit Access: Using Randomized Supply Decisions to Estimate the Impacts in Manila." *SSRN Electronic Journal* (2009).

Karlan, Dean S. "Using Experimental Economics to Measure Social Capital and Predict Financial Decisions." *American Economic Review* 95, no. 5 (2005): 1688–99.

Katz, Michael B. and Stern, Mark J. "Poverty in Twentieth-Century America." *America at the Millennium Project Working Paper #7* (2001): 3.

Katz, Michael B. *The Undeserving Poor: America's Enduring Confrontation with Poverty, Fully Updated and Revised.* Oxford: Oxford University Press, 2013.

Kaur, Prabhjot and Dey, Soma. "Andhra Pradesh Microfinance Crisis and its Repercussions on Microfinancing Activities." *India Global Journal of Management and Business Studies* 3, no. 7 (2013): 695–702.

Khandker, Shahidur R. "Savings, Informal Borrowing, and Microfinance." *The Bangladesh Development Studies* 26, nos. 2/3 (2000): 49–78.

Khandker, Shahidur R. "Microfinance and Poverty: Evidence Using Panel Data." *Bangladesh World Bank Economic Review* 19, no. 2 (2005): 285.

Kibreab, Gaim. "The Myth of Dependency Among Camp Refugees in Somalia 1979–1989." *Journal of Refugee Studies* 6, no. 4 (1993): 321–49.

Klein, Naomi. *The Shock Doctrine: The Rise of Disaster Capitalism*. New York, NY: Picador, 2007.

Klieman, Kairn A. "U.S. Oil Companies, The Nigerian Civil War, and the Origins of Opacity in the Nigerian Oil Industry, 1964-1971." *Journal of American History* 99, no. 1 (June, 2012): 155–65.

Kottak, Phillip C. "Culture and Economic Development." *The American Anthropologist* 92, no. 3 (1990): 723–31.

Krane, V., Andersen, M. B., and Strean, W. B. "Issues of Qualitative Research Methods and Presentations." *Journal of Sport and Exercise Psychology* 19 (1997): 213–18.

Kruglanski, Arie W. *Lay Epistemics and Human Knowledge: Cognitive and Motivational Bases.* New York: Plenum, 1989.

Krugman, Paul. "Republicans and Race." *New York Times*, November 18, 2007. www.nytimes.com/2007/11/19/opinion/19krugman.html.

Labov, William and Joshua Waletzky. "Narrative Analysis: Oral Versions of Personal Experience." *Journal of Narrative and Life Story* 7, nos. 1–4 (1997): 3–38.

Lado, Cleophas. "Some Aspects of Rural Marketing Systems and Peasant Farming in Maridi District, Southern Sudan." *Transactions of the Institute of British Geographers* 13, no. 3 (1988): 361–74.

Lahaye, Estelle, Rizvanolli, Ralitsa, and Dashi, Edlira. "Current Trends in Cross-Border Funding for Microfinance." *CGAP*, November, 2012.

Lapavitsas, Costas. "Financialised Capitalism: Crisis and Financial Expropriation." *Historical Materialism* 17, no. 2 (2009): 114–48.

Lapavitsas, Costas. *Profiting Without Producing: How Finance Exploits Us All.* London: Verso, 2013.

Larson, Dave. *Searching for Differences: Microfinance Following Conflict vx. Other Environments.* Bethseda: Development Alternatives, 2001.

Leahy, Anna. *Constituents of Matter.* Kent State University Press, 2007.

Ledgerwood, Joanna. *Microfinance Handbook: An Institutional and Financial Perspective.* Washington, DC: The World Bank, 1999.

Leon, Josh. "Poverty Capitalism: Interview with Ananya Roy." *Foreign Policy in Focus* (2011).

Levé, Guy. *The Encyclopedia of Card Play Techniques at Bridge.* Toronto: Master Point Press, 2007.

Lewarne, Stephen and Snelbecker, David. "Economic Governance in War Torn Economies: Lessons Learned from the Marshall Plan to the Reconstruction of Iraq." *USAID* (2004).

Lewis, C. K. *The Four Loves.* New York: Harcourt, 1991/1960.

Lewis, David. "Anthropology and Development: The Uneasy Relationship." In *A Handbook of Economic Anthropology*, edited by James G. Carrier (pp. 472–486). Cheltenham and Northhampton: Edward Elgar, 2005.

Linked In. "Finance South Sudan Limited LinkedIn Profile." Accessed January, 2016. https://www.linkedin.com/company/finance-south-sudan-limited.

Luttrell, Cecilia and Quiroz, Sitna. "Understanding and Operationalising Empowerment." ODI Working Paper (2009). http://www.odi.org/sites/odi.org.uk/files/odi-assets/publications-opinion-files/5500.pdf.

Mac Ginty, Roger. *No War, No Peace: The Rejuvenation of Stalled Peace Processes and Peace Accords.* London: Palgrave Macmillan, 2016.

Mader, Philip. "Rise and Fall of Microfinance in India: The Andhra Pradesh Crisis in Perspective Strategic Change." *Briefings in Entrepreneurial Finance* 22, no. 1–2 (2013): 47–66.

Malkki, Liisa. *The Need to Help: The Domestic Arts of International Humanitarianism.* Durham and London: Duke, 2015.

Manning, Willard G. "Health Insurance and the Demand for Medical Care." *RAND Health Insurance Experiment Series*, 1987.

Marulanda, Beatriz and Otero, María. "The Profile of Microfinance in Latin America in Ten Years: Vision and Characteristics." *Boston MA: ACCION International* (2005).

Marwood, B. V. "Juba Conference 1947 Conference Recordings." EP/SCR/1.A.5/1 (June, 1947). Retrieved in 2010 from http://www.gurtong.net/LinkClick.aspx?fileticket=OBZpercent2B7v1SXispercent3Dandtabid=124.

Maurer, Bill. *Mutual Life, Limited: Islamic Banking, Alternative Currencies, Lateral Reasoning.* Princeton: Princeton University Press, 2005.

Maurer, Bill. "The Anthropology of Money." *Annual Review of Anthropology* 35 (2006): 15–36.

Mauss, Marcel. *The Gift: Forms and Functions of Exchange in Archaic Societies.* London: Lowe and Brydone Printers, 1967.

Mawdsley, Emma, Townsend, Janet G., and Porter, Gina. "Trust, Accountability, and Face-to-face Interaction in North-South NGO Relations." *Development in Practice* 15, no. 1 (2005): 77–82.

Mcintosh, Craig, Janvry, Alain, and Sadoulet, Elisabeth. "How Rising Competition Among Microfinance Institutions Affects Incumbent Lenders." *The Economic Journal* 115, no. 506 (2005): 987–1004.

Menkhaus, Ken. "Vicious Circles and the Security-Development Nexus in Somalia." *Conflict, Security and Development* (2004).

Merleau-Ponty, Maurice. *The Visible and the Invisible.* Evanston, IL: Northwestern University Press, 1968.

Ministry of Finance and Economic Planning. *GoSS Aid Strategy 2006–2011.* Government of Southern Sudan, 2007.

Mitchell, Timothy. *Rule of Experts: Egypt, Techno-Politics, Modernity.* Berkeley, CA: University of California Press, 2002.

Mittal, Anuradha and Mousseau, Frederic. "Understanding Land Investment Deals in Africa." Presentation at The Oakland Institute, South Sudan, October 19, 2011.

Moi, P. "Dual Exchange Rate Privileged a Few – Tisa." *The New Nation.* October 5, 2014. Web. Accessed December, 2014. http://www.newnationsouthsudan.com/component/k2/dual-exchange-rate-privileged-a-few-tisa.html.

Montgomery, Richard. "Disciplining or Protecting the Poor? Avoiding the Social Costs of Peer Pressure in Micro-credit Schemes." *Journal of International Development, Special Issue, Sustainable Banking with the Poor* 8, no. 2 (1996): 289–305.

Morais, Neavis and Ahmad, Mokbul Morshed. "NGO-led Microfinance: Potentials and Challenges in Conflict Areas." *Journal of International Development* 23, no. 5 (2011): 629–40.

Morduch, Jonathan and Haley, B. *Analysis of the Effects of Microfinance on Poverty Reduction.* Working Paper No. 1014. New York: New York University Press, 2002.

Morduch, Jonathan. "The Microfinance Promise." *Journal of Economic Literature* 37 (1999): 1569–614.

Morvant, Solène. "MFI's Clients Borrowing Strategies and Lending Groups Financial Heterogeneity Under Progressive Lending: Evidence from Rural Mexico." *Economic and Political Weekly* 31, no. 2 (2007): 193–216.

Mosley, Paul and Hulme, David. "Microenterprise Finance: Is There a Conflict Between Growth and Poverty Alleviation?" *World Development* 26, no. 5 (1998): 783–90.

Moyo, Dambisa. *Dead Aid: Why Aid Is Not Working and How There Is a Better Way for Africa.* New York: Farrar, Straus and Giroux, 2009.

Murray, Charles. "Does Welfare Bring More Babies?" *Public Interest* (Spring, 1994).

Myrdal, Gunnar. *Economic Theory and Underdeveloped Regions.* London: University Paperbacks, Methuen, 1957.

Nagarajan, Geetha. *Developing Microfinance Institutions in Conflict Affected Countries: Emerging Issues, First Lessons Learnt and Challenges Ahead.* Geneva: Enterprise and Cooperative Development Department, ILO, 1997.

Nagarajan, Geetha. *Microfinance in Post-Conflict Situations: Towards Guiding Principles for Action.* Geneva: Enterprise and Cooperative Development Department, ILO, 1999.

Nagarajan, Geetha and McNulty, Michael. *Microfinance Amid Conflict: Taking Stock of Avfailable Literature.* Accelerated Microenterprise Advancement Project, 2004. http://pdf.usaid.gov/pdf_docs/Pnade302.pdf.

Nama, Nosisana and Swartz, Leslie. "Ethical and Social Dilemmas in Community-based Controlled Trials in Situations of Poverty: A View from a South African Project." *J. Community. Appl. Soc. Psychol. Journal of Community and Applied Social Psychology* 12, no. 4 (2002): 286–97.

Navajas, Sergio, Schreiner, Mark, Meyer, Richard L., Gonzalez-Vega, Claudio, and Rodriguez-Meza, Jorge. "Microcredit and the Poorest of the Poor: Theory and Evidence from Bolivia." *World Development* 28, no. 2 (2000): 333–46.

Nawaz, Shah. "Microfinance and Poverty Reduction: Evidence from a Village Study in Bangladesh." *Journal of Asian and African Studies* 45, no. 6 (2010): 670–83.

NBS. "South Sudan National Bureau of Statistics." The Republic of South Sudan NBS, Home (2010). Accessed http://www.ssnbss.org.

Ndulu, Benno, Chakraborti, Lopamudra, Ligane, Legohand, Rmachandran, Vijaya, and Wolgin, Jerome. *Challenges of African Growth: Opportunities, Constraints and Strategic Directions.* Washington, DC: The World Bank, 2007.

Neha, Sud. "Equity Bank Group and IFC Team up to Expand Access to Finance in East Africa." *World Bank Group* (2012). http://ifcext.ifc.org/IFCExt/Pressroom/IFCPressRoom.nsf/0/AC89C97D0C72E6F0422579D000611D73.

Ngor, Mading. "South Sudan Pound Rises after Qatari Bank Import Deal." *Thomson Reuters* (September 6, 2012). Accessed December 13, 2014. http://www.reuters.com/article/2012/09/06/us-southsudan-pound-idUSBRE8850WX20120906.

Nobel Prize. "Joseph E. Stiglitz — Biographical." Nobel Media AB, 2014. (January 17, 2016). http://www.nobelprize.org/nobel_prizes/economic-sciences/laureates/2001/stiglitz-bio.html.

Nobel Prize. "The Nobel Peace Prize 2006." *Nobelprize.org.* Accessed November, 2017. http://www.nobelprize.org/nobel_prizes/peace/laureates/2006.

Obi, Cyril. "Oil as the 'Curse' of Conflict in Africa: Peering through the Smoke and Mirrors." *Review of African Political Economy* 37, no. 126 (2010): 483–95.

OECD. *Report on International Engagement in Fragile States: South Sudan.* OECD Publishing, 2011. https://www.oecd.org/countries/southsudan/48697972.pdf.

OFAC. *South Sudan Sanctions Program.* Washington, DC: Office of Foreign Assets Control, 2015. http://www.treasury.gov/resource-center/sanctions/Programs/Documents/southsudan.pdf.

Ohanyan, Anna. *NGOs, IGOs, and the Network Mechanisms of Post-conflict Global Governance in Microfinance.* New York, NY: Palgrave Macmillan, 2008.

Okeny, Kenneth. "The 1947 Juba Conference." *Northeast African Studies* 13, no. 1 (1991): 39–58.

Olson, Mancur. *The Rise and Decline of Nations: Economic Growth, Stagflation, and Social Rigidities.* New Haven: Yale University Press, 1982.

Orso, Cristina Elisa. "Microcredit and Poverty. An Overview of the Principal Statistical Methods used to Measure the Programme Net Impacts." *POLIS Working Paper* No. 180 (February, 2011).

Ostrom, Elinor. *Governing the Commons: The Evolution of Institutions for Collective Action.* Cambridge: Cambridge University Press, 1990.

Owens, John. "Studying the Past, Looking to the Future: USAID's Microfinance Experiences over the Past 25 Years: An Impression from the Field." *USAID's Microfinance Consortium.* (May, 2014.) https://www.microlinks.org/studying-past-looking-future-usaid's-microfinance-experiences-over-past-25-years-impression-field.

Oxfam America. "Smart Development in Practice. Field Report from Southern Sudan." *Smart Development in Practice Field Reports.* Oxfam Publishing, 2009.

Paris, Roland. *Building Peace after Civil Conflict.* New York: Cambridge University Press, 2004.

Parker, Joan. *Microfinance in Post-Conflict Countries: Towards a Framework for Action.* Geneva: Enterprise and Cooperative Development Department, ILO, 1999.

Peshkin, Alan. "In Search of Subjectivity—One's Own." *Educational Researcher* 17, no. 15 (1998): 17–21.

Pitt, Mark M. and Khandker, Shahidur R. "The Impact of Group Based Credit Programs on Poor Households in Bangladesh: Does the Gender of Participants Matter?" *Journal of Political Economy* 106, no. 5 (1998): 958–96.

Piven, Frances Fox. "Foreword to Schram, S. F." In *Words of Welfare*, edited by Sanford Schram (p. xii). Minneapolis and London: University of Minnesota Press, 1995.

Platteau, Jean-Philippe and Gaspart, Frédéric. *Disciplining Local Leaders in Community-Based Development.* Centre for Research on the Economics of Development (CRED). Namur, Belgium: University of Namur, 2003.

Population Census Council. *5th Sudan Population and Housing Census - 2008.* Khartoum: Central Bureau of Statistics, 2009.

Prahalad, C. K. and Hart, Stuart L. "The Fortune at the Bottom of the Pyramid." *Strategy + Business: Corporate Strategies and News Articles on Global Business, Management, Competition and Marketing.* Booz and Company (2002). http://www.strategy-business.com/article/11518?gko=9a4ba.

Prahalad, Coimbatore K. *The Fortune at the Bottom of the Pyramid: Eradicating Poverty through Profits.* Upper Saddle River, NJ: Wharton School Publications, 2006.

Prendergast, John. "Blood Money for Sudan World Bank and IMF to the 'Rescue.'"*Africa Today* 36, nos. 3/4 (1989): 43–53.

Public Law. "Microenterprise for Self-Reliance and International Anti-Corruption Act of 2000." § H.R. 1143 (106th) (2000).

Pugh, Michael. "The Political Economy of Peacebuilding." *International Journal of Peacebuilding* 10, no. 2 (2005): 23–42.

Pugh, Michael C., Turner, Mandy, and Cooper, Neil. *Whose Peace?: Critical Perspectives on the Political Economy of Peacebuilding (Critical Perspectives on the Political Economy of Peacebuilding).* Palgrave Macmillan UK, 2008.

Putnam, Robert D. "Bowling Alone: America's Declining Social Capital." *Journal of Democracy* 6, no. 1 (1995): 65–78.

Rahman, Aminur. *Women and Microcredit in Rural Bangladesh: An Anthropological Study of Grameen Bank Lending.* Boulder: Westview Press, 1999.

Rahnema, Majid. "Poverty" in *Wolfgang Sachs The Development Dictionary* 2nd edition. London and New York: Zed Books, 2010, p. 185.

Rauf, Shahnaz and Mahmood, Tahir. "Growth and Performance of Microfinance in Pakistan." *Pakistan Economic and Social Review* 47, no. 1 (2009): 99–122.

Ravallion, Martin, Chen, Shaohua, and Sangraula, Prem. "Dollar a Day Revisited." *World Bank Economic Review,* 23, no. 2 (2009).

Reed, Larry R., Laegreid Gatti, Lisa, and Awimbo, Anna. *Vulnerability: The State of the Microcredit Summit Campaign Report.* Microcredit Summit Campaign, 2013.

Reed, Larry R. *State of the Campaign Report.* State of the Campaign, 2015. https://stateofthecampaign.org/read-the-full-2015-report/.

Refugees International. "South Sudan: Urgent Action Needed to Avert Collapse." Refugees International (2009). http://www.refugeesinternational.org/policy/field-report/south-sudan-urgent-action-needed-avert-collapse.

Renden, Mattijs, Andelaars, Emma, and Jansson, Resi. "The (im)possibility of Financial Inclusion in South Sudan." *The Broker* (2013). http://www.thebrokeronline.eu/Blogs/Spurring-economic-transition/The-im-possibility-of-financial-inclusion-in-South-Sudan.

Rhyne, Elisabeth. "The Yin and Yang of Microfinance: Reaching the Poor and Sustainability." *MicroBanking Bulletin* 2, no. 1 (1998): 6–8.

Richmond, O. P. "The Dilemmas of Subcontracting the Liberal Peace." in *Subcontracting Peace: The Challenges of the NGO Peacebuilding*, edited by O. P. Richmond and H. Carey (pp. 19–36). Burlington: Ashgate, 2005.

Richmond, Oliver. "'Beyond Liberal Peace? Responses to "Backsliding."' In *New Perspectives on Liberal Peacebuilding*, edited by Edward Newman, Roland Paris and Oliver Richmond (pp. 54–77). Tokyo: UN University Press, 2009.

Robinson, Marguerite S. *The Microfinance Revolution: Sustainable Finance for the Poor.* Washington, DC: The World Bank, 2001.

Rodrik, Dani. *Goodbye Washington Consensus, Hello Washington Confusion?* Cambridge, MA: Harvard University, 2006.

Roodman, David. "Charting Growth." http://www.cgdev.org/blog/charting-growth using data from http://www.mixmarket.org/mfi/trends/products_and_clients.total_borrowers/2005-2009 (2011).

Roodman, David and Morduch, Jonathan. "The Impact of Microcredit on the Poor in Bangladesh: Revisiting the Evidence." *Journal of Development Studies* 50, no. 4 (2013): 583–604.

Roodman, David and Qureshi, Uzma. "Microfinance as Business." *Center for Global Development 2*, Washington, DC (2006).

Rosenberg, Richard. "Microcredit Interest Rates." *CGAP Publications*. no. 1, 1996.

Rosenstein-Rodan, P. N. "Problems of Industrialisation of Eastern and South-Eastern Europe." *The Economic Journal* 53, nos. 110/111 (Summer 1943): 202–11.

Rowlands, Jessica. *Questioning Empowerment: Working with Women in Honduras*. Oxfam Publishing, 1997.

Roy, Ananya. *Poverty Capital: Microfinance and the Making of Development*. New York and London: Routledge, 2010.

Rutherford, Samuel. "The Poor and Their Money: An Essay about Financial Services for Poor People." Institute for Development Policy and Management University of Manchester (January, 1999).

Saad-Filho, Aflredo and Fine, Ben. "Thirteen Things You Need to Know About Neoliberalism." *Critical Sociology* 43, nos. 4–5 (2016): 685–706.

Sachs, Jeffrey and Andrew Warner "Economic Reform and the Process of Global Integration." *Brookings Papers on Economic Activity* 1 (1995): 1–18.

Sample, Bob. *How RESULTS Activists Collaborated With Microcredit Leaders and High Government Officials to Build the Microfinance Movement*. Washington, DC, Results Education Fund (September, 2006).

Sandrai, Adel. "Devaluation of South Sudanese Pound: A Sound Economic Policy in Unsound Economic Environment." *The Sudd Institute*. (2013).

Sanjay, Alok Kumar and Gupta, Vivek, "Gyandoot: Trying to Improve Government Services for Rural Citizens in India eTransparency" Case Study No. 11 (2000). http://www.egov4dev.org/transparency/case/gyandoot.shtml.

Sanyal, Paromita. "From Credit To Collective Action: The Role Of Microfinance In Promoting Women's Social Capital And Normative Influence." *American Sociological Review* 74, no. 4 (2009): 529–50.

Satish, P. "Mainstreaming of Indian Microfinance." *Economic and Political Weekly* 40, no. 17 (2005): 1731–9.

Schnall, Marianne. "Conversation with Natalie Portman." *Feminist.com*, Resources. Accessed http://www.feminist.com/resources/artspeech/interviews/natalieportman.html.

Schram, S. F. *Words of Welfare*. Minneapolis and London: University of Minnesota Press, 1995.

Schüklenk, Udo. "Protecting the Vulnerable: Testing Times for Clinical Research Ethics." *Social Science and Medicine* 51, no. 6 (2000): 969–77.

Schuler, Sidney, Syed, Hashemi Ruth, Badal and Shamsul, Huda. "Men's Violence Against Women in Rural Bangladesh: Underdetermined or Exacerbated by Microcredit Programmes?" *Development in Practice* 8, no. 2 (1998): 148–57.

Schwittay, Anke. *New Media and International Development: Representation and affect in microfinance.* New York: Routledge, 2014.

Seibel, Hans Dieter. "Islamic Microfinance in Indonesia: The Challenge of Institutional Diversity, Regulation, and Supervision." *Journal of Social Issues in Southeast Asia* 23, no. 1 (2008): 86–103.

Selby, Jan. "The Myth of Liberal Peace-Building." *Conflict, Security and Development* 13, no. 1 (March, 2013): 57–86.

Sen, Amartya. *Development as Freedom.* New York: Knopf, 1999.

Sharma, Manohar and Zeller, Manfred. "Repayment Performance in Group-based Credit Programs in Bangladesh: An Empirical Analysis." *World Development* 25, no. 10 (1997): 1731–42.

Sheehan, Genevieve. "Microfinance as a Pathway to Peace and Reconciliation: A Case Study from Sri Lanka." *International Perspectives on Peace and Reconciliation.* Melbourne: University of Melbourne, 2003.

Simons, Gary F. and Fennig, Charles D. *Ethnologue: Languages of the World* 20th edition. Dallas, TX: SIL International, 2013.

Sinclair, Hugh. *Confessions of a Microfinance Heretic.* San Francisco: Berrett-Koehler, 2012.

Singh, Anoop, Belaisch, Agnès, Collyns, Charles, De Masi, Paula, Krieger, Reva, Meredith, Guy, and Rennhack Robert. "Stabilization and Reform in Latin America: A Macroeconomic Perspective on the Experience Since the Early 1990s." *International Monetary Fund.* Occasional Paper (2005).

SIPRI. "Stockholm International Peace Research Institute." SIPRI, Home. (2013). Accessed www.sipri.org.

Smith, Adam. *The Wealth of Nations*, Book 1. London: Methuen and Co, 1776.

Smith, David. "South Sudan President Accuses Officials of Stealing $4bn of Public Money." *The Guardian* (2012).

Soares De Oliveira, Ricardo. "Illiberal Peacebuilding in Angola." *Journal of Modern African Studies* 49, no. 2 (2011): 287–314.

Soursourian, Matthew and Dashi, Edlira. *Current Trends in International Funding for Financial Inclusion.* CGAP Donor Brief, World Bank Group. Washington, DC: CGAP Publishing, 2015. http://documents. worldbank. org/curated/en/756341467995103982/Current-trends-in-international-funding-for-financial-inclusion.

Special to New York Times. "New York Times Welfare Queen' Becomes Issue in Reagan Campaign." *ProQuest Historical Newspapers: The New York Times* (1976): 51.

Standing, Guy. "Social Protection." In *Deconstructing Development Discourse: Buzzwords and Fuzzwords*, edited by Cornwall, Andre and Eade, Deborah (pp. 53–67). Oxford: Oxfam/Practical Action, 2010.

Steen, Margaret. "Natalie Portman: Microfinance Lifts Families Out of Poverty." *Stanford Graduate School of Business* (2007).

Stewart, Frances and FitzGerald, Valpy. "Introduction: Assessing the Economic Costs of War." In *War and Underdevelopment*, Vol. 1, edited by Frances Stewart, Valpy FitzGerald, and Associates. Oxford: Oxford University Press, 2001.

Stiftung, Bertelsmann. *South Sudan Country Report.* Gütersloh: Bertelsmann Stiftung BTI, 2014.

Stiglitz, Joseph E., Sen, Amartya, and Fitoussi, Jean Paul. *Mis-Measuring Our Lives: Why GDP Doesn't Add Up*. New York: The New Press, 2010.

Stiglitz, Joseph E. "Peer monitoring and credit markets." *The World Bank Economic Review* 4, no. 3 (1990): 351–66.

Stockman, Farah. "The Wild West in South Sudan: Cowboy Capitalists Rush into World's Newest Nation, as Locals Struggle — and Politicians Take a Cut." *The Boston Globe* (June 9, 2013). http://www.bostonglobe.com/opinion/2013/06/08/cowboy-capitalists-rush-into-south-sudan/Mkk9CBw5idzolS3C38F1BJ/story.html_2013.

Stone, Diane. "The Policy Research Knowledge Elite and Global Policy Processes." In *Non-state Actors in World Politics*, edited by D. Josselin and W. Wallace. New York: Palgrave, 2001.

Sud, Neha. "Equity Bank Group and IFC Team up to Expand Access to Finance in East Africa" Washington, DC: International Finance Corporation, 2012.

Sudan Tribune. "East Africans Drive Business in 'Boom Town' Juba." *The Sudan Tribune*, 2006. http://www.sudantribune.com/spip.php?article16175.

Sudan Watch. "MicroSave-Africa - USAID Sponsors Southern Sudan's First Microfinance Conference." *Sudan Watch* (blog), last modified August 1, 2010, http://sudanwatch.blogspot.com/2010/08/microsave-africa-usaid-sponsors.html.

Swibel, Matthew. "The World's Top Microfinance Institutions." *Forbes*, 2007. http://www.forbes.com/2007/12/20/top-microfinance-philanthropy-biz-cz_ms_1220intro.html.

Swidler, Ann and Susan Cotts Watkins. "'Teach a Man to Fish': The Doctrine of Sustainability and Its Effects on Three Strata of Malawian Society." *World Development* 37, no. 7 (2009): 1182–11.

Tamazuj, Radio. "South Sudan Importers Discouraged by Dollar Scarcity." *Radio Tamazuj*, December 13, 2014. https://radiotamazuj.org/en/article/south-sudan-importers-discouraged-dollar-scarcity.

Tepperman, Jonathan. "Brazil's Antipoverty Breakthrough: The Surprising Success of Bolsa Família." *Foreign Affairs*, 2016. https://www.foreignaffairs.com/articles/brazil/2015-12-14/brazils-antipoverty-breakthrough.

The Brian Lehrer Show. "A New Look at 'The Undeserving Poor." Produced by Courtney Stein. New York Public Radio, November, 2013.

Tosh, J. "Sources of Economic Change in a Cinderella dependency: the Southern Sudan." *Institute of Communication Studies, COLR* 77 (8), London (1978).

Trading Economics. "South Sudanese Pound 2008–2014." Trading Economics, South Sudan. http://www.tradingeconomics.com/south-sudan/currency.

Udry, Christopher, "Risk and Insurance in a Rural Credit Market: An Empirical Investigation in Northern Nigeria" *The Review of Economic Studies* 61, no. 3 (1994): 495–526.

UK DFID. *Statistics on International Development*. Department for International Development, National Statistics, 2013. https://www.gov.uk/government/uploads/system/uploads/attachment_data/file/254277/Statistics_on_International_Development_2013a.pdf.

Uma, Julius N. "South Sudan: 10,000 Micro-businesses at Risk of Collapse." *Sudan Tribune*, 2010.

UN. "Resource Mobilisation for Peacebuilding Priorities: The Role of the Peacebuilding Commission." Peacebuilding Commission, United Nations. (April 6, 2011).

UNCDF. "UNCDF in South Sudan." UNCDF, South Sudan. Accessed October, 2015. http://www.uncdf.org/en/South-Sudan.

UNCDF. "History." UNCDF, History. Accessed October, 2015. http://www.uncdf.org/en/history.

UNDP. *United Nations Human Development Report*. United Nations Development Programme, 2008. Accessed June 20, 2009. http://hdr.undp.org/statistics.

UNDP. "Building an Inclusive Financial Sector in Southern Sudan" Project Document. 2010.

UNDP. "Human Development Reports." UN Development Programme, Income Gini Coefficient (2013). Accessed http://hdr.undp.org/en/content/income-gini-coefficient.

USAID. *A Guide to Economic Growth in Post-Conflict Countries*. Office of Economic Growth, Agriculture and Trade. Washington, DC, 2009.

USAID. *Spring Review of Small Farmer Credit*. vol. 1–20. Washington, DC, 1973.

USAID. *Sudan Agricultural Enterprise Finance Program (AEFP) Tenth Quarterly Report. USAID January 1, 2005 – March 31, 2005*. Chemonics International Inc. Nairobi, Kenya, April 2005. *http://pdf.usaid.gov/pdf_docs/Pdacf003.pdf*.

USAID. *Sudan Agricultural Enterprise Finance Program Final Report*. Chemonics International Inc., 2008.

USAID. *Guide to Economic Growth in Post-Conflict Countries Report*. 2009.

USAID. Sudan: Monthly Update July 2010. Usaid.gov/

USAID. "USAID and Banks Launch Partnership To Expand Farmers' Access To Credit In South Sudan." Press Release (2012).

USAID. "USAID Launches Loan Partnership with South Sudan Private Banks." *Sudan Tribune*, 2012. http://www.sudantribune.com/spip.php?article44404.

Valdivia, Martin. "Business Training Plus for Female Entrepreneurship? Short and Medium-Term Experimental Evidence from Peru." PIERI Working Papers, 2014.

Vander Weele, Ken and Markovich, Patricia. "Managing High and Hyper-Inflation in Microfinance: Opportunity International's Experience in Bulgaria and Russia." *Microenterprise Best Practices* (2001).

Vatta, Kamal. "Microfinance and Poverty Alleviation." *Economic and Political Weekly* 38, no. 5 (2003): 432–33.

Von Pischke, John D. *Finance at the Frontier: Debt Capacity and the Role of Credit in the Private Economy*. Washington, DC: World Bank Publications, 1991.

Vuni, Isaac. "South Sudan Parliament Throw Outs Census Results." *Sudan Tribune*, 2009. http://www.sudantribune.com/spip.php?article31746.

Wallerstein, Immanuel. *The Modern World-System: Capitalist Agriculture and the Origins of the European World-economy in the Sixteenth Centenary*. University of California Press, 1974.

Warner, Wellman Joel. *The Wesleyan Movement in the Industrial Revolution*. Longmans, Green and Company, 1930.

Watts, Michael. *Crude Politics: Life and Death on the Nigerian Oil Fields*. Niger Delta Economies of Violence Working Paper No. 25: (2009).

Weber, Max. *The Protestant Ethic and the Spirit of Capitalism.* Taylor and Francis e-Library, 2005.

Williamson, John. "Did the Washington Consensus fail?" Outline of speech at the Center for Strategic and International Studies Washington, DC, 2002. https://pi ie.com/commentary/speeches-papers/did-washington-consensus-fail.

Wilson, Tamsin. "Microfinance During And After Armed Conflict: Lessons From Angola, Cambodia, Mozambique And Rwanda" Concern Worldwide and The Springfield Centre For Business In Development March 2002.

Woolcock, Michael J. V. "Social Capital and Economic Development: Toward a Theoretical Synthesis and Policy Framework." *Theory and Society* 27, no. 2 (1998): 151–208.

Woolcock, Michael J. V. "Learning from Failures in Microfinance: What Unsuccessful Cases Tell Us About How Group-Based Programs Work." *American Journal of Economics and Sociology* 58, no. 1 (1999): 17–42.

World Bank, United Nations and International Monetary Fund. *Framework for Sustained Peace, Development and Poverty Education in Sudan Staff Assessment of Progress*. Joint Assessment Mission for Sudan, 2006.

World Bank. "About the MDTFs." World Bank, Sudan Multi-Donor Trust Funds (2013). http://web.worldbank.org/WBSITE/EXTERNAL/COUNTRIES/AFRI CAEXT/SUDANEXTN/EXTAFRMDTF/0,,contentMDK:20850935~menuP K:2193691~pagePK:64168445~piPK:64168309~theSitePK:2193668,00.html.

World Bank. "Doing Business 2011: Making a Difference for Entrepreneurs." Washington, DC: The International Bank for Reconstruction and Development, 2010.

World Bank. "How Social Capital is Measured?" http://web.worldbank.org/WBSITE/EXTERNAL/TOPICS/EXTSOCIALDEVELOPMENT/EXTTSOCIALCAPITA L/0,,contentMDK:20185164~menuPK:418217~pagePK:148956~piPK:216618~theSitePK:401015,00.html Accessed December 10, 2015.

World Bank. "Project Information Document (PID) Appraisal Stage: *Private Sector Development Project Report* no. AB 6781. September, 2011. http://www-wds.worl dbank.org/external/default/WDSContentServer/WDSP/IB/2011/09/28/0000018 43_20110930131437/Rendered/PDF/South0Sudan0PSDP0PID9.23.11.pdf.

World Bank. "South Sudan Overview." (2015). Washington, DC: World Bank. http: //www.worldbank.org/en/country/southsudan/overview.

World Bank. "Emergency Project Paper On A Proposed Grant In The Amount Of US $9 Million To The Republic Of South Sudan For A Private Sector Development Project (2012) Washington, DC: World Bank.

World Bank. "Sudan at a Glance." World Bank Development Data (2009). http://dev data.worldbank.org/AAG/sdn_aag.pdf.

World Bank. "World Bank Open Data." World Bank, Data (2013). http://data.worldbank.org.

World Bank. "World Bank Open Data." World Bank, Data (2014). http://data.worldbank.org.

Wydick, Bruce. "Can Social Cohesion Be Harnessed to Repair Market Failures? Evidence from Group Lending in Guatemala." *Economic Journal* 109, no. 457 (1999): 463–75.

Yongo-Bure, Benaiah. *Economic Development of Southern Sudan.* Lanham, MD: University Press of America, 2007.

Yunus, Muhammad. *Banker to the Poor: Micro-lending and the Battle Against World Poverty.* New York: Public Affairs, 1999.

Zelizer, Viviana A. *The Social Meaning of Money: Pin Money, Paychecks, Poor Relief, and Other Currencies.* Princeton: Princeton University Press, 1999.

Žižek, Slavoj. *First as Tragedy, Then as Farce.* London: Verso, 2009.

Index

About the Author

Dr. Crystal Murphy is assistant professor of political science and director of the master's in international studies program at Chapman University.

www.ingramcontent.com/pod-product-compliance
Ingram Content Group UK Ltd.
Pitfield, Milton Keynes, MK11 3LW, UK
UKHW041423091026
15587UKWH00023B/236

9 781498 577380